# Weep Not for Your Children

# Religion and Violence

Series Editors
Lisa Isherwood, University of Winchester, and Rosemary
Radford Ruether, Graduate Theological Union, Berkeley,
California

This interdisciplinary and multicultural series brings to light the
ever increasing problem of religion and violence. The series will
highlight how religions have a significant part to play in the
creation of cultures that allow and even encourage the creation of
violent conflict, domestic abuse and policies and state control that
perpetuate violence to citizens.

The series will highlight the problems that are experienced by
women during violent conflict and under restrictive civil policies.
But not wishing to simply dwell on the problems the authors in this
series will also re-examine the traditions and look for alternative and
more empowering readings of doctrine and tradition. One aim of
the series is to be a powerful voice against creeping fundamentalisms
and their corrosive influence on the lives of women and children.

Published:
*Reweaving the Relational Mat*
*A Christian Response to Violence against Women from Oceania*
Joan Alleluia Filemoni-Tofaeono and Lydia Johnson

*America, Amerikkka*
Elect Nation and Imperial Violence
Rosemary Radford Ruether

Forthcoming:
*In Search of Solutions: The Problem of Religion and Conflict*
Clinton Bennett

*Meditations on Religion and Violence in the United States*
T. Walter Herbert

*Shalom/Salaam/Peace*
*A Liberation Theology of Hope in Israel/Palestine*
Constance A. Hammond

# Weep Not for Your Children

*Essays on Religion and Violence*

*Edited by*
Lisa Isherwood and
Rosemary Radford Ruether

LONDON    OAKVILLE

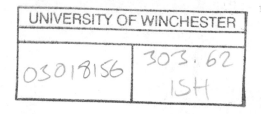
Published by Equinox Publishing Ltd.
UK: Unit 6, The Village, 101 Amies St., London SW11 2JW
USA: DBBC, 28 Main Street, Oakville, CT 06779

www.equinoxpub.com

First published 2008

British Library Cataloguing-in-Publication Data
A catalogue record for this book is available from the British Library.

ISBN-10   1 84553 243 0      (hardback)
          1 84553 244 9      (paperback)
ISBN-13   978 184553 243 7   (hardback)
          978 184553 244 4   (paperback)

Library of Congress Cataloging-in-Publication Data

Weep not for your children : essays on religion and violence / edited by Lisa Isherwood and Rosemary Radford Ruether.
    p. cm. — (Religion and violence)
Includes bibliographical references and index.
ISBN 1-84553-243-0 (hb) — ISBN 1-84553-244-9 (pb)
1. Violence—Religious aspects. 2. Good and evil. I. Isherwood, Lisa. II. Ruether, Rosemary Radford. III. Series.
BL65.V55W44 2007
201'.76332—dc22
                    2006015894

Typeset by S.J.I. Services, New Delhi
Printed and bound in Great Britain by Lightning Source UK Ltd, Milton Keynes, and Lightning Source Inc., La Vergne, TN

# CONTENTS

*Rosemary Radford Ruether* is the Carpenter Professor of Feminist Theology at the Graduate Theological Union in Berkeley, California. For 28 years she was the Georgia Harkness Professor of Applied Theology at the Garrett Theological Seminary and Northwestern University in Evanston, Illinois. She is the author or editor of a number of books dealing with feminist and liberation theologies.

*K. Renato Lings* is a Danish national, currently working in Denmark as a translator/interpreter, teacher, lecturer, and writer.

*Lisa Isherwood* is Professor of Feminist Liberation Theologies and Director of Theology at the University of Winchester. She is an executive editor of the international journal, *Feminist Theology*, and co-founder of the Britain & Ireland School of Feminist Theology. She has authored or edited a number of books.

*Marcella Maria Althaus-Reid* is an Argentinian theologian. She holds the Chair of Contextual Theology in the School of Divinity, the University of Edinburgh. Prof. Althaus-Reid has published extensively in the area of Liberation Theology and Queer theory.

*Agnes Rafferty* is an activist through the Britain & Ireland School of Feminist Theology and UK contact person for the European Society of Women in Theological Research.

*Nicole Soleto* is a graduate of Harvard Divinity School and campaign and media coordinator for Call to Action, a Catholic organisation working for social justice. Nicole is the author of *Women Healing from Abuse* (Paulist Press, 2006).

*Thalia Gur-Klein* has an MA in English Literature from the University of Leiden and an MA in Jewish Studies from the University of Amsterdam; she is currently working on a PhD.

*Victoria Rollins* received her doctorate from the University of Exeter and campaigns churches to seek an end of violence to women.

*Monica Mahler* is Research Associate and Visiting Faculty in the Women's Studies in Religion Program at Harvard Divinity School. She holds a Ph.D. in Christian Ethics from Union Theological Seminary and M.Div. from Harvard Divinity School.

*Carol Adams* is the author of the pioneering work *The Sexual Politics of Meat* and more recently *The Pornography of Meat*.

*June Boyce-Tillman* is Professor of Applied Music at the University of Winchester. She has published widely in the area of education, particularly music and religious education. She is the author of *Unconventional Wisdom* (2007); *Constructing Musical Healing: The Wounds that Sing* (2000) and *The Creative Spirit: Harmonious Living with Hildegard of Bingen* (2001). June is a hymn writer – 'A Rainbow to Heaven' (2006) – and a performer and creator of one woman shows on religious themes.

# Introduction

## Lisa Isherwood

We do not have to go as far back as the Crusades to be reminded of the link between religion and violence or to realize that people have always viewed that link quite differently. George W. Bush we are reminded was told by God to invade Iraq and despite the rhetoric around the action, that of salvation and redemption, we continue to be faced with the stark reality of that action—death and suffering on a scale that we will probably not fully know until many years from now when it is deemed politically alright to tell the truth. There are those in the Muslim world who saw the bringing down of the Twin Towers as a religious act, one aimed at making a brutal point about the realities of western capitalism and its own brutal/genocidal regime. The circle seems endless and the way in which we view things is quite obviously dictated by where we reside on that ever spinning wheel.

These are 'big acts of violence' and they sometimes mask those actions that are just as brutal and destructive but can be, in the common mind, put to one side as of less importance. What is it after all that ten women will have been raped in the time it took you to read this when seen alongside the millions of the Holocaust and the tens of thousands of the Killing Fields. Well, we suggest that it is something and that all these acts have common roots in patterns of religious and theological thinking that have been infected by destructive and pervasive dualism and the social and political reality of patriarchy that such thinking so easily accommodates, if not helps to create. We hope the articles in this book suggest how we may step outside the circle in order to find other ways of looking and ways of thinking again about the traditions we inhabit and the patterns of thought that they encourage.

This book does not focus much on war although there are two articles that examine aspects of it, the way in which the concept of the Just War has been misused and the resistance of Jewish women during the Holocaust. It does however deal with many aspects of institutionalized violence and attempts to expose the erroneous theological thinking behind such reality. What we are attempting to do is draw attention to the everyday acts of violence that pass almost unnoticed by the faithful or at least are placed into the category of faith filled acceptance. We are suggesting that some violence is done by the traditions themselves in the name of faith and that the acceptance of faith often numbs the faithful and stops the outrage that is required in order to seek a solution and more life enhancing ways of being.

Of course, an enduring example of how faith can blind to issues of justice and perpetuate rather than stop suffering is with the evergreen problem of homosexuality. This issue also highlights more than most that very opposing views can be held springing from the same set of scriptures. The churches seem forever exercised by this issue and some belief that they would be better off thinking about global warming and here, of course, is the crunch. Indeed they would be better off thinking about such big questions, if and only if, they would withdraw the venomous statements about gay and lesbian people that they so easily spew out. Otherwise they have created a problem that leads to, in many cases, unfulfilled lives of gay and lesbian people, at least lives unacknowledged as fully human and as worthy of the blessings of church and state as any others. The rate of teenage gay and lesbian suicide is much higher than that of straight teenagers and physical violence to gay and lesbian people is still within societies and at times enshrined in law, that is to say homosexuality is still a crime in many countries which carries a prison, if not a death, sentence.

While some countries, recently Spain and Britain, are acting to ensure that same sex partners have equal pension and inheritance rights through the introduction of civil partnerships, the Vatican and the Church of England are issuing battle cries against this 'ideology of evil'. Reacting to Spain's legalisation of gay marriage cardinal Alfonso Lopez Trujillo, head of the Pontifical Council on the Family, declared the law a great iniquity and called for Christians to resist accepting it even if that meant breaking the law of their country. There is nothing surprising in this since it was Ratzinger himself who produced the document in 1986, agreed to by John Paul II that declared all homosexuals to be 'intrinsically morally evil. Is this not violence? Declaring, with such divine authority, about the innate character of millions of people worldwide, suggesting that they are evil, that they pervade decent society and like a cancer should be cut out! He seems to have learnt well from the Nazi propaganda machine of his youth, if this was said these days about the Jews there would be outrage, there is a hush in many quarters where we would expect more when the recipients of such venom are gay and lesbian people. This is institutional violence and it breeds internal and external homophobia both of which can be deadly. The legacy of homophobia that John Paul II has left the Catholic Church will, I imagine, not be mentioned when his sainthood is conferred because after all he did such great things on the world stage!

The Catholic Church is not alone in its desire to make the lives of gay and lesbian people difficult and at times intolerable. The Church of England response to civil partnerships being introduced in the UK was to issue a statement which 'relying on scripture, tradition and reason' declared that marriage is between a man and a woman, most tellingly because it is central to the health and stability of human society. Marriage carries a huge responsibility and so much economic reality on its ever decreasing shoulders! While couched in more inclusive terms that Vatican statements have historically been, the Church of England leaves us in no doubt that there is no equality here but a great deal of compassion. This too smacks of violence, the kind that through its 'big heart' nonetheless relegates people to second-class citizenship and the psychological damage as well as civil damage that this can do to them. The report acknowledges that homophobic violence exists but does not take radical steps to ensure that the church is part of the cure and not in any way part of the violence. Such polite engagement with real issues and an almost apologetic insistence on exclusion is characteristic of much church reaction and does nothing to change the world. Let us be in no doubt that an incarnational religion engages with the world in order that a change may come about, a change in which justice may be seen and not just spoken about.

I think in the present day the issues of homosexuality and domestic violence both illustrate the way in which the churches, mired down in scripture, tradition and the erroneous reason that sometimes springs from these two dubious bedfellows is almost powerless to change anything. We are faced with classic examples of good people being co-opted into bad systems through the power of those systems to overawe and make small of the individuals. That Christian churches should be such powers is a scandal given the origins of the Jesus movement. Incarnational religion declares the human/divine power and glory of the individual; it calls forth life in abundance and promises heaven on earth. Are we really saying that the God who dwells in heaven *is* the abusing God that some of the tradition has placed before us? The authors in this book ask us not to forget that religion and violence are often linked and to never take our eyes off how central core beliefs can affect the world, for the bad as well as the good.

## The Articles

Rosemary Radford Ruether lays before us the continuing violence of many forms of the religious right in relation to women and reproductive and abortion rights. She illustrates how the targeting of women's reproductive rights is a political as well as religious agenda and a potentially lethal one for women who may die due to lack of access.

Renato Lings reminds us that violence is done to texts in order to pursue an agenda that can do violence to marginal groups of people—a double atrocity. He is meticulous in demonstrating how this occurs and he provides ways in which we may do it differently.

Lisa Isherwood argues that the very nature of the creation of gender and the ways in which it is held in place within society does violence to women and men. She illustrates her argument through the use of Christian marriage as an example. There is nothing natural about gender let alone divinely commanded; indeed, the divine desire is for the full embrace of our humanity and not the clinical removal of parts of ourselves in the name of gender conformity.

Marcella Althaus-Reid continues the notion of the harmful effects of redemption theology by considering the relationship between Christian debt economy and global debt economy. By placing before another social model, that of *anyi* as practiced in Peru she opens up the possibilities of the *anyi Messiah*, one who operates on gift and mutuality rather than debt/redemption. Moving, as she does, from real situations, the lunchtime crucifixions of those suffering under the global economy she takes us to ask whether Christ could survive a non-redemption theology?

Agnes Rafferty continues the reflection on religious symbols through asking how we may nurture our desire through the symbols we use and thus end violence. She reminds us that religious symbols and language are being used in the present for the continued violence in Iraq, not by those seen as the 'evil doers' but rather by Bush and Blair who imagine themselves to be the saviours. Rafferty highlights the crucial importance of finding meaning in symbols and not allowing them to be co-opted by oppressors.

Nicole Soleto very starkly reminds us that those theologians who may only be interested in whether war is just or not have overlooked the place of women during war. She is realistic that violent conflict is with us for the foreseeable future but asks that theologians consider women when dwelling on the rules of combat. As we know women are raped almost as a matter of course during conflict but Soleto shows that domestic violence also increases before, during and after conflict—the home also becomes the battleground. Women then are at risk even before and after the external conflict. Why was this never considered, why are the health issues of women raped and infected with STD's and AIDS not considered to be war crimes or of note on the theological stage? The answer, the patriarchal background and framing of just war theories.

Thalia Gur Klein demonstrates how women responded to the atrocities of the holocaust but also extends that analysis to investigate how 'righteous women' continue to carry that response into the present day. She considers the work of two women poets from the Holocaust as well as the work of more contemporary women. This article shows how the effects of war are carried through generation and how they too require a religious response even in a secular society.

Victoria Rollins engages with an all too familiar theme that of domestic abuse but asks why the churches do not respond. She is daring in her analysis of the problem as an everyday genocide of women, which can be understood through parallels with the Holocaust. She is ever mindful of not being offensive to Holocaust sufferers and the strength of her article is that it illustrates how private abuse does indeed bear comparison with public and large scale genocide — the moods and motivations behind both are the same she claims.

Monica Mahler moves us to Latin America and to what she claims is, feminicide, that is the social phenomena akin to genocide, that involves the killing and maiming of thousands of women. This she sees as socially sanctioned through social, cultural and legal structures. It is not random and as such has roots in religious as well as secular symbols and systems. Indeed she reminds us that feminicide is nothing new for Christianity which sanctioned the murder of millions of women during the burning times of the witch hunts. Her article highlights the connections and shows how women are attempting to overcome these connections through affirming women's spirituality as the basis for social transformation.

Carol Adams takes us in a new direction by showing how God talk is connected to the sexual politics of meat eating, a politic of domination and ultimately ecological destruction. She illustrates for us what violence we sanction through the callous approach to animals which we consider to be lower than us in an imagined and purely man-made hierarchy.

June Boyce-Tilman is not pouring calming music on our troubled souls but rather showing how church music, usually associated with inner and outer peace, has in fact been used to perpetuate violence. This is done not simply in the way of being triumphalist but through an exclusion of experience that is considered to be beyond the boundaries of acceptable musical or cultural practice.

You have gathered here some interesting reflections on the area of religion and violence it is difficult to ask you to enjoy some of the deeply disturbing material that you will encounter. The authors ask that you respond, that you be moved to thought and action by what you read since in that way things do become different.

# Religion, Reproduction and Violence against Women

## Rosemary Radford Ruether

A major form of violence to women and abuse of women's bodies through the centuries has been the denial of women's sexual and reproductive agency. A key element of patriarchal control over women from its beginning has been the shaping of women as passive instruments of men's sexual and reproductive demands. In this pattern of thought women's should not be able to decide when and with whom they will have sex and when and under what circumstances they will be impregnated and bear a child. Men have, of course, actively sought to restrict access to the bodies of women they 'own' from other men. Women have been locked up, veiled, interdicted from free movement outside the domestic sphere so their sexuality would be available only to the man who 'owns' and has a right to 'use' them.

The right of sexual access to these women by the owner-male has generally been understood as unrestricted. That is, he should be able to have sex with her whenever he wants, regardless of her own desires and bodily wellbeing. She should not be able to refuse his advances. This is reflected in the traditional legal view that a husband cannot be convicted of raping his wife, since he has a right to sex with her whenever he wants, regardless of her wishes. Likewise, she should not be able to decide when she wants and does not want to get pregnant and to use and demand the use of methods of contraception, although he might do so if he does not want her to get pregnant. Such decisions should belong solely to the man, not the woman in the relationship.

It is sometimes assumed that knowledge of contraception is a recent modern discovery and so this was not an option before the mid-20th century. But this is not the case. Many aboriginal women had knowledge of herbal abortifacients and ways of preventing pregnancy. Ancient Egyptian papyri from 1900–1100 BCE describe a variety of ways of preventing or terminating pregnancy.[1] Arabs knew a primitive type of inter-uterine device used to prevent camels from becoming pregnant on journeys. Knowledge of these methods were widely known to women of different classes, prostitutes and slaves, as well as married matrons, in the Greco-Roman world at the time of the rise of Christianity. It is patriarchal religion, particularly Christianity, that has been the major force for rejecting contraception and abortion in Western society and repressing knowledge and use of such methods of reproductive choice.

The major theologian for arguing these anti-contraceptive views and making them mandatory in Western Christianity has been Augustine (354–430 BCE). As a student in his late teens Augustine took a concubine and lived with her for eleven years while he completed his studies and established his career, as was common for men of his class who preferred a steady sexual companion to visiting prostitutes. They had one son, Adeodatus, shortly after the relationship began and had no further children thereafter. Since Augustine also affiliated at this time with the Manichaean sect that advocated conception—based on their view that as few souls as possible should be allowed to enter bodies through birth[2] —one can assume that he, in fact, practiced some kind of contraceptive sex during these many years in which he was clearly sexually active with his common-law wife, but produced no further children. The method of contraception used by the Manichees was periodic abstinence, based on the infertile period of the woman, ironically the one method that modern Catholicism now allows.[3]

After his conversion of Catholic Christianity, Augustine adopted celibacy as the higher spiritual vocation and repudiated his planned marriage with a socially desirable wife, having previously repudiated his concubine and mother of his child in preparation for this marriage. As a bishop Augustine wrote a number of treatises against the morality of the Manicheans and on marriage, celibacy, sex and reproduction that represent his critical reflections on his own sexual

1.　See John T. Noonan, *Contraception: A History of its Treatment by the Catholic Theologians and Canonists* (Cambridge, MA: Harvard University Press, 1966), pp. 9–10.
2.　Noonan, *Contraception*, pp. 108–26.
3.　Noonan, *Contraception*, p. 120.

experience.[4] For Augustine his inability to control his own sexual urges and his accommodation of his sexual needs through taking a concubine (and, briefly, a second one, while he waited for his marriage) represented his most heinous sin and the manifestation of the 'fallen' condition of 'mankind'. Western sexual ethics has been deeply influenced by this Augustine heritage.

Although Augustine accepted that women's souls were made in the 'image of God' and hence had the capacity for salvation, he believed that in woman's 'feminine' nature, her psychophysical 'nature' as wife and producer of children, woman was created by God to be subordinate to the male. By taking the lead in disobedience to God, Eve violated this subordination and became the cause of the Fall and the entrance of sin into the world. She is then to be doubly subjugated, both as an expression of her originally intended subordination and as punishment for her primacy in sin. The true Christian woman voluntarily accepts her place as one of silence and submission, even in abusive relationships, for example with a husband who beats her, and thereby shows that she is truly on the path of redemption. Only after death, when sex and procreation have been transcended, will women be equal to men according to their spiritual merits. But here on earth women's subordination has not been changed but rather reinforced by the Church.

Augustine also developed a peculiar doctrine of sex and reproduction in relation to his views of original creation and the fall into sin. He believed that in God's intended original creation, in the Garden of Eden, there would have been sex and reproduction, but without either sexual pleasure or the rupture of the women's hymen. Sex between the man and the woman would have been a purely 'rational' act on the man's part, 'like a farmer sowing his seed in a field'. The ejaculation of the man's seed into the woman's womb would not have been accompanied by an organism, or as Augustine would put it 'any filthy rush of sensual pleasure'. Concupiscence or pleasure in the sexual act would have been absent.

Women also would have remained virginal, losing their virginity neither in the sexual act or subsequent birth of children, a peculiar

4.    Augustine's main treatises against the Manicheans are *The Morals of the Manichees* and on *The Morals of the Catholic Church*. In both of these he details his objection to their views of avoiding conception. His major treatise where he lays out his sexual morality are *The Good of Marriage* and *Marriage and Concupiscence*. See Noonan, *Contraception*, pp. 119–39.

view that suggests something less than fully physical about these processes. That virginal sex and reproduction would have been the original and ideal form of human sex is reduplicated in the teaching that Mary, Jesus' mother, reproduced in this way, thereby recovering the original innocence and goodness of Eve.

But this sinless sex and reproduction was not to be. Eve, by taking the initiative in eating the forbidden fruit and persuading her husband, Adam, to eat as well, violated and inverted the proper relation between female and male. Adam sinned too by following his wife's lead, thereby negating his own position as his wife's 'head'. This disobedience to God threw the primal couple into a state of sin. The effects of sin are three-fold, for Augustine. First, humanity lost its original immortality which it would have possessed if it had remained united with the will of God. Secondly, it lost its original freedom to do the will of God. It became entrapped in self-will in which every act is an expression of its own ego. Humans are unable to extricate themselves from this sinful self-will by themselves, but can only be saved by special acts of grace that transform self-will into obedience to God, given only to a limited number of the elect.[5]

Finally, the sexual act was corrupted so that it now can only happen in tandem with concupiscence or sexual pleasure. This involuntary 'rush' of sexual pleasure in the (male) sexual act Augustine identifies with the essence of sin. He thinks of such experiences of 'concupiscence' or sexual organism entirely from a male point of view, quite oblivious as to what women might experience in the sexual act. For Augustine this union of ejaculation and sexual organism marks every sexual act as sinful and as the means by which original sin is transmitted to the child.

The only exception to this rule was Jesus, conceived by God without male participation in a woman who remained virginal in the conception and birth. In late medieval thought Mary also comes to be seen as an exception to the transmission of original sin through the sex act, since although she was conceived by the sexual act of her parents, God intervened in the moment of her conception to impede the transmission of 'sin' along with her father's seed by

5. For Augustine's views on original creation, fall and redemption, see particularly his treatise 'On Original Sin', 'On the Grace of Christ', 'On the Predestination of the Saints', and 'On the Gift of Perseverance'. For a summary of his views, see Rosemary Ruether, *Women and Redemption: A Theological History* (Minneapolis, MN: Fortress Press, 1998), pp. 71–77.

which she was conceived; i.e. the doctrine of the Immaculate Conception.[6]

From these peculiar views Augustine derives his ethics of sex and reproduction. Every sexual act is sinful and transmits sin to the child, even within marriage. The child born in original sin is redeemed in baptism and God's electing grace. Although every sexual act is sinful, the goodness of procreation itself, pronounced by God in the beginning ('And God blessed them, and God said to them, 'be fruitful and multiple and fill the earth': Gen. 1.28) remains, although it has been superceded by the better good of celibacy. Procreation belongs to the order of creation, but celibacy to the higher order of redemption. Ideally, every Christian should choose to be celibate in anticipation of that heavenly order 'where there will be no marrying or giving in marriage' (Lk. 20.35). But for those who are unable to choose this high state, they should marry, as Paul said, 'It is better to marry than to burn (with sexual passion)', 1 Cor. 7.8.

Sex outside of marriage is totally sinful and tantamount to 'pure fornication', having no purpose other than sexual pleasure. Although sex in marriage is also sinful, it is 'forgiven' or only venially sinful, if it is undertaken purely for the purpose of reproduction of children, seeking as much as possible to disdain the resulting sexual pleasure. But this also means that any sex within marriage that seeks to avoid reproduction also is totally sinful and equivalent to fornication. Although Augustine concedes that sexual pleasure might be a secondary good if it keeps the couple loyal to each other and prevents the male from straying after other sexual partners outside of marriage, but it is never a good in itself, but only when there is no active prevention of conception.

From this view derives the basic teaching in Western Christianity that sex is allowable only within heterosexual marriage and so long as the sexual act remains 'open' to conception, (even if conception is not actually possible because of the wife's infertility. This allowance of sex when the married couple is infertile for the sake of 'fidelity' would be the basis of the Catholic Church's allowance in modern times of the contraceptive method of periodic abstinence, in which the couple has sex only during the wife's infertile period).

6. For a description of the development of this doctrine, see Rosemary Ruether, *Goddesses and the Divine Feminine: A Western Religious History* (Berkeley, CA: University of California Press, 2005), pp. 159-64.

Medieval Christianity would reinforce this Augustinian tradition. From the eighth to the twelfth centuries it was monastic penitential literature, intended to guide confessors in the guidance of penitents, that occasionally condemned contraception, mainly forms of potions used by women.[7] However in the late eleventh to the thirteenth centuries canon law revived Augustine's writing on sexuality and enforced strict views that sex was essentially sinful due to its unavoidable 'concupiscence'. It was allowed or venially sinful only in marriage and when no impediment was made to conception. But even here, too much pleasure in sex was sinful. Some writers even suggested that any pleasure in sex was sinful.[8] In the sixteenth and seventeenth centuries this hostile view of sexual pleasure was somewhat alleviated by some Catholic writers who saw sexual pleasure as a secondary good in marriage, but here too only if conception was not impeded.[9]

Despite these long ages of repression, knowledge of contraception did not disappear in the West. Medical treatises from antiquity that contained methods of contraception were preserved in the Arab world and transmitted from there to the West. These treatises were read in medieval medical courses, although these would not have been accessible to most lay people.[10] For ordinary women the major source of information on methods of contraception and abortion would have been through folk medicine, passed down mainly from woman to woman.[11]

In the nineteenth and twentieth centuries in Western Europe there were several developments that elevated anti-contraception from a traditional but not particularly central issue of moral theology to a virtual crusade against women's reproductive agency on the part of the Roman Catholic Church. From the late eighteenth to the second half of the nineteenth centuries there was a rapid decline of the birthrate in France. The birthrate fell to at or below replacement level with average family size below two children per couple. This happened without any major public campaigns in favor of birth control or new methods of contraception, apparently through the

---

7. See Noonan, *Contraception*, pp. 143–70.
8. Noonan, *Contraception*, pp. 173–99.
9. Noonan, *Contraception*, pp. 303–83.
10. Noonan, *Contraception*, pp. 200–31.
11. See Linda Gordon, *Birth Control in America* (New York: Penguin, 1990), pp. 26–46.

widespread adoption of *coitus interruptus*. This change also reflects a widespread assumption of the right of humans to control natural processes and a rising skepticism toward church authority after the French Revolution.[12]

In the late nineteenth and early twentieth centuries public campaigns in favor of birth control began in England and United States, together with a new advocacy of sexual pleasure as a good in itself, particularly women's capacity and right to sexual pleasure. This issue had been traditionally ignored in a religious teaching that focused on the male organism as the source of sexual pleasure (despite the fact that women typically had been condemned by the clergy as dangerously lusty). The new birth control movement was accompanied by a considerable development of new or better methods, such as the diaphragm, thin rubber condoms and spermicidal jellies.

In the United States the birth rate had been declining steadily in the second half of the nineteenth century, even without new methods or a birth control campaign, primarily through the practice of *coitus interruptus* and due to a Victorian women's culture of affected coldness to sexual activity (to which they resorted when they decided that they wanted no more children). By the 1870s, this was causing alarm that the white Anglo-Saxon Protestant middle class birth rate was falling drastically at a time when there was greatly increased immigration of Catholics from Ireland and from Eastern and Southern Europe. Male leaders began to fear that WASP's were losing the 'race war' to more fertile blacks and Catholics. Some medical writers began to claim that higher education was bad for women, causing them to divert their bodily energy to their brains, causing them to become infertile![13] Thus white women's quest for education and cultural advancement was blamed for the falling birth rate of WASP middle class women.

The result of these alarms was the passage of state and federal laws forbidding sending through the mail service any drug or medicine that prevented conception, their importation into the United States, manufacture in the United States or their advertisement through the mail service. Anthony Comstock, a Protestant moral reformer, was a particular promoter of such laws.

12. Noonan, *Contraception*, pp. 387-95.
13. See C.J. Barker-Benfield, *The Horrors of the Half-Known Life: Male Attitudes toward Women's Sexuality in Nineteenth Century America* (New York: W.W. Norton, 1976).

The federal statute with the above provisions, passed 3 March 1873, thus became known as the Comstock law. Margaret Sanger and other promoters of birth control in the early twentieth century were jailed and their clinics closed under these laws. These laws were slowly modified in the 1930s and 40s but not fully repealed until 1958. By this time it was the Catholic hierarchy rather than Protestants that were the primary group trying to maintain such laws in the United States.[14]

Although Protestant churches from the time of the Reformation to 1900 had generally accepted the traditional Augustinian anti-contraceptive view, this was gradually changing in the twentieth century. A major break took place in 1930 when the Lambeth conference of the bishops of the world Anglican Church conceded the morality of the use of contraception within marriage. This decision was stated in a highly conservative manner, advocating abstinence as the 'primary and obvious method', and only where this was not possible were other methods allowed.

This decision by the Anglicans, together with the falling French birthrate and widespread advocacy of birth control worldwide, galvanized the Vatican into action. Although there had been sporadic condemnation by national episcopacies before, the papal encyclical *Casti Connubii*, issued by Pius XI December 31, 1930, was intended to define once and for all the Catholic teaching on this matter. The encyclical reiterated the cumulative Catholic tradition on sexuality and marriage, ruling out not only *coitus interruptus*, but also barrier methods of contraception.[15] Acts of contraception were declared 'intrinsically evil' in every instance.

Such a judgment constitutes an extraordinary example of moral absolutism that goes far beyond judgements against other 'sins'. For example, in the Catholic moral tradition even killing is not seen as intrinsically evil in every case, since there can be mitigating circumstances, such as just war and self-defense, when killing is allowed. Stealing can be justified if there is no other way to obtain food to prevent starvation. Why such absolutism on this matter of contraception? Does the Catholic Church seem to lose its sense of moral perspective when it comes to questions of sexuality?

Total rejection of contraception was modified slightly in 1951 when Pius XII accepted the 'rhythm' method for family planning

14. Noonan, *Contraception*, pp. 412–13.
15. Noonan, *Contraception*, pp. 446–49.

(periodic abstinence through use of the woman's sterile period).[16] Nevertheless, from the 1930's through the 50s a crusade against contraception, including the use of the confessional to query penitents as to their possible use of contraception, came to be seen as characteristic of Catholicism. It was as though the control of marital sexuality at whatever cost to women's health and wellbeing, as well as that of their families, had become the central article of faith and practice for Catholic Christianity.

By 1960 the issue of contraception had become not only obsessive but explosive among Catholics. When the new Pope, John XXIII, announced his plan to assemble a council to 'update' Catholicism, many reform-minded Catholics were determined that the traditional view on contraception be among the teachings to be revised. Four books testifying to dissenting views among Catholic moral theologians and married lay leaders were rushed into print and circulated at the council by 1964. These were *Contraception and Holiness*, edited by Gregory Baum, a Canadian Augustinian theologian; *Contraception and Catholics*, by Louis Dupre of Georgetown University; a collection of essays edited by William Birmingham, editor of the lay journal *Cross Currents*, *What Modern Catholics think about Birth Control*; and a collection of personal testimonies edited by lay theologian Michael Novak, *The Experience of Marriage*.[17]

When the council opened in 1962 doubts about the unchangeability of the traditional teaching was spreading to leading reform bishops, such as William Bekkers, Bishop of s'-Hertogenbosch, Holland, and Cardinal Leo Joseph Suenens of Brussels. With a United Nations conference on population coming up in 1964 John XXIII was concerned that the Catholic Church should have a credible position. When a conservative Franciscan theologian, Ermengildo Lio, prepared a document on marriage, *De Castitate*, for consideration at the council which simply repeated the traditional teaching, Suenens urged the Pope to form a small commission to study the birth control issue in depth.[18] The first six members of the

16. Noonan, *Contraception*, pp. 445–46.
17. These four books all appeared in 1964 and were distributed at the Second Vatican Council.
18. See Robert McClory, *Turning Point: The Inside Story of the Papal Birth Control Commission* (New York: Crossroad, 1995), pp. 38–41.

commission, which included a demographer, a sociologist, an economist, and two medical doctors, were handpicked by Suenens.

When John XXIII died in June, 1963, his successor Paul VI decided to continue and to enlarge the commission. However the commission did not really grasp the possibility of real revision of the traditional teaching until 1964. By that time there had been several decisive interventions on the floor of the council, as well as articles by bishops, such as Thomas Roberts, challenging the tenability of the past views and calling for reform. Paul VI enlarged the commission to 58 members, including five women. The commission had a majority of lay people with representatives from every continent. There were 16 theologians, but most of the group were experts in other areas, doctors, psychologists, demographers and economists.

There were three married couples, from French Canada, France and the United States. The first two were involved in 'natural' family planning clinics, while the U.S. couple, Pat and Patty Crowley, were leaders of the international Christian Family Movement. The Crowleys decided to solicit letters from their CMF constituents on their experience with 'natural' family planning and its effects on their sexual life and family wellbeing. They were aghast at the stories of suffering and hardship which they received, tales of unplanned pregnancies despite careful efforts to observe the 'rules', economic and physical hardship, loss of health, caused by many children closely spaced, feelings of fear of sexuality and resentment against one another which couples felt in trying to enforce the sexual regime of periodic abstinence.

The Crowleys took a hundred of these letters with them to report to the commission as evidence of the problems of the method. Later they would enlarge their inquiry into a systematic survey with over 3000 respondents from eighteen countries worldwide. They received the same responses of ineffectiveness, anxiety and hardship. The French-Canadian couple, Dr Laurent and Mrs. Colette Potvin, surveyed their constituents with much the same results. These reports were all the more impressive, since they did not come from marginal or alienated Catholics, but from those seeking to be the most faithful.

These reports from the actual experiences of married couples with the 'rhythm' method made a strong impact on the assembled celibate male scholars, many of whom had never heard such testimony before. Their own growing doubts about the theoretical tenability of the teaching was deeply reinforced thereby. The commission drafted a final report of their findings in a meeting from April to June of 1966 which accepted the view that if the general orientation of a marriage was open to reproduction, this did not mean that every sexual act had to be open. Within this framework of committed love and desire for children, any method of contraception which is medically and psychologically sound and accessible to the couple is acceptable.

This document, titled 'Responsible Parenthood', passed by a vote of 52 to 4 of the members of the commission. By this time the Pope had added another group of sixteen bishops and cardinals to give final authority to the meeting. The report also passed this group by a vote of 9 to 3 with 3 abstentions. Together with a pastoral introduction explaining how the church's doctrine could 'develop' on this topic, this was the report delivered to the Pope on June 28, 1966.[19]

However the conservative head of the Holy Office, Cardinal Alfredo Ottaviana, together with John Ford, leader of the group of four who had voted against the report, were determined to undermine it with Pope Paul VI. They had drafted a protest against the final report which they then further developed to bring to the Pope as an alternative to the final report. This has been called 'the minority report', but this name is misleading since the commission had specifically decided to submit only one final report that represented the overwhelming majority. Ford and Ottaviana, together with Ermenegildo Lio, author of the original conservative document rejected for discussion at the Council, argued that the authority of the traditional teaching was so constant that it was infallible.[20]

Thus, their position relied not on answering the arguments raised in the Commission, but on the assertion of static, unchangeable teaching authority. They also sought to persuade the Pope that if the Church changed its teaching on this subject, it would lose all credibility as an authoritative teacher for church members. This argument was particularly persuasive for Paul VI who was deeply worried about the question of authority. Apparently it did not occur to these men that *not* changing the teaching, when it had already lost credibility with both Catholic intellectuals and lay people, might

19. McClory, *Turning Point*, pp. 114, 127–29.
20. McClory, *Turning Point*, pp. 110–11, 129–32.

cause a much greater loss of credibility, while acknowledging that the church's teaching could adapt to new knowledge and social conditions might restore confidence in the church's teaching authority.

The confrontation between these two different worldviews is piquantly illustrated by an exchange between the Spanish Jesuit Marcelino Zalba, and Patty Crowley at the close of the commission when it was evident that the majority would recommend change. Zelba commented that if the church changed its teachings on contraception, 'What then with the millions we have sent to hell, if these norms were not valid'. Crowley, astonished that Zelba would see this as a problem, responded, 'Father Zelba, do you really believe that God has carried out all your orders'. A momentary stunned silence, followed by some chuckles, followed this exchange.[21]

This exchange succinctly sums up the crux of the problem in the relationship of church authority to sexual violence against lay people's, especially women's, reproductive agency. Central to this relationship is not concern for the wellbeing of women, children or the maintenance of love between a couple. Rather the key issue for such men is the maintenance of their unquestioned power to define the sexuality of lay people and to exert the ultimate sanctions of eternal hell fire if they do not obey. Implicitly, this assumes not only that they know God's will fully, but also that God is an instrument of their power. They are empowered to define sexual sin and its punishment, and God is at their disposal to carry out their orders. That their definitions may have nothing to do either with the realities of sexual relations or with God was unthinkable for Zelba, while it was obvious to Crowley.

Unfortunately the two years between 28 June 1966 and July, 1968 saw the undoing of three years of careful work to critique the failings in theory and practice of the traditional teaching and to forge an alternative with integrity. A few men working in secret persuaded the Pope to reject the overwhelming majority opinion of his own commission and to reaffirm the traditional teaching without modification. This is what appeared in the encyclical, *Humanae Vitae*, published on 29 July 1968.

The response of the majority members of the commission was one of shock. Several spoke critically of the decision. Charles Curran,

21. McClory, *Turning Point*, p. 122.

moral theologian at Catholic University, who had already faced down an effort to fire him for his mildly dissenting views on birth control, drafted a critique of the encyclical which would eventually be signed by 600 Catholic theologians worldwide. Cardinal O'Boyle of Washington D.C. came down brutally on the dissenters. Curran and 23 other dissenters were suspended, as well as thirty parish priests who expressed their disagreement. Most ended up leaving the priesthood. Worldwide most bishop's conferences responded ambivalently, without fully endorsing the encyclical and speaking vaguely of the rights of conscience, if people did not agree with it.[22]

Many Catholic lay people decided to leave the church, but most decided that they could remain Catholics and not accept this particular teaching. Regular church attendance and financial giving among American Catholics dropped sharply between the late 1960s and 1980s, largely due to the response to the encyclical.[23] Polls taken in subsequently years have showed that 80 per cent of American Catholics believe you could be a good Catholic and not accept this teaching, a fundamental paradigm shift in relation to church teaching authority from that which had prevailed for centuries.[24] The betrayal by the Vatican of its own consultative process was disastrous for its own credibility, leading some church observers to conclude that the encyclical lacks validity because it clearly has not been 'received' by the overwhelming majority of the Catholic people.[25]

The hard-liners who clung to the traditional teaching, theologians, bishops and some lay-people, were not deterred by this overwhelming dissent. They were prepared to see themselves as the 'faithful remnant' who maintained the 'truth' against an apostate world that sought to invade the bastion of church. Although Pope Paul VI remained anguished by his own decision, he was to be followed (after the short papacy of John Paul I), by a Pope that had no doubts. This was the former Archbishop of Krakow, Karol Wojtyla, who became John Paul II in 1978. Wojtyla had actually

22. McClory, *Turning Point,* , pp. 140–46. See also Philip Kaufman, *Why You Can Disagree and Remain a Faithful Catholic* (New York: Crossroads, 1991).

23. McClory, *Turning Point,* p. 148. See also Andrew Greeley, *American Catholics Since the Council: An Unauthorized Report* (Chicago: Thomas More, 1985).

24. This is the argument of Robert Blair Kaiser's book on the Birth Control Commission, *The Politics of Sex and Religion* (Kansas City, MO: Leaven Press, 1985).

25. McClory, *Turning Point,* pp. 149–50.

been one of the sixteen bishops named to the Birth Control Commission in its last phase, but declined to ever attend. Thus he did not participate in any of the conversations that led to an alternative view by the majority.

John Paul II accepted completely the view that the traditional teaching was not only unchangeable but infallible and took every opportunity to extol the teaching upheld in *Humanae Vitae*. Upholding a strict view that every act of contraception is intrinsically evil became a litmus test for advancement to any leadership position in the church as bishop, seminary president or head of a religious order (along with rejection of women's ordination). In his major encyclical on moral theology issued in 1993, *Splendor Veritatis*, not only is the view that every act of contraception is essentially evil upheld, but any dissent or even critical discussion are disallowed.

Addressing himself, not to the Catholic people, but to the Catholic bishops, the Pope decreed that no institution can be called Catholic, whether a school, a medical facility or a counseling service, that does not uphold this teaching. Thus the stage was set for a full scale purge of any dissenters in the church, particularly priest theologians, but not excluding the persecution of the occasional woman religious, layman or woman who held a leadership position in a Catholic institution.

Even though the vast majority of lay Catholics can privately dissent by simply behaving otherwise in their personal sexual lives, while declining to submit to church discipline through the confessional, the Catholic church's teaching nevertheless continues to have enormously deleterious effect through its influence on local, national and global public policy. In many predominately Catholic countries where the Catholic hierarchy maintains a strong influence on political leaders, contraception is not readily accessible and abortion is illegal. This causes women to resort to illegal abortions causing a high level of death and injury due to unsafe abortions.

The Catholic Church maintains a virtual stranglehold on Catholic hospitals, not only in Catholic countries but also in countries such as the United States. As a result not only is abortion not allowed to be done in the hospital, but contraception, including emergency contraception for victims of rape, is not accessible. The Catholic Church also lobbies against family planning programs made available to poor women through Title X of the Public Health Service Act. It is estimated that these publicly supported clinics have helped women prevent 20 million unwanted pregnancies over the last two decades and hence greatly reduce the recourse to abortion.

Family planning funds as a part of U.S. international aid have also been greatly reduced over the last 15 years. George Bush also reimposed the 'Global Gag Rule' on his first day in office in 2001, barring any overseas family planning organization from receiving U.S. family planning funds if it advocates for legal and safe abortion even with its own funds. In reimposing this rule Bush was seeking to 'pay his dues' to Catholic as well as right-wing Protestant political support. Cutting insurance coverage for contraception is also an area where Catholic influence has been felt in state and federal policy.[26]

The Catholic Church has also sought to play a major role in blocking family planning, accessible contraception and legal and safe abortion in international population conferences sponsored by the United Nations. In the UN conference on Population and Development, held in Cairo, Egypt in 1994 the Vatican sought to play a major role in preventing advocacy of any element of sex education, contraception, family planning and safe abortion, in alliance with some of the most reactionary Islamic countries, as well as a handful of conservative representatives of Catholic states, such as Nicaragua and Malta.

International policy on population has greatly changed in the last twenty years, rejecting coercive imposition of population control in preference for broad ethical guidelines that empower women's education and community health. That women's rights, including women's reproductive rights, are an integral part of human rights was a major principle of the draft documents of the conference. The Vatican had no understanding of these changes, but instead tried to appeal to a rhetoric of hostility to Western imperialism and feminism to sway third world and Islam nations against women's reproductive rights.

Disgusted with the obstructionist role played by the Vatican at the Cairo conference and subsequent UN conferences on population and development, some international NGOs, led by the U.S. and Latin American network, Catholics for a Free Choice/Catolicas por el Derecho a Decidir, inaugurated the 'See Change' campaign to promote the idea that the Vatican qua the Holy See should not be

26. See 'Family Planning Under Attack' on catholicsforcontraception.org

represented at the UN as if it were a state, but rather should be present as an NGO like any other religious organization.[27] Although this campaign seems unlikely to succeed any time soon, it has at least spotlighted the negative views and disproportionate power exercised by the Vatican at UN meetings.

A depressing development for those who seek justice for women and all people worldwide has been the reactionary trends in both political and religious movements of the last forty years. In the nineteen sixties and seventies liberation and feminist theologies were rising in the churches, the Catholic church seemed poised on the edge of a major movement toward democratization, and progressive politicians seemed open to support for more just, egalitarian and ecologically sustainable policies, nationally and internationally. The eighties into the twenty-first century has seen a devastatingly reactionary trends in both global religion and politics, led by fundamentalist trends in religion (particularly Catholic, Protestant and Muslim) and heightened militarism and imperialist economic exploitation led by the United States. Significantly, reactionary religion and politics have formed a particularly unholy alliance, represented by George W. Bush's sanctification of imperial war. Women's reproductive rights have become the central targets of this unholy alliance of right wing religion and politics.

The Bush Administration depends heavily on the Christian Right (Protestant and Catholic) for political support and from the first catered to the anti-woman's reproductive rights ideology of the Christian Right in social policy and judicial appointments. In selecting John Ashcroft, a conservative evangelical, as his attorney general, George W. Bush chose a man, who as attorney general and then governor of Missouri opposed contraceptive insurance coverage and had signed a bill declaring that human life begins at conception. As U.S. Attorney General, Ashcroft has continued to follow a hard line not only against abortion but also against forms of contraception. For example, he pressured the U.S. Food and Drug Administration to deny over-the-counter sales of emergency contraception in drug stores, even though this medication is recognized as safe. He has subpoenaed the medical records of women who have had abortions and his Justice Department has argued in court that the law need not honor doctor-patient confidentiality.

27. See www.seechange.org

At the beginning of his first administration Bush also named anti-choice Wisconsin Governor Tommy Thompson Secretary of the Department of Health and Human Services. Thompson opposes abortion and has signed bills declaring that life begins at conception. Bush also has continually appointed anti-choice men and women to represent the United States at international population conferences and as judges to U.S. circuit courts. By appointing a series of such persons to vacancies in circuit courts, he had packed these courts with judges hostile to family planning, women's reproductive rights and abortion, even at the earliest stage of fetal development. Bush also sought to strip contraceptive coverage from the Federal Employees Health Benefit Plan.

Bush reversed U.S. support for the Cairo Agreement (1994 UN conference on Population and Development) that couples and individuals have a right to freely determine the number and spacing of their children and to have the information and the means to do so. Bush sent Christian Right representatives to follow-up UN conferences on population and development. The anti-choice Christian Right delegates appointed to represent the United States at the Asian/Pacific Conference on Population and Development in December 2002 tried to dismantle sex education programs, ban condom use for HIV/AIDs prevention and block programs to prevent and treat unsafe abortions.

Bush has continually supported 'abstinence only' sex education policies and appointed representatives that promote these policies as the only acceptable form of family planning. This has also been applied to HIV/AIDs funding. Patricia Funderburk Ware who supports 'abstinence only' policy to prevent HIV/AIDs was appointed to head the Presidential Advisory Committee on HIV/AIDs. This has also been applied to U.S. funding for AIDs prevention in Africa. In March of 2003, U.S. funding for AIDs prevention in Africa, promised in Bush's State of the Union address in January of that year, was effectively gutted by applying the global 'gag rule' to these funds. No agency that receives funds from the United States can counsel on abortion or contraception, including the use of condoms as a method to avoid contracting AIDs. Two hundred million dollars was cut from funding programs for women's reproductive health in Afghanistan and $3 million in aid for the World Health Organization was frozen to prevent research on mifpristone, a pill that prevents the implantation of a fertilized egg used in emergency contraception.[28]

The rhetoric of the Bush Administration and that of the Catholic and Protestant Christian Right has focused on abortion from the first moment of conception as the great 'crime against humanity' of our time, with very little interest in the fate of the newborn after birth. They pose as the great defenders of the 'innocent fetus'. But it should be obvious that the best method for lowering the level of abortion, as well as preventing injury and death to mothers, is effective and accessible contraception coupled with sexual education that encourages its knowledge and use. But blocking sex education, promoting the fantasy of 'abstinence only' as the only way to prevent unwanted conceptions, and blocking emergency contraception, these religious and political forces are in reality promoting the increase of abortion, together with injury and death to the women who desperately seek abortion under illegal and unsafe conditions.

With the election of Joseph Ratzinger as Pope Benedict XVI there seems little hope for rethinking these disastrous policies in global Catholicism. Ratizinger was John Paul II's hatchet-man in enforcing reactionary views against contraception and abortion. There seems to be little doubt that Ratzinger shares the view that contraception is intrinsically evil in every instance, even in marriage.

He has also been key in sanctioning any theologian who breaks ranks on these teachings. It was Ratzinger who officially stripped Charles Curran of his ecclesiastical permission to teach as a Catholic theologian in August of 1986.While rigidly judgmental about the sexuality of lay people, Ratzinger continues the policies of protecting sexually abusive priests. In a confidential letter to all Catholic bishops Ratzinger ordered that church investigations into child abuse by priests should be kept secret, thus seeking to prevent such allegations from being taken up by courts of law.[29]

The denial of reproductive agency to women is one of the perduring and most egregious forms of violence to women, causing millions of deaths, physical injuries, loss of health and destruction

28. This information on the Bush Administration and reproductive rights comes from J. Berstein, 'The Bush Administration's Assault on Women, a Chononology', *NARAL*, 24 February 2003.

29. See Jamie Doward, 'Pope "obstructed" sex abuse inquiry', *The Observer*, 24 April 2005; see http://observer.guardian.co.uk/international/story/0,6903,1469055,00.html.ying

of human development. By denying women the moral right and the ability to choose when they will have sex and when the sexual act will impregnate them, women's lives are continually destroyed. Desperately seeking abortions under illegal and unsafe conditions, they die or are permanently injured. They are forced to submit to unwanted sex and/or unchosen pregnancies that prevent their educational development and capacity to live fuller lives.

Children are also denied the possibility of being welcomed into families where their birth is chosen and their education and loving care is possible. All these disastrous consequences for women for children, for humanity in general and its relation to world resources are denied by insisting that such passive acceptance of pregnancy and childbearing is woman's 'natural' fate and duty. Religion has been and continues to be the primary source of shaping and enforcing this ideological justification of violence to women.

# Removing the Sexual Cobweb:
## To 'Know' in a Text of Terror

*K. Renato Lings*

Biblical scholarship has not been immune from violence in both its methods and applications. I hope to demonstrate that violence can be done to a text through the rough handling of language and cultural background. In addition we are all aware of how the application of biblical scholarship in theology and ethics can lead to violent treatment of individuals and communities. This is evident in the matter of homosexuality where the texts are constantly referred to when arguing for excluding and dehumanizing theology and church behaviour. I wish to argue that less violence to the text can lead to less excluding theology.

This article sets out to explore the possibility of reading the Hebrew verb ידע in Judges 19 from a non-sexual perspective. It examines the context for the presence of other verbs expressing physical assault and locates two, namely, ענה and עלל. An examination of Hebrew verbal grammar points to the great difficulties created by a sexual interpretation of ידע. The article points out some of the ways in which post-biblical tradition has sown confusion among Bible translators. Similarly, many English renderings of נבלה, the Hebrew term for 'folly', appear to be problematic. A non-sexual interpretation of ידע is likely to lead to a reappraisal of the ways in which the narrative mirrors an ancient androcentric culture. A non-sexual focus enables readers to engage with a highly sophisticated plot with a strong political message.

## Introduction

Judges 19–20 is a narrative which a lot of people find unpalatable. The brutality of this story, in which a young, defenceless woman is mortally wounded through sexual assault, is certainly shocking. This should not surprise us, as it is likely to be an integral part of the original agenda. As I understand the ancient context, this tale was written as a scathing attack on King Saul, his hometown Gibeah, and his tribe Benjamin. The narrator seems to have been in the service of David given that the thrust of the story is clearly pro-Davidic and pro-Judah.[1]

Instead of engaging with this fundamental aspect, however, scholars have for a long time read the story in conjunction with Sodom and Gomorrah.[2] While these two narratives certainly have thematic similarities, they address very different audiences and contexts. One thing they have in common is under-researched, namely, their political nature.[3] Unfortunately, modern Bible translators and commentators tend to depoliticize the plots. One way that this is achieved is by giving cross-references between this narrative, Genesis 19, and Leviticus 18 and 20. Through this subtle procedure, these diverse texts become interlocked within a specific

---

1. According Marc Zvi Brettler, *The Book of Judges* (London and New York: Routledge, 2002), the book has been shaped 'toward particular goals that I would broadly identify as political' (p. 104). Similarly, 'it should be connected to political issues in ancient Israel' (p. 105). The activities described in Judges are 'fundamentally political' (p. 109). The final chapters, of which this narrative is an important part, present a 'strong pro-Davidic political message' and 'a strong anti-Saul basis' (p. 115). A similar view is taken by Yairah Amit in *The Book of Judges: The Art of Editing* (trans. Jonathan Chipman; Leiden, Boston, Köln: E.J. Brill, 1999), p. 342: 'I would accept … viewing the section of the concubine in Gibeah as an attack against the tribe of Benjamin in general, and the town of Gibeah in particular. As such, it serves the anti-Saul and pro-Davidic polemic'. Amit expounds this point on pp. 348–49. Tammi Schneider repeatedly alludes to the David/Saul polemic. See *Judges* (Collegeville, MN: The Liturgical Press, 2000), pp. 169, 246, 249, 258, 269, 271, 274.

2. A recent example is Michael Carden's *Sodomy: A History of a Christian Biblical Myth* (London: Equinox, 2004). See also Steven Greenberg's *Wrestling with God and Men. Homosexuality in the Jewish Tradition* (Madison: University of Wisconsin Press, 2004). See also Weston W. Fields, *Sodom and Gomorrah: History and Motif in Biblical Narrative* (Sheffield: Sheffield Academic Press, 1997). The latter includes a discussion of the destruction of Jericho.

3. Fields, *Sodom and Gomorrah*, p. 71 says of Gibeah: 'the story would never have even been told had not the narrator wanted to make a statement about Gibeah and the Benjaminites'.

sexual agenda.[4] Thus, post-biblical tradition has severed Judges 19–20 from its historical roots.[5] The sophisticated political fiction of Gibeah has been recast in a sexual mould, as a result of which it has been used to stigmatize same-sex relationships.[6] To remove the confusion generated by this sexual cobweb spun over the centuries is going to take a very long time. This essay is intended as an initial modest step in this direction.[7]

In recent decades, the story has been reread from a feminist perspective. Phyllis Trible has provided a suitable label: Gibeah is indeed a *text of terror*.[8] While feminist approaches represent an important innovation, they have not liberated the text from the iron grip in which the sexualization of the Hebrew verb ידע, 'to know', has held it for nearly two millennia.[9] In this essay I pursue

4.  For example, this is the policy of CEV, ESV, GNB, NIV, and NWT. See also Robert A.J. Gagnon, *The Bible and Homosexual Practice: Texts and Hermenentics* (Nashville: Abingdon Press, 2001), pp. 43–44, 91–97.

5.  It is beyond the purview of this essay to present a detailed historical account of this process. It would have to survey the translations offered by all available early Bible versions including the *Septuagint* (Greek), *Targum* (Aramaic), *Peshitta* (Syriac), and *Vulgate* (Latin).

6.  This text is commonly known as the Gibeah Outrage or the Crime of Gibeah. In this essay I use the name of Gibeah to denote the narrative extending from Judges 19.1 to 20.13.

7.  I am grateful to John Banks, Sandra Jacobs, and Eric Kay for their contributions to these pages in the form of very helpful comments and suggestions.

8.  Phyllis Trible, *Texts of Terror: Literary-Feminist Readings of Biblical Narratives* (London: SCM Press, 1984).

9.  Mieke Bal, *Death and Dissymmetry: The Politics of Coherence in the Book of Judges* (Chicago and London: University of Chicago Press, 1988), p. 53 offers a sophisticated version of this notion: 'we are used to interpreting the biblical expression "to know" as a simple, if euphemistic, synonym for sexual intercourse... "to know" does not mean sex, but sex means "to know". The importance of sex is the knowledge which comes as a result... I do not think that the Hebrew expression for sexual intercourse is a euphemism, an expression that softens the crudeness of its content. I think that it is a specification that sharpens the content'. Bal applies this approach to the predicament of the Levite, which she classifies as 'the threat of homosexual rape' (pp. 92, 119, 157–59), and 'this humiliation of him' (p. 93). Cheryl Exum, *Fragmented Women: Feminist (Sub) versions of Biblical Narratives* (Sheffield: Sheffield Academic Press, 1993), concurs: 'the rape of the Levite himself' 'and the threat to rape the man' (p. 182); cf. pp. 183, 186, 195. Schneider, *Judges*, declares that 'to know' is 'a clearly sexual term' and that it refers 'to knowing the man sexually' (pp. 260, 267, 268). She confidently goes on to make an extraordinary assertion: 'since the Hebrew is rather straightforward there are no philological issues to discuss' (p. 262). This contradicts my own research, which sheds light on three facts: (1) the roles of ידע in the Hebrew Bible are under-researched; (2) the issue is of great philological interest; (3) ידע is not a sexual verb.

three goals: (1) to discuss the linguistic reasons why ידע is better understood from a non-sexual perspective; (2) to document some of the distortions wrought by sexual translations of ידע; and (3) to propose a contextual and intertextual reading of Gibeah based on the biblical material. For my philological explorations I am in agreement with the principle expressed by Bal:

> We need to be aware of the insufficiency of our language to account for the past, anchored as it is in a specific ideology of gender-relations' (p. 86). She proposes to "reduce anachronism and the fallacy of taking the present as norm" (ibid.). Not taking these problems into account 'contributes to the slightly condescending view of the past that inspires negative translations of concepts that are neutral or positive in context (p. 88).

On this basis, I have chosen to search for the 'neutral' and 'positive' concepts embedded in the narrative. I assume they can be teased out by examining the nuances of the Hebrew language. I also assume that the narrator is a skilful communicator and that what the protagonists of this story do and say is in accordance with the cultural norms in which they found themselves immersed.

## 'Knowing' versus Sexual Assault

It is worth pointing out that the popular saying 'to know in the biblical sense' is based on a deeply ingrained misunderstanding. The vast majority of modern Bible readers and commentators firmly believe that ידע is a sexual metaphor. However, my current research indicates that there is no philological evidence to underpin this interpretation of ידע.[10] It is based on unverified, long-held assumptions, not on careful scrutiny of the linguistic data. In effect, ידע is not a sexual verb, neither in Judges nor in Genesis. Instead, it sometimes is a technical term to depict the formalization of a marriage contract.[11] In addition, it is important to notice that the Hebrew Bible routinely expresses sexual relations inside and outside

10. My research (as yet unpublished) examines all occurrences of ידע in the books of Genesis and Judges.

11. Such is the case of Gen. 4.1, 4.17, 4.25 (renewed commitment), and 19.8. All these examples suggest a formalized husband/wife scenario. This should be compared with a number of situations in Genesis, in which non-marital sexual relations are described. Often ידע is present, but it clearly plays a non-sexual role, cf. Gen. 19.33, 35; 38.16; 39.8.

of marriage by means of other common verbs, notably בוא + the preposition אל, 'go into', and שכב + את or עם, 'lie down with'. The book of Judges provides two such examples from Samson's relationships with Philistine women, and the book of Genesis contains no fewer than thirty instances.[12]

In short, it is fair to say that the Gibeah text does not deal with sex. It is far more accurate to speak of sexual violence in a context of gender inequality.[13] The narrator expresses this adequately through the use of two Hebrew verbs, namely, ענה, 'humiliate' (19.24, 20.5), and עלל, 'abuse', the latter with the preposition ב attached (19.25). Grammatically speaking, neither verb appears in the basic conjugation known as *Qal* (*Kal*). In this simple conjugation, ענה means 'to be bowed down', often in the sense of being 'oppressed'.[14] To perform an aggressive role, ענה has to move to another space in the Hebrew verbal paradigm. This space is supplied by the intensifying conjugation called *Pi'el* (Intensive Mood). In the process, the meaning of ענה changes to 'oppress' or 'humiliate'. Such is the case of the two occurrences in 19.24 and 20.5. As for עלל, the Hebrew Bible records no instances in the *Qal* Conjugation. However, עלל takes on an aggressive function when operating in several intensifying conjugations. One of these is known as *Hithpa'el* (Reflexive Mood). Here ב + עלל means to 'mock' or 'vex', which matches the occurrence in 19.25.

The situation of ידע is different. In the Gibeah text it occurs twice, namely, in 19.22 and 19.25. The current sexual reading of 'know' in 19.22 is not present in the early sources.[15] It is not reflected in the *Septuagint* (LXX), the first known translation into Greek of the

---

12. In 15.1 Samson wants to 'go into' his wife the Timnite woman. In 16.1 he meets a woman in Gaza to whom he 'goes in'. The 30 sexual occurrences of these verbs in the book of Genesis are divided evenly: 15 of בוא and 15 of שכב.

13. Exum, *Fragmented Women*, p. 181 discusses 'a gender-motivated subtext, not a conscious misogynistic design on the part of the narrator'.

14. Frequently ענה expresses a social concern. In a number of cases, it reflects the nexus between oppression—including psychological affliction—and poverty, cf. Thomas D. Hanks, *God So Loved the Third World. The Bible, the Reformation and Liberation Theologies the Biblical Vocabulary of Oppression* (Mary Knoll, NY: Orbis Books, 1983), pp. 15-17, 37-38, 87, 97, 107. In other words, 'poor' in the context of the Hebrew Bible often equals 'oppressed' and 'humiliated'.

15. The only biblical interpretation of Gibeah is located in Hosea 10.9. The prophetic reflections on the story are embedded in a denunciation of idolatry, wickedness, injustice, and arrogance, cf. Hos. 10.2, 5-8, 12-15.

Hebrew Bible.[16] Similarly, it is absent from the interpretation offered by Josephus.[17] The sexual approach to Gibeah is more recent; it seems to have begun in the early centuries of the Common Era. It is certainly present in Jerome's Latin *Vulgate* translation, in which ידע is rendered *ut abutamur eo*, 'so that we may abuse him'.[18] I see no reason to follow Jerome's lead in this case. In effect, his rendering of ידע is highly problematic in the light of the Hebrew verbal paradigm. In 19.22 the word נדענו, 'we shall know him', is not modified in any way. Apart from the added ligature נ and object suffix ו, 'him', this is the first person plural of ידע in *Qal*, the Simple Conjugation, whose role is factual. In this position, ידע commonly denotes knowledge, understanding, experience, or acquaintance, as well as covenantal and contractual relationships.

In some cases, the Hebrew paradigm admits a certain intensification of ידע. Judges 8.16 provides an obscure example in the *Hiph'il* (Causative) Conjugation. In this passage ידע seems to mean 'cause to know', i.e., 'show'.[19] Another intensifying conjugation is the Cohortative (not represented in Judges), in which ידע means 'investigate'.[20] Apart from these, examples are few and far between. It cannot be overemphasized that ידע in Judges 19 functions within its normal range, which is provided by *Qal*. Jerome's rendering of 19.22 gives the erroneous impression that ידע is intensified to the maximum through a different conjugation. His approach contradicts the logic of Hebrew verbal grammar and stretches ידע beyond recognition.

For all of these reasons, I find it much more accurate to interpret the 'knowing' requested in 19.22 from a non-sexual perspective.

16. For an English version, see *The Septuagint Bible* in the translation of Charles Thomson (1954). The LXX appeared in the third to second centuries BCE, cf. Ángel Sáenz-Badillos, *A History of the Hebrew Language* (Cambridge: Cambridge University Press, 1993), p. 81.

17. Josephus, who lived in the first century CE, did not think the Levite was threatened with sexual assault; cf. Carden *Sodomy*, p. 76; Fields *Sodom and Gomorrah*, p. 63.

18. Jerome prepared his translation in the late fourth and early fifth centuries, cf. Alister E. McGrath, *Historical Theology: An Introduction to the History of Christian Thought* (Oxford: Blackwell Publishing, 1998), p. 146.

19. The meaning of the Hebrew is uncertain. Perhaps it is to be taken as 'teach a lesson', given the hostility underlying the scene. However, this material is too fragile to draw any conclusions from it. A much clearer example of ידע in *Hiph'il* is found in Gen. 41.39, where the meaning is 'make known', 'show', or 'teach'.

20. The book of Genesis provides two occurrences: 18.21 and 19.5.

This has consequences for the way in which the text is read. Below I offer my own reading by means of a literal translation of key parts of the Gibeah narrative.

## A Literal Translation

JUDGES 19

22   … [The] men of the town, who were sons of worthlessness, surrounded the house and were pounding on the door. And they spoke to the elderly master of the house, saying, 'Bring out the man who has come into your house so that we may *know* him' [ונדענו].

23   Out to them went the man, the master of the house, and said to them, 'No, my brothers, please *do not be evil* [אל־תרעו נא]; seeing that this man has come into my house, do no such folly.

24   'Behold, [here are] my unmarried daughter and his concubine. Them let me bring out now, and *humiliate* you them [וענו אותם] and do to them what is good in your eyes. But to this man do nothing. That is folly.'

25   But the men would not listen to him. And the man seized his concubine and pushed [her] out to them. And they *knew* her [וידעו אותה] and *made sport of her* [ויתעללו־בה] all night long …

JUDGES 20

5   'Against me rose the masters of Gibeah. They surrounded the house against me in the night. Me they meant to kill, and my concubine they *humiliated* so that she died.'

### Translating ידע

For many centuries, Bible translators have accepted the post-biblical approach to ידע. It is still the primary gateway to the Gibeah text provided by contemporary English Bible translations. For the two occurrences of ידע in 19.22 and 19.25, I have undertaken a statistical survey of thirty versions. Only nine versions (30 per cent) have respected the neutrality of the Hebrew ידע by rendering it as 'know' in both cases.[21] NKJV has deviated by inserting the word 'carnally' into 19.22. Two versions suggest 'have intercourse' for both occurrences.[22] GWT discards all ambiguity and chooses 'have sex'. Four versions speak of 'sex' or 'intercourse' in 19.22 but take the

21. AB, ASV, ESV, JP17, KJ21, LITV, RSV, TMB, WEB.
22. NJB, NWT.

leap into physical assault in 19.25: 'they forced [her] to have sex/ sexual relations' (NCV, NLB), 'they abused' (NLT), and 'they assaulted' (NEB). Eight versions suggest sex, intimacy, relations or intercourse for 19.22 and 'rape' for 19.25.[23] JB and NAB prefer 'abuse' in 19.22; by contrast, JB opts for 'intercourse' and NAB for 'relations' in 19.25. Finally, three versions offer violent choices for both occurrences, including 'amuse ourselves with', 'take our pleasure with', 'rape', 'took by force', and 'violated'.[24]

This brief overview has made it clear that 70 per cent of modern Bible versions are inclined to read ידע from a sexual perspective in at least one of the two occurrences. Below I have presented this material in two tables. Table One classifies the English translations of ידע in 19.22. The first column is divided into four categories according to the approaches taken by the translators. The Neutrality category leaves the interpretation of ידע open, whereas Ambiguity is not entirely open but contains at least a suggestion of a sexual reading. The Sex category reflects language that is clearly sexual, while Force includes either violent sex or physical assault. The second column shows the diversity among the versions and puts their interpretations in italics. The third and fourth columns represent numerical distribution and percentages based on a total of thirty modern versions, all of which were published after the year 1900.

Table 1 reveals that within the majority of 70 per cent, 27 per cent retain some ambiguity in their renditions of ידע. However, 30

**Table 1:** Modern Approaches to ידע in 19.22

| Category | ידע 19.22 | Versions | Percentage |
|---|---|---|---|
| Neutrality | *Know* | 9 | 30.0 |
| Ambiguity | *Have intercourse* | 5 | 17.0 |
| | *Have relations* | 1 | 3.3 |
| | *Be intimate* | 1 | 3.3 |
| Sex | *Know carnally* | 1 | 3.3 |
| | *Have sex* | 8 | 26.6 |
| Force | *Amuse ourselves with* | 1 | 3.3 |
| | *Take our pleasure with* | 1 | 3.3 |
| | *Abuse* | 2 | 6.6 |
| | *Rape* | 1 | 3.3 |
| Categories: 4 | Variations: 10 | 30 | 100 |

23. CEV, GNB, JP99, NASB, NET, NIV, NRSV, REB.
24. BBE, CCB, JM.

per cent are purely sexual, and 17 per cent have added the notion of aggression as they indicate sexual violence.

Table 2 has a similar structure and presents the ways in which the same versions deal with the second occurrence of ידע in 19.25.

A comparison between Tables One and Two reveals that, as Bible translators move from 19.22 to 19.25, something happens to their perception of ידע. First, the number of translation variations has risen from ten to twelve.[25] Second, a considerable repositioning among the categories has taken place. Thus, the Neutrality category has increased slightly, i.e., from nine to ten versions. However, Ambiguity shows a clear decrease from seven to four versions. A dramatic shift is found in the Sex category, which from nine has dropped to one. Another remarkable feature is the spectacular rise in the Force category. From five versions in Table One, Table Two lists no fewer than fourteen. Conceivably this is a direct consequence of the eruption of sexual violence in 19.25.

This exercise has made it clear that the textual approaches taken by most modern versions differ from the style of the Hebrew narrator. While the latter uses the same verb for both 19.22 and 19.25 and consistently keeps it within the factual *Qal* Conjugation, only nine English translations—30 per cent—follow this path. Such an anomalous situation invites critical reflection. First of all, it would

**Table 2:** Modern Approaches to ידע in 19.25

| Category | ידע 19.25 | Versions | Percentage |
|---|---|---|---|
| Neutrality | *Know* | 10 | 33.3 |
| Ambiguity | *Had intercourse* | 3 | 10.0 |
| | *Had relations* | 1 | 3.3 |
| Sex | *Had sex* | 1 | 3.3 |
| Force | *Forced to have sex* | 1 | 3.3 |
| | *Forced to have sexual relations* | 1 | 3.3 |
| | *They took [her] by force* | 1 | 3.3 |
| | *They abused* | 1 | 3.3 |
| | *They violated* | 1 | 3.3 |
| | *They assaulted* | 1 | 3.3 |
| | *They raped* | 7 | 23.3 |
| | *They wantonly raped* | 1 | 3.3 |
| | [Not translated] | 1 | 3.3 |
| Categories: 4 | Variations: 12 (+ 1) | 30 | 100 |

25. The option of James Moffatt (JM) is missing, which is a regrettable oversight on the translator's part. I have tentatively placed this omission with the Force category given JM's choice of 'rape' for 19.22.

appear that the majority either ignores or disregards the repetition of ידע. From a literary perspective, this is problematic. Biblical Hebrew narrators believe in the rhetorical function of significant repetition.[26] In spite of this, many translators make different choices for the two occurrences; in several cases the choices are very different indeed. Secondly, the impression produced by these two tables is one of widespread contradiction—if not confusion—among the translators. For example, it is far from clear how being 'intimate' can be made interchangeable with 'assaulted'. Moreover, 'knowing' someone in the sense of making their acquaintance is difficult to reconcile with 'wantonly raping' them.

By contrast, the narrator is even-handed throughout. In both cases the context of ידע is highly dramatic, but the Hebrew style remains balanced. The repeated deployment of a neutral verb such as ידע amid the tension of 19.22 and the brutality of 19.25 is, in my view, a deliberate—and successful—form of laconic understatement. The very presence of ידע adds a touch of reality to the prose in both verses. This is how some people may speak when they want to meet a stranger. Even their mistreatment of the concubine contains this element. The fact that they 'knew' her is not a euphemistic comment on the narrator's part. Rather than innuendo, in this passage ידע is likely to echo what is actually being said. In other words, this is indirect speech. The men in the mob are saying to the young woman, *'Come here, baby, let us get to know you'*. What reinforces this hint at churlish merrymaking is the fact that the following verbal construction is ויתעללו־בה. It may well be translated 'they made sport of her' or 'they had fun at her expense'.[27]

26. Cf. Carol Meyers, *Discovering Eve: Ancient Israelite Women in Context* (New York and Oxford: Oxford University Press, 1988), p. 90; Robert Alter, *The World of Biblical Literature* (London: SPCK, 1992), p. 146; Mary Phil Korsak, *At the Start: Genesis Made New* (trans. Mary Phil Korsak; New York: Doubleday, 1993), pp. 223, 235; Everett Fox, *The Five Books of Moses, Genesis, Exodus, Leviticus, Numbers, and Deuteronomy. A New Translation with Introductions, Commentary and Notes* (New York: Schocken Books, 1995), pp. x, xix, xxi–xxii.

27. Modern scholars perceive a straightforward case of massive gang rape. However, the philological nuances suggested by the Hebrew narrator indicate a more complex scenario. The fact that it went on all night seems to indicate some crude form of party with a certain structure to it—and possibly a generous supply of wine. It is imaginable that the concubine was made to play mouse in 'cat and mouse' and similar games. Exactly how an ancient audience would perceive this scene is perhaps a matter of speculation, but the language employed hints that the participants took their pleasure with the young woman in a number of ways, and that sex/rape was a major ingredient.

Regrettably, most translators fail to follow this literary technique. Under the omnipresent influence of post-biblical tradition, they increase the intensity of their language, which often reaches the level of overstatement. It would appear that the horror they are perceiving has shocked them and caused them to resort to a style comparable in the modern world to that of tabloid newspapers. As their emotions take over, translators lose sight of Hebrew grammar. In effect, they have raised their renditions of ידע to levels of intensification unheard of in the verbal paradigm. They have virtually made the neutral ידע interchangeable with the two real carriers of the violence in this text, namely, ענה and עלל. Readers who are not familiar with biblical Hebrew will never suspect that any form of knowing or acquaintance is taking place.

### Translating 'Do not be evil'

There are other reasons for feeling concerned about the careless way in which ידע is treated by translators. Below I look at the response of English Bible versions to the first mention of 'evil' in this story, which takes the form of the verb רעע, 'to be evil'. The phrase is אל־תרעו נא, 'please do not be evil' (19.23). The renditions offered by thirty modern versions are shown in Table 3. I will begin by dividing these thirty versions into several groups according to their word choices. In Group One there are two

Table 3: 'Please do not be evil'

| Version | אל־תרעו נא 19.23 | Version | אל־תרעו נא 19.23 |
|---|---|---|---|
| AB | Do not commit such outrage | NASB | Do not act so wickedly |
| ASV | Do not so wickedly | NCV | Don't be so evil |
| BBE | Do not this evil thing | NEB | Do nothing so wicked |
| CCB | Do not treat him badly | NET | Don't do this wicked thing |
| CEV | Don't commit such a horrible crime | NIV | Don't be so vile |
| ESV | Do not act so wickedly | NJB | Do not be so wicked |
| GNB | Don't do such an evil, immoral thing | NKJV | Do not act so wickedly |
| GWT | Don't do anything so evil | NLB | Don't do such an evil thing |
| JB | Do not commit this crime | NLT | Don't do such an evil thing |
| JM | No vice! | NRSV | Do not act so wickedly |
| JP17 | Do not so wickedly | NWT | Do not do anything wrong |
| JP99 | Do not commit such a wrong | REB | Do nothing so wicked |
| KJ21 | Do not so wickedly | RSV | Do not act so wickedly |
| LITV | Do not do evil | TMB | Do not so wickedly |
| NAB | Do not be so wicked | WEB | Do not act so wickedly |

versions: 'Do not do evil' (LITV) and 'do not do anything wrong' (NWT). LITV has kept very close to the Hebrew, while NWT has added the word 'anything'. This slightly removes it from the original, but the outcome is still recognizable. Both versions are accurate in that they leave the interpretation of the phrase open, which matches the narrative style of this early part of the pericope.

The uniting element in Group Two is the word 'so'. Seventeen versions share this choice: 'Do not so wickedly',[28] 'do not act so wickedly',[29] 'don't do anything so evil' (GWT), 'do nothing so wicked' (NEB, REB), 'do not be so wicked' (NAB, NJB), 'do not be so evil' (NCV), and 'don't be so vile' (NIV).

The presence of 'so' in all these renditions is intriguing. The main question to be raised is what aspect of the Hebrew the word 'so' is meant to reflect. Unfortunately there is no equivalent word in the original sentence. All we find next to 'do no wrong' is the particle נא, which is more adequately translated 'please'. By attaching the adverb 'so' to English adjectives such as 'wicked', 'evil', and 'vile', as well as to the corresponding adverbs, the translators are augmenting the force of these adjectives. 'So wicked' is more forceful than just 'wicked'. In addition, by its very nature 'so' implies that something specific has been identified in the speaker's mind. This indicates a gap between the indefinite, toned-down style of the Ephraimite in the Hebrew text and the strident 'so wicked' and 'so vile'. While the biblical narrator keeps his options open, these English versions seem to have thrown caution to the wind and settled at this early stage for a particular interpretation. The exact nature of this interpretation is not made explicit, but judging from their renditions of ידע in 19.22, they presumably think that the scenario is male–male sexual assault.

Group Three assembles six versions: 'Do not commit such a wrong' (JP99), 'don't do such an evil thing' (NLB, NLT), 'don't do such an evil, immoral thing' (GNB), 'do not commit such outrage' (AB), and 'don't commit such a horrible crime' (CEV). Two features characterize this group. First, all versions have preferred to use a noun such as 'thing', 'wrong', 'outrage', and 'crime'. Second, they have attached the determiner 'such'. JP99 comes close to the original except for the unwarranted 'such'. NLB and NLT offer a similar performance. Here an indefinite 'evil thing' would have sufficed

28. ASV, JP17, KJ21, TMB.
29. ESV, NASB, NKJV, NRSV, RSV, WEB.

on its own, but preceded by 'such' it becomes definite. The insertion of this word is a form of amplification. The tendency is exacerbated in GNB. In addition to 'such', this version has introduced another new element in the form of 'immoral'. In other words, GNB has not translated but engaged in emphatic paraphrase.

For its part, AB sticks to one noun, namely, 'outrage'. However, the problem here is that 'outrage' belongs in a stronger language category than 'wrong' or 'evil thing'. AB's combination of 'commit such outrage' adds an unmistakable element of moral indignation. Again it seems that the translator has made up his mind about what is going on, leaving aside all uncertainty. Unfortunately, he is also moving ahead of the Hebrew narrator. Finally, CEV cements the tendency to paraphrase. While the word 'commit' is not too far removed from the style of the Hebrew, the rest of CEV's phrase stands out as an exaggeration. First of all, it is inappropriate to use 'such' here. Second, it is unclear why the word 'horrible' has been inserted. Third, the word 'crime' is considerably stronger than either 'wrong' or 'bad thing', as it has legal connotations. In the original text no specific 'crime' is being discussed at this stage. In CEV, however, it is on the verge of taking place. Taken as a whole, Group Three seems to have made up its mind: the mob of Gibeah is bent on male–male rape.

Group Four contains three versions: 'Do not this evil thing' (BBE), 'don't do this wicked thing' (NET), and 'do not commit this crime' (JB). Many of the previous considerations apply to this group. The main characteristic is the attachment of the demonstrative 'this'. The effect it has on the sentence is similar to the distorting role of 'such' in Group Three. The performance of BBE and NET would be perfectly adequate without the intrusive 'this'. However, its presence lends the impression that the translators have a specific act in mind. This procedure clearly limits the scope for interpretation. JB takes the problem a step further. Not only does the word 'this' create difficulties, but also the word 'crime' is loaded. As long as the narrator has not yet defined the wrong perceived by the Ephraimite — but not by a first-time reader — there is no justification for a conscientious translator to jump to conclusions. Clearly JB is not attuned to the deliberate ambiguity created by the Hebrew narrator.

Group Five has only two versions: 'Do not treat him badly' (CCB), and 'no vice!' (JM). In the case of CCB, it is an open question how the word 'him' got into the equation. This choice raises two important grammatical questions. The Hebrew verb תרעו is intransitive. In other words, it takes no direct object, unlike the transitive English verb 'treat'. In addition, the text has no pronoun or suffix meaning 'him'. The logical conclusion is that CCB invented it. The underlying reason for the anomaly seems to be the common sexualization of ידע. This very problem is clearly also at the heart of James Moffatt's version. Instead of translating, JM has opted for a revealing paraphrase. As the words 'no vice!' are put into the Ephraimite's mouth, it turns him into a prudish moralizer. This jars with the no-nonsense style of the original. While JM makes his host sound worried about male–male sex, the Hebrew narrator suggests a concern for social etiquette, fairness, and common sense.

The above survey has shown that only two out of thirty Bible versions have remained true to the original, namely, LITV and NWT. JM has resorted to all-out paraphrase. The remaining twenty-seven versions have gone the way of amplification. This amounts to 90 per cent of the total. Except for CCB it has become clear that to render the Hebrew phrase אל־תרעו נא, the most popular approach is to insert a determiner or demonstrative in the form of 'so', 'such', or 'this'. Undoubtedly these English versions misinterpret the original in several ways. First, to buttress a flawed interpretation they graft a textual element that does not belong there. Second, this extraneous element transforms an earnest, but fairly subdued, Hebrew exhortation into a moralistic exclamation. The latter betrays the translators' horror at the threat of male–male sexual assault, which in fact is non-existent. The end result is deeply problematic. The near-explicit message with which unsuspecting readers are left differs considerably from the cryptic ambiguity of the original. In this manner, the post-biblical distortion is perpetuated.

## Translating 'Folly'

The third and final translation problem I will discuss in relation to the sexualization of ידי in Judges 19 is in both verses 23 and 24. This is the significant repetition of the crucial Hebrew term נבלה, which is 'foolishness', 'folly', or 'senselessness'. The root from which this word derives is נבל, 'fool'. The latter term particularly denotes the unwise person who may also be ignorant, thick-headed, indiscreet, and hot-tempered. Frequently the Hebrew Bible describes foolishness and folly as an ethical concept related to ungodliness and injustice.[30]

Both terms are defined in the book of Samuel. Referring to her husband Naval (נבל), a woman named Abigail explains to David: נבל שמו ונבלה עמו, 'Fool is his name, and folly is with him' (1 Sam. 25.25). This example shows that both נבל and נבלה are used in a sense that is derogatory, but not excessively so. They fall within the admissible range when it comes to characterizing a close family member. Another significant example is found in 2 Sam. 13.11-14. This is the scene in which David's daughter Tamar struggles to convince her rapist of the foolishness—נבלה—of his intent. Thus she tells him: 'do not do such folly' (v. 12). Moreover, she reminds him that, if he goes ahead, this act of iniquity will change his reputation and make him כאחד הנבלים בישראל, 'like one of the fools in Israel'. As she uses both נבל and נבלה, it is clear that her language does not reflect visceral horror at the looming disgrace. Instead, Tamar adopts an intelligent strategy based on arguments. Physically she is weaker than Amnon (v. 14). She instinctively realizes that the only forms of defence available to her are reasoning and persuasion. Unfortunately for her—and for himself—Amnon is unwise enough to behave like one of the fools in Israel. In effect, this act of folly will cost him his life.[31]

In other words, these are common terms which do not belong at the more extreme end of the spectrum. The fact that both Tamar and the old Ephraimite employ נבלה indicates that the word fits within a category that makes it suitable for negotiation. In their respective predicaments, both are the underdogs and they know it. So they wisely try to appease their opponents by convincing them of the folly of their intent. At the same time, they certainly want to avoid antagonizing them by insulting them with excessively strong, moralistic language. This fact is important to bear in mind for my examination of English Bible versions below.

In the context of 19.23-24, I have commented upon the puzzle that, while being told that the 'sons of worthlessness' are behaving foolishly, we are not told of the exact nature of the alleged folly. Thanks to the artful construction of the narrative, it is advisable to remain open to the possibility that this curious detail may well be

30. Cf. Kenneth D. Mulzac, 'Fool' in *Eerdmans Dictionary of the Bible* (Knotsville: Eerdmans, 2000), pp. 467–68.
31. See 2 Sam. 13.22–29.

part of the literary refinement of a sophisticated writer. Often what is left unresolved can be as effective—or even more so—than a direct statement.

The repetition of נבלה indicates its rhetorical importance. First, the elderly Ephraimite uses this word emphatically. He is trying to impress on the townsmen that what they are after makes no sense. Second, even if modern readers do not fully understand, he is likely to be readily understood by the mob of Gibeah. Indeed, the word נבלה is an integral part of the Ephraimite's persuasion technique. He wants to convince the mob to act neither badly nor foolishly. Such vocabulary seems appropriate for the delicate situation the elderly man is in. His fairly diplomatic choice of words reveals that while he opposes the demand with which he has been presented, he wishes to remain on speaking terms with the people he is addressing. After all, an incomer is vulnerable and has to make sure that his continued presence in the city is acceptable.

Below I am going to examine two significant features of English Bible versions. First, I am interested in evaluating the extent to which the translators attain the same literary nuances for נבלה as those suggested by the Hebrew narrator. Second, I want to reach a clear impression of the degrees of consistency attained by the translators. The thirty English renditions of the dual occurrence of נבלה are shown in Table Four.

A close inspection soon makes it clear that the group following the lead of the original is small. There are only four versions. The choices made are 'folly' (ASV, WEB), 'act of folly' (NASB), and 'godless thing' (GWT). To include GWT here seems justified. In the world of the Hebrew Bible, the concepts of 'senseless' and 'godless' often go together. All four versions enjoy the benefit of rhetorical consistency as they reflect the significant repetition of the original.

Only one additional version, namely, KJ21, has opted for the literal translation 'folly' in 19.23. However, its style changes in 19.24 to 'vile thing', which is far more moralistic. From here onwards, sadly, all literal translation ends. It might be argued that NWT has retained a trace of נבלה in its two choices, where at least 'folly' and 'foolish thing' are represented. Unfortunately, however, this is outweighed by the emotional edge of the added adjective 'disgraceful'. In all other cases, the translators have distanced themselves from נבלה and have entered into the realm of another noun, namely, רעה, 'evil' or 'wickedness'. The latter does appear in

**Table 4:** 'Folly'

| Versions ⇩ | נְבָלָה 19.23 | נְבָלָה 19.24 |
|---|---|---|
| AB | Senseless disgrace | Senselessly disgraceful thing |
| ASV | Folly | Folly |
| BBE | Wrong | Thing of shame |
| CCB | *Evil* | *[Not translated]* |
| CEV | *[Not translated]* | *Horrible thing* |
| ESV | Vile thing | Outrageous thing |
| GNB | Evil, immoral thing | Awful thing |
| GWT | Godless thing | Godless thing |
| JB | Infamy | Infamy |
| JM | Wanton crime | So wanton a crime |
| JP17 | Wanton deed | Wanton thing |
| JP99 | Outrage | Outrageous thing |
| KJ21 | Folly | Vile thing |
| LITV | Grave sin | Wicked thing |
| NAB | Crime | Wanton crime |
| NASB | Act of folly | Act of folly |
| NCV | Terrible thing | Terrible thing |
| NEB | Outrage | Outrage |
| NET | Disgraceful thing | Disgraceful thing |
| NIV | Disgraceful thing | Disgraceful thing |
| NJB | Infamy | Infamy |
| NKJV | Outrage | Vile thing |
| NLB | Terrible thing | Terrible thing |
| NLT | Shameful | Shameful thing |
| NRSV | Vile thing | Vile thing |
| NWT | Disgraceful folly | Disgraceful, foolish thing |
| REB | Outrage | Outrage |
| RSV | Vile thing | Vile thing |
| TMB | Folly | Vile thin |
| WEB | Folly | Folly |

the text, but not until the different context of 20.12 and 13. All we find in 19.23 and 24 is נבלה.

Among the versions in Table Four the dominant tone is judgmental. Many of the terms listed express outrage and horror. However, none is appropriate for an isolated, beleaguered sojourner who is struggling to negotiate a way out of an acute crisis. The often-vehement language that the versions are putting into his mouth would perhaps be fitting for use by the prosecution in courtroom proceedings. Such is indeed the scenario in 20.1-13, in which נבלה occurs twice (20.6, 10) in reference to the actual crime perpetrated in 19.25. But for an elderly Ephraimite facing overwhelming odds, to use such challenging words is not only unrealistic but also out of character. Throughout this narrative, the style of the Hebrew narrator is slightly understated, which is part of the refinement. By contrast, the vast majority of modern translators have used overstatement. Evidently their linguistic analysis is blurred by the sexual cobweb in which tradition has shrouded ידע. In 19.23-24 the translators do not appear to see the word נבלה. What must be on their minds is an imaginary crime of male–male rape that never happened, neither here in this text nor anywhere in the Bible.

Not only have all traces of 'folly' mysteriously disappeared in most cases. To make matters worse, the ways in which many translators treat נבלה are incongruous. About half of the versions represented in Table Four propose two different renditions of one Hebrew term. In other words, where the narrator is consistent, these versions are inconsistent. Given the importance of significant repetition in Classical Hebrew, this deviation from the original is both remarkable and regrettable.

Undoubtedly, נבלה is treated very carelessly. While a fair number of these versions achieve some form of consistency, many betray a rather strong emotional involvement on the translator's part. Such emotion is not exactly present in the original 'folly'. What is worse, the translators make the resident alien of Gibeah sound like a prudish moralizer, which in the Hebrew narrative he is not. He is a man who is trying to appease his fellow-citizens, while he disagrees with their intent. The very strong language offered by some Bible versions lacks the firm, but subdued, authenticity that characterizes the original.

## The Post-biblical Approach

Returning to the crucial role played by ידע, the above explorations have demonstrated that the sexual cobweb is the cause of most of the translation problems detected so far. Indeed, to use another analogy, the post-biblical approach to ידע may be likened to the ice sheet covering a frozen lake. It only allows the observer to see one aspect of the lake and restricts the options for manoeuvring on it. To explore what is under the surface takes an effort.

The post-biblical approach has assigned a role to ידע for which it is not equipped. Historically, male same-sex relations have been read into this text despite the fact that ידע has nothing to contribute to any debate on homosexuality. What is more, the post-biblical agenda is completely sexual, and the unnamed protagonists are treated as historical individuals. In particular, the Levite has often been described in very unflattering terms for his alleged role in the crime. He is criticized for being callous and cruel, and there have been hints at voyeurism and sadism.[32] To a lesser extent the host (the Ephraimite) has received similar treatment.[33] Little information is given in the text about the concubine, but her story is treated as factual.[34] Her father is disliked because he lets his daughter depart with the Levite for the second time. The father's hospitality toward the Levite is regarded as excessive, and the Levite is criticized for being too easily manipulated by such extravagant generosity.[35]

Likewise, the dramatic nightly scene in Gibeah is viewed as an example of uncontrollable male lust which is sated thanks to the dubious complicity of the Ephraimite and the Levite. The main victim is a woman who, in the view of modern commentators, is betrayed by the men who are supposed to offer her protection.[36] The narrator is regarded with suspicion. He is likely to be male, and his treatment of the concubine causes discomfort.[37] In summary, modern readers feel revulsion at what they perceive as a horror story, whose main purpose is to intimidate women.[38] Table Five shows some of the key problems generated by the sex/violence approach to ידע in the post-biblical era.

32. Bal, *Death and Dissymmetry*, pp. 55, 124–26, 236; *Fragmented Women*, p. 196.

33. Trible, Texts of Terror, p. 41.

34. Exum, *Fragmented Women*, p. 201: 'my first step has been to claim that a crime has been committed. Proving it depends upon taking the woman's word for it'. Schneider, *Judges*, does not entertain the possibility of fiction despite the fact that 'neither protagonist's name was important enough to record' (p. 268), and 'the characters...are nameless, with relationships to each other which are confused and difficult to understand with any precision' (p. 269). Bal, *Death and Dissymmetry*, p. 29, concedes that 'women who are here "taken and given" cannot be considered full characters in the narratological sense. They do not act, they do not have the slightest subject-position, and they are not individualized'.

35. Bal, *Death and Dissymmetry*, p. 166.

36. Bal, *Death and Dissymmetry*, pp. 61, 92, 93, 119, 123, 125, 184, 185; Exum *Fragmented Women*, p. 195. Schneider, *Judges*, pp. 261, 261, 268, 269. Exum 1993 also views the concubine's fate as a form of punishment; cf. pp. 179, 181, 183, 189, 200.

37. Exum, *Fragmented Women*, pp. 187, 188, 191.

38. Exum, *Fragmented Women*, pp. 179, 181, 183, 189, 190, 192.

**Table 5:** The Post-biblical Approach to ידע

| *Focus, Characteristics, and Outcome* |
| --- |
| ידע as agent of sex and violence |
| Crucial verb: ידע |
| Male homosexuality |
| A sexual agenda |
| Individuals |
| The Levite |
| The Ephraimite |
| The concubine and her father |
| A bossy man of Bethlehem |
| The Levite versus the girl's father |
| Male lust |
| Men versus women (gender) |
| The narrator |
| Literary manipulation |
| Horror and revulsion |

Among commentators, only sporadically are some of the risks attached to the post-biblical approach acknowledged. One such risk factor is the fomenting of hostility to the Hebrew Bible. Many Bible readers are disgusted at what they perceive as gratuitous sexual cruelty, which leads them to reject the Hebrew Scriptures. Furthermore, from this position to anti-Jewish sentiment there is but a short distance.[39]

It is fair to say that, since the day of its composition, four distinct groups have been at the receiving end of the terror of Gibeah. The first to be targeted were the people of Benjamin. Second, the terrible fate of the concubine also made it oppressive of women. Third, in post-biblical times gay men became the primary target. As I write, anti-gay readings are still very common.[40] In recent years, a fourth category has been added. Two of the male protagonists in

39. Bal, *Death and Dissymmetry*, p. 159 speaks of 'cheap indignation motivated by anachronistic ethnocentrism'. Müllner 1999 with: Ilse Mullner, 'Lethal Differences: Sexual Violence as Violence Against Others in Judges 19' in Athalya Brenner (ed.), Judges: A Feminist Companion to the Bible (Sheffield: Sheffield Academic Press, 1999), p. 129 observes that 'texts from the Jewish tradition are sometimes used as sole historical reference, thus functioning as scapegoats'. Similarly, 'both the selection and the interpretation of the texts reflect the anti-Judaic pattern which misjudges the Judaic tradition as particularly patriarchal' (p. 130). Müllner points out 'the difference between narration and history'. Not taking this into account betrays 'a basic lack of understanding about interpretive pluralism in Jewish traditions'.

40. Cf. Gagnon, *The Bible and Homosexual Practice*, pp. 74, 91 n. 25.

particular — the travelling Levite and his host in the town of Gibeah, the old Ephraimite — are being singled out as villains.[41]

The latter process seems to be the outcome of the modern Western propensity to read biblical narratives as stories of individuals. This causes the main focus to be on the perceived villains and victims. Lyn Bechtel (1998) has noticed the discrepancies between the Hebrew Scriptures and a large number of modern interpreters (pp. 108, 126).[42] She explains it by locating the Bible within a communal culture, whereas modern western approaches are coloured by the prevailing individualism (pp. 109-112).[43] This insight is based on the fact that the Hebrew writers are primarily concerned with communities such as tribes, cities, and nations, while today's scholars are much more likely to engage with the protagonists. According to Bechtel, 'the shift away from group orientation and toward individual orientation' occurred in the Greco-Roman period. Carol Meyers has observed the same phenomenon: 'The contemporary focus of western life on the individual … is one crucial area of distinction between the biblical mindset and our own'.[44]

## Towards a Biblical Approach to Gibeah

Returning to the image of the frozen lake, if the ice crust is removed, the underlying water comes to light and a more complete picture of the lake is brought about. Water is more versatile than ice and can be accessed in a number of different ways. In addition, it allows for an in-depth exploration of the lake. If an analogous procedure is applied to Judges 19, the panorama changes. As soon as ידע is allowed to play its original non-sexual and non-violent role, a

41. Alter, *The World of Biblical Literature*, p. 113: 'the wayfaring Levite behaves like anything but an angel'. See also Bal, *Death and Dissymmetry*, pp. 47, 91–93, 119, 125–26, 157, 159, 184–85, 189–90, 236; Exum, *Fragmented Women*, pp. 179, 181, 183, 186, 191, 196–97; Schneider, *Judges*, pp. 247, 259–64, 266–69, 271, 273, 275. The Ephraimite is criticized by Bal, *Death and Dissymmetry*, pp. 92–93, 119–20; Exum, *Fragmented Women*, p. 183; Schneider, *Judges*, p. 275.

42. Lyn Bechtel, 'A Feminist Reading of Genesis 19:1–11', in Brenner *Genesis: A Feminist Companion to the Bible* (Sheffield: Sheffield Academic Press, 1998), pp. 108–28.

43. See also Lyn Bechtel, 'Shame', in Letty M. Russell and Shannin Clarkson (eds.), Dictionary of Feminist Theologies (London: Mowbray), pp. 259–60, where she mentions 'group-oriented societies such as ancient Israel' (p. 260).

44. Meyers, *Discovering Eve*, p. 71.

number of issues come to the surface, which are likely to be among the ones addressed at the time of composition.

First of all, when יד is restored to its basic function, it can be appreciated for the ways in which it interacts with the two verbs on which the violent part of the action hinges. The heterosexual assault can be seen as the driving force behind the mob scene in Gibeah. The narrator's political agenda involves several tribes of Israel. In biblical times, the story seems to have dealt with conflicts between the communities to which the mythological or fictional characters belonged. In my view it makes good sense to read Judges 19-20 as a political pamphlet in which the polemic is encoded in narrative form. Thus, the Levite symbolizes the landless tribe of Levi, and the old sojourner embodies the northern tribe of Ephraim.[45] The narrator turns Gibeah—hometown of Saul—into an image of the tribe of Benjamin. For her part, the concubine— who is from Bethlehem, hometown of David—represents the tribe of Judah. The Benjaminites (Saul) are portrayed as villains, whereas Judah (David) is cast in the dual role of victim (the concubine) and appointed avenger.[46]

The concubine's father and the Ephraimite represent the ancient virtue of patriarchal hospitality. In some cases this consisted in a contest of wills, in which the host would seek to prevail upon his guest to make him stay as long as possible, and at other times it would mean going to extremes to protect him.[47] The towns of Bethlehem and Gibeah are portrayed as contrasts. Bethlehem illustrates the concepts of generosity and hospitality in opposition to Gibeah, which is depicted as the emblem of iniquity. This makes Gibeah and Benjamin comparable to the Canaanites in that their conduct is viewed as unworthy of Israelites.

Similarly, the social problems generated by an androcentric culture come to the forefront, including the ways in which women become pawns at the hands of the men to whom they belong. The

45. Müllner, 'Lethal Differences', p. 136 draws attention to the fact that the social situation of the Levite is in many ways comparable to that of the Ephraimite. His is 'a state of relative powerlessness'. Both men are incomers in someone else's territory (19.1, 16).

46. Judah leads the battle against Gibeah, cf. 20.18.

47. 19.3-9, 17-24. As stated by Exum, *Fragmented Women*, p. 182, this concern overshadows any other, including gender aspects: 'the gender issue becomes submerged in issues of concern to men: hospitality and codes of behaviour'.

literary technique displayed in the text can be appreciated, including the numerous inter-textual references to the books of Genesis, Samuel, and Chronicles. Likewise, the shocking effect that the Gibeah outrage still has on modern readers is another testimony to the literary skills of an educated, sophisticated narrator.

What follows is an interpretation of some aspects of the story as I perceive them. My approach endeavours to be biblical in the sense of showing respect for the narrator's style and concerns. In addition to its political symbolism, Gibeah also reveals important aspects of social conventions and male psychology in an androcentric culture.[48] I have already discussed the Hebrew phrase אל־תרעו נא. The speaker is the old Ephraimite. He has taken the wayfaring Levite into his house for the night along with his two travel companions. In the phrase 'do not act badly, please', or 'please do not be evil', there is no clear indication as to what kind of wrongdoing the Ephraimite is noticing. However, his language indicates that he takes the situation very seriously. The way in which he chooses his words suggests several possible interpretations.

First, the host may be objecting to the request for having the Levite brought outside the house.[49] This he is loath to do given that he himself has invited the Levite in (19.20-21). For a man of honour in the patriarchal sense, it would be shameful to expel a male guest at any time, and even more so late in the evening, given the dangers associated with dark streets.[50] Second, he is perhaps unwilling to expose the Levite to a potentially unpleasant encounter with some men of questionable reputation. They have just been characterized as 'sons of worthlessness' (19.22). Their desire to 'know' the stranger is ambiguous and possibly ominous.

Both of these considerations are likely to be on the Ephraimite's mind. He certainly refuses to co-operate with these dubious citizens

---

48. The terms 'patriarchy' and 'patriarchal' have been the object of considerable debate. In relation to ancient Israel, Meyers recommends 'androcentric', which connotes the sense of 'male centred' or 'male dominated' (*Discovering Eve*, pp. 24, 39, 43, 169). Exum uses 'androcentric' in her discussion of Gibeah, see *Fragmented Women*, pp. 177 and 179.

49. I am indebted to Elizabeth Duke for this insight.

50. Fields comments on the 'lack of protection in public places, especially at night' (*Sodom and Gomorrah*, p. 99). Similarly, 'night' spells 'danger' (p. 103). By letting this episode occur during the night, 'the narrator evokes an ominous and sinister feeling in his audience' (p. 107). In effect, 'night and violence, danger and darkness were inseparably joined' (p. 108).

of Gibeah. As head of a household, he feels the need to assert himself and make the point that the Levite is under his care. Any dealings with the visitor have to be brokered by the host. At the same time, the Ephraimite treads carefully. As an immigrant his legal status is likely to be precarious. Numerically he, his household and his guests in combination are no match for the mob. The number of men outside is unspecified, but if they are able to surround the house (19.22), they are likely to outnumber the people inside. From the Ephraimite's perspective, there is no point in trying to defend the integrity of his home through physical force. If a scuffle should ensue, he will be the loser. In other words, it benefits him to get along with these townsmen, and the best he can do is try to weather the storm by negotiating a solution.

While he disagrees with their intent, the Ephraimite is at pains to remain on speaking terms with the men at his front door. So he addresses them courteously as אחי, 'brothers'. In contrast to the rude directness of their language, he uses the polite word נא, 'please'. Wisely he does not scold them, as this would be counterproductive, but shows restraint as he exhorts them not to be 'evil' or to do no 'wrong'. Thus, the moderate tone of the Ephraimite's language is part of his strategy. He is acutely aware of being under pressure. There are no law enforcement officials around, to whom he might appeal for protection. He is left to his own devices. From that disadvantageous position he tries to strike a deal.

Up to this point only a few of the elements that play a part in this tense situation have been introduced. The narrator uses a minimalist technique that may be described as gradual or deferred disclosure. The information that readers need for completing the picture has so far been partial. The missing element is not provided until 20.5. Here it becomes clear why the riffraff of Gibeah demand to speak to the Levite. Their agenda is simple: they want the concubine. She may well be an attractive woman. They have all seen her in the public square upon her arrival. Because she belongs to him they need to talk to the Levite, her lord and master. Now, finally, the missing bit of the puzzle slips into place: these men of Gibeah are threatening to kill him if he does not let them take their pleasure with the concubine.

This is an indirect allusion, by which the narrator deftly compares Gibeah—an Israelite city—with the Egyptians and Philistines mentioned in Genesis. On two occasions Abraham chooses to pass

Sarah off as his sister and use her as good-will ambassador to the local king. His son Isaac does the same with his wife Rebekah.[51] In each case the men fear that they may be killed because of the beauty of their wives. The Gibeah narrator has picked up this theme from Genesis and developed it.[52] In fact, this is the only incident in the Hebrew Bible in which it is taken to its ultimate consequences. Both Sarah and Rebekah enjoy divine protection, thanks to their being involved in the covenant between YHWH and their husbands. By contrast, while the Levite may have priestly status, he is not Abraham, and neither he nor his anonymous concubine has received any divine promise.

In this manner, the Gibeah narrative offers the twist of letting the 'sons of worthlessness' behave like non-Israelites. The Levite has sought shelter in Gibeah to avoid the risk of spending the night with the people of Jebus, a Canaanite city (19.11-14). However, this precautionary measure has been of no avail. The implication is that the men of Gibeah conduct themselves in a manner unworthy of Israel.[53] The full nature of their challenge to the Levite is never stated directly, but the death threat emerges through his brief summary of events in 20.5. This explains why the old Ephraimite takes the unusual step of involving his young daughter. Conscious of his hosting responsibilities, he is also in solidarity with the Levite, with whom he has just bonded thanks to their common geographical background in the hill country of Ephraim.[54] This sentiment may well be augmented by his respect for the Levite's priestly status. If his guest has to make such a tremendous sacrifice, his sense of patriarchal honour urges the Ephraimite to make a similar gesture. He cannot prevent the disaster, but he can try to mitigate the plight of his guests to the best of his ability. He does not want the concubine to face the threatening mob alone. From his beleaguered perspective, the only conceivable way forward is to let his own household carry

---

51. Gen. 12.10–20; 20.1–18; 26.6–11.

52. Alter, *Biblical Literature*, p. 112 has noted the linguistic interconnectedness of Judges 19 and parts of Genesis: 'the only plausible inference is that the author of Judges 19 had a minute textual familiarity with Genesis'. While Alter focuses specifically on Sodom and Gomorrah, I posit that such familiarity extends to the entire Abraham cycle in Genesis.

53. Judg. 19.30; 20.6, 10, 13.

54. 19.1, 16, 18.

part of the burden. So he causes his daughter to be at the concubine's side and proposes to let the two of them leave the house together.

This procedure may seem outlandish to modern observers, but perhaps in an ancient androcentric culture it makes sense. At the same time, the Ephraimite is fully aware that this enterprise comes at a cost. As he tells the rabble outside to 'humiliate' the two women (19.24), he is not simply extending a blank cheque for them to satiate their unbridled lust. His choice of words implies that he is pointing out some of the consequences. In fact, he is reminding these men of Gibeah that rape will lead to social degradation for both victims. A defiled concubine is likely to be considered unsuitable for normal married life.[55] If the host's daughter is violated, her humiliated condition will make it impossible to find her a husband.

The book of Samuel contains illustrative examples of both situations. When King David's daughter Tamar becomes a rape victim, it is described three times through the verb ענה as her 'humiliation'.[56] The outcome is dramatic. From being a beautiful, desirable young woman she is transformed overnight into a mere phantom. Following the moment of her misfortune, she exits to become a nonentity. All we know about the rest of her life is that it bears the marks of tragedy:

> So Tamar remained, a desolate woman, in her brother Absalom's house.[57]

The other example begins in 2 Sam. 15. Faced with the uprising of his son Absalom, David decides to flee, leaving ten concubines behind to look after the royal house in Jerusalem (15.16). It seems clear that these servant wives are given this role because they are expendable. If anything happens to them, it will not be a major disaster. Soon thereafter, Absalom takes possession of Jerusalem. His chief adviser also encourages him to take carnal possession of his father's concubines:

> So they pitched a tent for Absalom upon the roof; and Absalom went in to his father's concubines in the sight of all Israel.[58]

55. Bal, *Death and Dissymmetry*, pp. 158, 185. Exum, *Fragmented Women*, p. 181 asks: 'what is the husband to do with his damaged goods?'
56. 2 Sam. 13.12, 14, 22.
57. 2 Sam. 13.20 (NRSV).
58. 16.22 (NRSV).

As a result of this public degradation, the fate of the ten women is sealed. Their having been defiled by Absalom means that they will never again be considered worthy of the king's sexual attention. As soon as David regains control of Jerusalem, one of his first acts is to make sure these concubines are locked up in a house under guard, living for the rest of their lives 'as if in widowhood'.[59] (2 Sam. 20.3).

Returning to Gibeah, the seriousness of these considerations explains why the Levite makes a swift move as soon as he realizes what is going on. He proceeds to push his concubine outside before the Ephraimite has had the time to fetch his daughter. His motivation is threefold. First, his own life is in the balance. Second, he is fully aware that the hell raisers standing at the door are after his concubine. They are not interested in the Ephraimite's daughter, which explains the phrase 'the men would not listen to him' (19.25). Third, the Levite does not want to cause any disgrace to the family that has been hosting him so generously (19.21).

In my view, these are some of the indirect ways in which the narrator depicts the ungodliness of Gibeah and Benjamin, the vulnerability of the elderly sojourner, and the dangers in which the Levite and the concubine find themselves immersed. According to the logic of the narrative, the blame for the ensuing tragedy falls squarely on Gibeah and the tribe of Benjamin, to whom the city belongs, and from whom it receives massive support.[60] Table Six summarizes the main outcome of a biblical approach to the Gibeah narrative.

### Conclusions

This essay has shown that the two occurrences of ידע in Judges 19 can be read from a non-sexual perspective. It has been demonstrated that the physical assault taking place is carried out through two other verbs, namely, ענה and עלל. Not only is the traditional sexual interpretation of ידע an improbability, but given the structure of the verbal paradigm of Biblical Hebrew, to turn a neutral verb such as ידע into an agent of sexual aggression is a grammatical impossibility. Post-biblical tradition has caused Bible translators to

---

59. 2 Sam. 20.3 (NRSV).
60. 20.5–6, 10, 12–15.

**Table 6:** A Biblical Approach to Gibeah

| *Focus, Characteristics, and Outcome* |
|---|
| ידע is non-sexual, non-violent |
| Three important verbs: עלל, ענה, and ידע |
| Heterosexual assault |
| A political agenda |
| Communities |
| The tribe of Levi |
| The tribe of Ephraim |
| The tribe of Judah |
| Patriarchal hospitality |
| Bethlehem versus Gibeah |
| The sinful tribe of Benjamin |
| Saul (Benjamin) versus David (Judah) |
| Gender in an androcentric culture |
| Literary sophistication |
| An artfully constructed, fictional crime story |

misrepresent ידע on several counts. To sustain a sexual reading, they have had to interpolate demonstratives and determiners, which are absent from the Hebrew. Similarly, their interpretations of נבלה lack the restraint of the original and come across as emotionally charged. If the sexual cobweb around ידע is removed, the narrative reveals several aspects of male psychology and social conventions in an androcentric culture, including gender imbalances and the vulnerability of women. This ancient tale sheds no light on the issue of male homosexuality in biblical times. Similarly, the Levite and his host are not cruel sadists but they themselves are pawns in a sophisticated plot whose political aim is to bring discredit on the city of Gibeah and the tribe to which it belongs. If the encoded political agenda is understood, the terror may be classified as artistic fiction rather than historical fact. Whatever the background, the Gibeah narrative is clearly biased against Benjamin: it only presents one side of the story.

# THE VIOLENCE OF GENDER: CHRISTIAN MARRIAGE AS TEST CASE

## Lisa Isherwood

Boys will be boys and Oh the ladies God bless them! Nothing wrong here we have been told simply noticing and rejoicing in the difference, a difference that makes the world a richer place and much more interesting. But is this true? I personally think that if it were true then much less effort would have to go into creating and maintaining that difference, an effort that Christianity has made almost from the beginning and one that advanced capitalism has happily colluded in. I wish to argue that the construction of gender is in itself violence to the person, as well as forming the foundation of many acts of gendered violence in both the public and private sphere. Far from being a God-given difference, gender is a social construction based on dominance and submission, unhealthy foundational aspects for any fully functioning sense of self. Gender it seems to me is not simply about knowing the difference but also about making the difference, a difference that can be harshly felt in the lives of women and men.

From Plato through to Irigaray we hear philosophers telling us that the body and what is inscribed upon it tell us more about social and political systems and control than about the fleshy mass itself. Gender is an early inscription—congratulations it is a boy—but one that is policed throughout life because left to ourselves we may slip. The reasons for this and what the creative outcomes may be is not the stuff of this article but rather the damage that strict binary opposites does in the lives of people. Butler suggests[1] that the

1. Judith Butler, *The Psychic Life of Power* (Stanford: Stanford University Press, 1997).

ascribing of gender places within us a deep sense of loss, a mourning, that we can not name and so suffer from all our lives—we are mourning that part of ourselves that has no space to flourish as it does not fit the ascribed gender role. We are in this sense dissected people cut off from all that we may be and carrying a great vacuum inside which is often filled by less than life giving alternatives. This is no small matter if true and one that clearly illustrates the damage that can be done to people through the rigid insistence on gender normality. This can be demonstrated if we turn to the work of Lacan[2] who leaves women in no doubt that in a symbolic order, one that is symbolised by the phallus, we are nothing more than an absence. An absence that needs to be filled, to be given meaning and direction by the phallus. Despite this direction we still do not have access to the world of language and so are always on the outside—the ascribing of gender then ensures that women have no world to inhabit. No room of our own where we speak the language of the mothers. Much to mourn here then, and much to feel the true loss of, as opposed to the loss we are said to feel.

This Lacanian analysis is, of course, challenged by women but the fact does seem to remain that the challenge is from outside, it is an analysis largely of recovery rather than totally creative possibilities. Irigaray and others demonstrate how this position in itself does damage to women at the psychic level as there appears to be no way to legitimize one's existence except through the phallus, which as Freud reminds us we do not have and spend energies to get by proxy, that is we lust after our father and want to have his baby. The baby, of course, being the substitute for the phallus. Jessica Benjamin has rather different views about how the early days of life affect us arguing that the basis of maleness is discontinuity, that is to say they are not their mothers and their very male identity has to be based in cold disconnection from their mother. However, she is still responsible for their survival and so Benjamin argues they objectify her into an object of their pleasure but not real in her own right. Her claim is that erotic domination has its roots in these early years and the anxiety that they can cause the male. By being viewed as mother object the woman is stripped of agency and becomes seen as empty with no meaning beyond the pleasure she gives. This pleasure becomes associated with

2.   Lacan in Alexandra Howson, *Embodying Gender* (London, Sage Publications, 2005), p. 22.

penetration by the phallus which Benjamin argues also acts as a counter to the real anxiety of being engulfed by the mother again[3]. The phallus then becomes the instrument of autonomy, and women have no object with which to overcome this phallic monopoly. Benjamin like many others has suggested that women need to be embodied and to resist through the uncovering of desire and erotic connection. It is easy to see how this so called private life of separation and lack of dependency by the male and cultivation of dependency by the female lends itself to many public systems which appear to thrive on autonomy and lack of connection. In short, the public world of church, state and economics mirrors the defective false sense of autonomy that the male attempts to assert due to his fear of being engulfed and overpowered by the maternal. I think it is already becoming clear, then, that the way in which gender division arises and the way we continue to view it is not without its harmful results. While it may appear that men get the better deal, I think we can also see that having to be the big, hard symbolic is not without its down side. James Nelson has given us a very clear picture of how the expectations of masculinity damage men too.

Like Benjamin and others I have argued many times before that sex and sexuality are central aspects of how we police gender [4] and the churches have been to the forefront in this policing. They have embedded roles and expectations so deeply within the culture that although we may well have forgotten the roots we are still affected by the assumptions. Recent research[5] amongst a cross-section of young women showed that their womanliness is assessed by how they react in sexual situations with men; the old expectations are largely still there. That is to say they are not expected to show or require too much sexual pleasure and the whole sexual scenario is focussed on his orgasm, the completion of which usually signals the end of 'sex'. The young women also reported that they did not have a language in which to talk about their own bodies and their pleasure. Some reported that if they did not fulfil the required

3.    Jessica Benjamin, 'Master & Slave. The Fantasy of Erotic Domination', in Ann Snitow (ed.), *Powers of Desire* (New York Monthly Review, 1983), pp. 280–99.

4.    Lisa Isherwood, *Erotic Celibacy: Queering Heteropatriarchy* (London: T. & T. Clark, 2006).

5.    Janet Holland, Caroline Ramazanoglu, Sue Sharpe and Rachel Taylor, *The Male in the Head* (London, The Tufnell Press, 1998).

behaviour patterns then they could expect violence. I have argued that how we are expected to act in our most intimate moments springs from a set of religious assumptions that read their own sources with gender construction on their minds. Women, from the beginning of the Christian story have been seen as the second and defective act of creation, the one who unmonitored will bring death and destruction. The passive receptor envisaged by Lacan had her roots deep in the Christian past in the primordial garden where the first readings of gender take place. Of course, they are suspect readings but that is beyond the scope of this article. What we can say here is that gender is not simply a difference, it affects life more deeply than that. It is kept in place by rigid systems one of which is the practice of heteropatriarchal sexuality and another is the compounding of that through the expectations on Christian marriage.

Despite many theological changes and some advances over the centuries the core of theological anthropology in relation to gender has remained largely untouched until the rise of feminist study. Even now Christian theology has trouble, indeed finds it almost impossible, to think outside very narrowly constructed gendered boxes. Of course, we see this clearly when we look to the conservative edges of the tradition where great attention is paid to the correct gender performance which will include dress and demeanour as well as position within family and church. The True Love Waits[6] campaign goes far beyond simply delivering virgins into marriage, it has a strict view on how those young men and women will act within their marriage and within their wider community. The ideas are based on strict complementarity, the notion that has plagued us since a certain reading of Genesis, and both are expected to act in strict accordance with these 'norms'. He will take the lead in all things and she will modestly support him through comfort and kindness; he will be a success in the workplace and she will support this through the bearing and rearing of children; he will be masterful and she will be glad of it! Interestingly, there is much talk in financial terms of the value of women's virginity and how it will be used within marriage—she becomes a commodity in the literature and perhaps also in reality. Certainly she will fulfil his sexual and emotional needs as this is her role in life. While this

6.   Jon Bicknell, *Sexy But True Love Waits* (London, Marshall Pickering, 1999).

may seem to be the extreme edge of the Christian tradition we actually do not have to go to the more conservative families to see how these gendered expectations affect living together.

### Christian Marriage: A Test Case?

I have always suspected that the weight placed on the idea of marriage by churches and governments has had an agenda that goes beyond that of 'morality'. Why I wonder has so much effort been put into the romantic myth and the notion that life is only full and complete once one is with one's other half. Well, it seems that some of the answer may be because the institution of marriage is a very good ground for the maintaining of gender which as we have seen underpins so much more than it at first appears to do. It is, of course, also a good nursery for the next generation to learn their gender too. Should Christian relationships be about underpinning the status quo? Was the early Jesus movement itself not rather anti such ideas and indeed it could be argued that marriage was not seen as a favourable option by them. If we accept Benjamin's suggestion that gender underpins our public institutions and the way they operate then surely Christians who can not be in favour of savage capitalism and the commodification of people and the earth that it entails, should not be in favour of any institution that fosters the rigid gender definitions we have.

As a sobering legacy for those who claim Christian marriage to be the pinnacle of human relationship we have Christian marriage manuals of the 1960s which read more like rapist manuals than lessons in loving mutuality. They encourage the muscular Christian to take his wife by force the first time so as to set the tone of the marriage and put in place the power relations. He is told she will object and may feel pain but will be glad of it in the end, as she can feel safe in the knowledge that he is in charge. Sex then used as a weapon to create and maintain the gendered roles within the marriage and far beyond into the public arena. The connection of this to the wider political scene can be shown through the objections of some Members of Parliament to the efforts of Marie Stoppes to provide safe contraception for women. One outraged Member of Parliament said such things would breed a generation of effeminate men who would not be able to discharge their duties in the Empire — a clear and rather Freudian link there I think! We see similar patterns promoted by the True Love Waits campaign, it is true they do not advocate the implied violence of the 1960s marriage manuals but they do make it clear that sex is something that the husband decides on and interviews with the young men show how they anticipate sex 24/7 once they are married. Where are the women and their desire in this I wonder?

If we turn to much more explicit cases of violence within marriage we see that Christian understandings of women as the secondary creation, issuing from the rib of Adam and placed here to be his helpmate are at the root of much of this behaviour. Woman is named by him along with everything else that he is to have dominion over and woman's role is understood as a complementary one. In addition, the secondary creation proves the defective status of women who by transgressing set the scene for centuries of mistrust, blame and the need to control the wild woman inside every woman. This is not simply the stuff of theological invention but has consequences in the real world. Those who work with abusers have found that the complementarity model as well as the authority model are foundational in acts of violence against women. Adam Jukes who works with both Christian and non-Christian men has found that men who are told that they need women to be whole, they need their other half, can become extremely frightened if their wives or partners show signs of independence. This threatens their own sense of self and many become violent in order to control the situation.[7] Despite papal rhetoric about the virtues of the complementarity model, it allows for a world of difference but equality, there is really nothing to recommend it. It divides us within ourselves and between ourselves in a very unhealthy manner and leads us into all kinds of insecurities and feelings of inadequacy if we do not have that all-important other half, who is, of course, of the opposite sex. It has never been a model that thrives on equality nor could it be since we live in an androcentric world which has divided genders in a violent and violence creating way.

Christian theology needs to seriously challenge this unhealthy model and encourage grounding in the incarnation that allows for a joyful embrace of our own completeness and incompleteness. It is the chaotic partialness of being alive that signals creative incarnation not an ideal form of wholeness that has to be mirrored in human

7.   Adam Jukes in Anne Borrowdale, *Distorted Images: Christian Attitudes to Women, Men and Sex* (London: SPCK, 1991), p. 108.

relations. Of course, this raises a very serious Christological challenge and one that the churches may not wish to embrace. There are questions here of autonomy and the situating of the divine in the messy incompleteness of life. We are in need of a Christology that encourages self-empowerment rather than the giving away of one's power to others. This is more difficult than it seems when the whole of Christian theology is based on the idea of surrender to God, Christ himself being understood to have given his will over as well. So, we begin to see the tangled web of theology and gender construction because in questioning the idea of complementarity which pervades even our secular ideas of gender we are thrown back to questioning not only foundational myths but the nature of the relationship between God and Christ. There is much at stake here and so it is no wonder that many Christians shy away from radical challenges.

Of course, the authority model is just as destructive and dangerous for women. Jim Wilson who works with batterers puts it plainly, 'domestic violence comes from two things; the authority you believe you have over your wife and the services you expect to get from her'.[8] It is therefore not surprising that Bible believing Christians are highly represented amongst batterers since they believe their wives should be submissive (1 Pet. 3.5-6) which gives them high expectations and a great deal of control. Susan Brocks Thistlewaite worked with fundamentalist women and found that levels of battering and rape where as high as in non-Christian families.[9] Yet the denial runs deep. In addition, Christian women will often accept the blame for the violence far more readily than non-Christian women. One participant in the Thistlewaite programmes summed up the feelings of many of the women by declaring that God gives women more pain, an allusion to Gen. 3:16. Further, the notion of conjugal rights is alive and well in many Christian homes despite legislation to the contrary. This does not in all cases lead to forced rape, although the Thistlewaite figures do show a significant amount, but rather to coercion through

8.   Jim Wilson in Borrowdale, *Distorted Images*, p. 107.

9.   Susan Brocks Thistlewaite, 'Every Two Minutes', in Judith Plaskow and Carol Christ, *Weaving the Visions: New Patterns in Feminist Spirituality* (New York: Harper Collins, 1989), pp. 302–11. Her statistics are taken from the United Methodist Church's Programme of Ministries with Women in Crisis, 1980/1981 and read as follows: 1 in 27 wives admitted they had been raped, 1 in 13 had been abused and 1 in 4 received verbal and emotional abuse.

emotional pressure and an expectation model that is just as abusive. Christian theology needs to nurture models of masculinity that thrive through mutuality and move away from the muscular Christianity of their fathers and grandfathers. It needs to address the issues that Benjamin places before us and in so doing will change both the personal and the political.

I think a starting point would be to image mutuality as sexy, it has not been portrayed as such as we see from all kinds of pornography from the mildest to the worst. There the dominance/submission model, of which Benjamin speaks, is alive and well. Instead of condemning it because it is sex it would be more constructive if the churches engaged in a debate about images that enhance relationship. Images that allow the performance of masculinity in non-aggressive/thrusting and dominating ways. The churches need to issue a challenge to the phallocentric world in which we live. A world that places great pressure on men to perform their sexuality/gender correctly. It is this performance model of ownership and conquest that feeds the culture of violence that woman suffers.

It is not only pornography that is full of crazy images of masculinity. Popular culture of all kinds is brimming over with the indestructible male facing and overcoming the odds. Man the saviour is played out from Robocop to Nintendo and the acts of non-emotional heroism are nauseating. What is a man to do when a mere woman stands up to him or refuses to play the damsel in distress? How is he to cope if she is in a well-paid job and he is not? His real world, that of sexually charged celluloid heroes, is under threat and the cause is the woman who does not know the rules. Many men who inflict violence on women name their feelings of resentment and inadequacy as the reason for the violence. It is a frightening fact of life that woman as threat may become woman as target. Even more frightening that woman is created as threat by a media, which is incapable of imaging masculinity beyond narrow boundaries. What are the churches doing to balance this? The answer is nothing. There are some gay theologians who are attempting to examine what it means to be male but their attempts are not being met with joy by the churches. In the shadow of the AIDS crisis predatory/performative and conquest models of sexuality had to be seriously reworked. In their place many men developed playful, full bodied and imaginative relationships, which took them beyond patriarchal expectations and rituals. They have found that less emphasis on performance has meant there is greater opportunity for mutuality and empowerment. This new pleasure seeking has brought many gay men to a deeper understanding of selfhood through a more honest engagement with others.[10] This is not a model that Christianity has actively encouraged, indeed at times in its history it has advocated the exact opposite, with men showing their dominance in the marital bed. There is a crisis in masculinity in our time, the old models of power over/dominance/submission will no longer do, and one of the results is an increase in violence to women. There is a desperate need for the churches to become more realistic about sexuality and gender relations and they could do worse than listen to voices from the margins where accepted norms have already been challenged.

A crucial part of any theology of gender that rethinks notions of masculinity has to be, not only the uncoupling of the erotic from violence, but also the halting of sexual scape-goating. Woman is not the devil's gateway and she is free to walk in the street or sit in her home as she pleases. The responsibility lies with the man to respect her space and to acknowledge his own feelings and why he has them. This is not evidenced in True Love Waits literature where young boys are explicitly told that they have 'a willy with a life of its own'. This distancing from one's own feelings and the idea that something other than oneself is in control does not lend itself to a good model of selfhood. The solution offered by True Love Waits is not very helpful either, Jesus is Lord of your willy—a model that still disempowers and allows for the scape-goating of women, who in league will the devil, may just overcome Jesus the willy guardian! Along with the scape-goating goes an unconscious possession mindset, which encourages men to think that all women are theirs for the taking, we belong to them. The standard male defence, that she did not mean 'No', graphically illustrates this.

Christian sexual ethics have over the years alienated people from their desires and this has led to a world in which we find it difficult to be present with our needs and desires, to own them as ours and to enjoy them. Desire can never be removed but it can become misplaced and misshapen. While both women and men have suffered

10. See Martin Stringer, 'Expanding the Boundaries of Sex: An Exploration of Sexual Ethics After the Second Sexual Revolution', *Theology and Sexuality* 8.1 (1997), pp. 27–43.

this Christian intrusion into their sexual psyches, men have had women to blame for desire and the guilt that can accompany it. This has, in my opinion, led to greater alienation and a fear of intimacy. This is clearly seen in the writings of many of the church fathers and some more contemporary notables, but is also worryingly shown in psychological research. Carol Gilligan shows that young men will often invent violent situations in order to avoid intimacy.[11] The situations can be bizarre such as aliens landing but nevertheless a significant number prefer this fantasy to the prospect of intimacy (not to be confused with sex). How have men become so alienated from their feelings and their bodies? While sex continues to be understood as 'something out there that takes possession of me' and it is her fault, the stage will continue to be set for violence of all kinds. Christianity urgently needs to embrace a more body friendly sexual ethic, one that moves away from dualistic fantasies and encourages real engagement with real bodies in a mutual and empowering way. This is not fostered in my opinion by the notion that sex is only for marriage where it will be tightly regulated by the norms of Christian morality—a morality that is based in the psychic dysfunction of the men who have over the centuries created it.

Selfless love which is an expectation of women in the True Love Waits version of marriage is for them underpinned by the theology of Jesus' suffering and death and is a problem for women. At its worst it leads to their death, emotionally and physically. However, before it reaches that point it sets the scene for non-reciprocal relationships and an acceptance of such patterns. These relationships overlook the lived experience of women and perpetuate the myth that love poured out by one can overcome the lack of love by the other. Even when there is no physical violence in a relationship this model does damage to the women as it is a rather self deprecating form of existence that does not seem to be in accordance with an Incarnational religion based in abundant life.

For Farley, 'just love' is an expression of the equal worth of those loved[12]. It is an affirmation of their needs and a refusal to reduce their space through sex defined stereotypes and prejudices. Along

11. Carol Gilligan, *In A Different Voice, Psychological Theory and Women's Development* (Cambridge, MA: Harvard University Press, 1982).
12. Margaret Farley, 'New Patterns of Relationship: Beginnings of a Moral Revolution', in Walter Burkhardt (ed.), *Woman* (New York: Paulist Press, 1977), p. 67.

with other theologians Farley is calling for a remoulding of Christian ethics to include justice in an ethic of love. Intimacy in relationship can no longer be an excuse for overlooking the demands of justice. This, of course, will require a new look at the unit we call family and a re-evaluation of its place in the public arena. In addition the question of power within the family will need urgent attention and may call for models that are both challenging and frightening. The Christian church has tended to adopt whatever model of family relationship was prevalent at the time, this is clearly seen with the adoption of the Roman model under Constantine. The time seems right to break loose from convention and engage in radical alternatives. What exactly would a justice seeking space of women, men and children look like in a world drowning under the worst excesses of patriarchy; abuse, sexism, capitalism and so on. Families pledged to equality, respect and counter cultural living would be a welcome change to the unimaginative units we call home! Surely, if a notion such as the Christian family is to continue it cannot simply underpin the status quo through the perpetuation of gendered behaviour and the violence to the person that entails, what is Christian about that?

I have attempted to show that the construction of gender does violence to the person in a multitude of ways and further that Christian marriage as proposed by certain aspects of the Christian church simply underpin that violent construction. I believe it is the place of an incarnational religion to proclaim, foster and celebrate the fullness of human/divine life and not to narrow it through politically expedient social constructions. There are many things in the world that exploit and damage people and if Benjamin is right many if not all these systems hinge on the early experiences of male children and how they react to them through the objectification of the mother and the way this fits into the creation and maintaining of gender. Gender then is no innocent natural phenomena, it is part of a much wider and pervasive problem, it is in reality the root of much of the violence both personal and public that we live under. Christian marriage, if we are to continue with it, needs then to be the nurturing ground of people who live outside the all pervasive confines of gender construction, who challenge the status quo from a base of just love and mutuality which rejoices in the as yet untapped fullness of the human/divine reality.

LUNCHTIME CRUCIFIXIONS:
THEOLOGICAL REFLECTIONS ON ECONOMIC VIOLENCE AND
REDEMPTION

*Marcella Maria Althaus-Reid*


Sobre la deuda, basta...
(Enough of talking about the debt...)
Roberto Lavagna, Argentine Minister of Economy (La NacionLine
2004: 1).

I'm looking at some photographs taken a few years ago in my
country, Argentina. The scene is a public park in a small town. A
group of people, some sitting and some standing are looking at six
medium-sized wooden crosses standing in the middle of the park.
Hanging on them are men and women, some old, some young,
patiently standing still, with arms and legs tied up with ropes to
the wooden bars. Visible for the passers by, there are handwritten
cards located under some of the crosses. Each one carries the name
and the social problems of the person who has voluntarily crucified
him- or herself, such as unemployment and the loss of savings during
the collapse of the national banks.

In one of the photographs, a priest can be seen amongst the
crowds. He is also waiting together with other people to be crucified
during his lunchtime. After they have completed their crucifixion
hour, another group made up of other neighbours with other sets
of cards will arrive to help each other to be tied to their crosses.

These were lunchtime crucifixions for times of economic crisis
under the Globalization process. These were twenty-first century
Golgotha scenes that lasted whole afternoons during days in which
people queue for mock crucifixions in a humble town park in

Argentina.[1] The message was clear. Wooden crosses expressed the reality of authentic crucifixions in the life of ordinary people suffering under the Market, the reality of external debts and the disregard for human life which pervades their prosecutors. Curiously, these crucifixions happened in *La Quiaca,* where months earlier a priest was deposed from his parish for putting a white headscarf on the head of the statue of the Virgin Mary, thus making of her a 'Mother of the Disappeared'.[2] As the Salvadorean theologian, Jon Sobrino, would say, these scenes may remind us that we are in the presence of the crucified people of Latin America (Sobrino 1976). However, these cruci/fictions are much more than theatrical performances. In other words, they may be partaking at some levels of the skills of a 'Theatre of the Oppressed',[3] but at some point they also engage with an unfortunate Christian pedagogy of violent debt, which has been passed from generation to generation of Latin American people. For behind those mock crosses there are the shadows of external debts, public debts as well as private, individual brokenness. The fact is that a whole theology of debt has been used in Christianity to mediate a relationship between people and God, and as a result of this, God and humanity have been reduced to be best understood around a specific economic axis and ethos. Such is the axis of debt and the ethos of redemption.

Using a discourse from ideology in theology, we may say that as it is in Heaven, so it is on Earth. Global Capitalism may be built around a similar axis of debt and redemption, although the cost of such redemption is a different one. Are we then supposed to understand the world in a relation of interdependence with an economic (market) worldview? In that sense then it would be

1.    The mock crucifixions as a means of protest still continue today. At the time of writing this article I have read that 110 unemployed workers in the border between Argentina and Bolivia have 'crucified' themselves in protest while nearly 300 people have gathered to show them support.

2.    'Mothers of the Disapeared' (*Madres de los Desaparecidos* or *Madres de Plaza de Mayo*) refers to a group of women from Argentina who protested against the military regimes of the 1970s demanding justice against the abductions of people suspected of opposing the regime. They are recognized for wearing a white scarf on their heads with the names and/or photographs of their missing relatives.

3.    Theatre of the Oppressed refers to the theatre techniques of Augusto Boal in Brazil, who has developed it as an instrument to facilitate social changes. Cf Augusto Boal, *Theatre of the Oppressed* (London: Pluto Press, 2000).

legitimate to ask if the doctrine of redemption partakes of a reductionist economic worldview which obscures an ideological process of inversion in Christian salvation.

## *Redemption as an Ideological Inversion*

Debt prepares the ground on which the seeds of conflict fall, watering the martial crop as it grows.
(Dan Smith in Selby 1997: 92).

If truth is always a concrete truth, we can also say that the truth in Christianity has been always in struggle against reification processes, that is, ideological statements which render people powerless while doctrines grow strong. Redemption is an economic metaphor for salvation, but what kind of salvation? If the medium is the message, the doctrine of salvation needs to be considered as based on a commercial culture of oppression, which blurs the borders between the understanding of the production of the means of life (and the regulation of relationships and affection as the result of that), and the kind of relationship expected from gods.

In Christianity, it means the relation between a creator God as a producer of life as a supreme good and a humanity subjected to a violent ontological external debt. Ideological inversions may be difficult to avoid in religious thinking, but the problem is that the doctrine of redemption may have been the earliest attempt by Christianity to sacralize an economic order based on debt. Here we could find the origin of what we can call a 'judicial theology', or a lawyer's account of the rights and wrongs of commercial spiritual transactions, but moreover, an ontological substratum where debt is part of the cultural, economic and religious horizon of expectations.

In other words, there is no understanding in Christianity of life without debt. Such a debt could be abolished (as in the redemptive act of Christ) but the expectation of debt survives ontologically ingrained in a Christian economy of relationship. Debt, in this case, is more foundational for Christianity than love, for it even precedes love. It was Chairman Mao who once suggested that to understand a system we should find a foundational contradiction in it. In the doctrine of redemption, the contradiction is grace or freedom. Why? Because the covenant or pact of Grace (the 'free' transaction as opposed to the commercial one) is heavily dependent on a theology of debt based on social agreements between contracting parties. God has then become the God of the good will, and the incarnation of a divine sponsor or 'surety' in Jesus. Grace (freedom) is precisely what is lacking here.

However, redemptionist doctrines do not come from the heavens but rather are the product of ideological formations, and moreover will require some postcolonial theological analysis, because our doctrine of salvation seems to be a product of the hybridity between an understanding of debt in the Hebrew Scriptures, the Christian event and Roman jurisprudence. This is where Giorgio Agamben's thought becomes illuminating. In his book 'Homo Sacer' III (1998) Agamben highlights the fact that theological categories are indebted to judicial ones. For instance, the problem is not what economic order is present in the thinking of redemption, but that an economic order has become the hidden narrative and 'Grand metaphor' of our relation with God. Moreover, that the economic order is subjected to the fluctuations of violent exchanges. In the symbolic crucifixions of the poor in Argentina we have the paradox of a people whose life moves around the key element of the present economic universe of the market: debt. What we have here is a piece of Roman jurisprudence, where the surety of a commercial transaction can be exercised in two different ways: a *fidejussor* and an *expromissor*. The *fidejussor* was the person who took responsibility to pay as a guarantee in case the original debtor didn't pay what was owed. The *expromissor* was a more generous guarantor who took upon themself the responsibility to pay no matter what (Agamben 1998: 16).

The problems with theological inversion are basically the following:

1. It tends to hide that there is an economic foundational violence in a religious discourse, which haunts any relationship of gratuity which Christianity had tried to establish with the Sacred. It came back to haunt economic expectations and tainted the discourses of the neoliberal 'no alternative' to Globalization.
2. It creates a judicial theology, depending on obligations.

This foundational economic violence means that the shadow of debt threatens Grace. Two distinguished British theologians have already questioned the deep implications of using the 'debt' metaphor in theology: Timothy Gorringe, in his book *God's Just Vengeance: Christ, Violence and the Rhetoric of Salvation* (1996); and

Bishop Peter Selby in his book *Grace and Mortgage* (1997). For Gorringe, the image of a God as part of a retributive strategy of justifiable punishment requires serious rethinking. For Selby, the message of forgiveness through Christ's act of redemption needs to be understood in all its depth, including the consequences that this may have for our current economic system. That is, the divine assurance of the good news of the Kingdom of God as a true economy of Grace and freedom, and 'the hope of a world where debt will not rule' (Selby 1997: 163). The debts have been forgiven. Someone (Christ) has paid the price with his blood.

However, we still need to further question the difficulties of having the master code of the debt narrative as foundational for our relationship with God and with the world. It may be argued that the indebted countries of the world, which are paying the price of usury more than of a genuine debt at this moment, are following the same bloody road. For the external debt has become quasi-ontological and it seems to require a multitude of human sacrifices to be redeemed. The amount of people sacrificed by the Global Capitalist system is of such magnitude in terms of suffering and numbers that can it only be comparable to the suffering of a tortured god dying on a cross. How different would it be to have a divine economic metaphor based on the gift economy of many countries such as Rwanda or Perú? It was Gorringe[4] who, following a Liberation Theology type of hermeneutic of suspicion, saw that revelation should be discerned in the world, and not only in a theological attempt to discern God's Word in the institutionalized church. The economic system is one of these areas in which the revelation of God is particularly visible, because economy is by nature a way of relationships, of loving exchanges and the production and distribution of life. To go outside an economy of redemption means to go outside an economy of debt. In our current market economy, that means to go outside the system. However, one does not need to consider the possibility or impossibility of a different economic system, if we consider how in other cultures not taken into account by western theologies, there are different models of economies which also are rooted in a spiritual model. What the redemption model does not acknowledge is that different forms of imagining love and relationship outside a narrow debt model as

4. For this point see Timothy Gorringe, *Discerning Spirit: A Theology of Revelation* (London: SCM Press, 1990).

the one Christianity has developed, may lead us to somehow different and more creative understandings of God and life outside the patterns of, for instance, work and debt and high property values in general which pervade Christian theology. Different forms of loving relationships mean also that we may value property in different ways, and thus, a sense of exchanging solidarity among men and women and not just relationships based on a debt economy might contribute to the rediscovering of the face of God in the current Capitalist system. It may also affect the structures of organization of the church.

## The Peruvian Economy of Tenderness

It may be that a theology of the land needs to stand against a theology of debt. In Latin America, issues of land have been at the forefront of the agenda of many churches and church inspired movements, such as The Landless Movement (*Movemento Sem Terra*), whose origins can be traced to the Ecclesial Base Communities. In the past years differences between *campesinos* and *hacendados* (peasants and landowners) in Latin America and in particular in Perú have been and continue to be tense. People have become divided along issues of land, property and production resources including technologies. However, even if relationships among *campesinos* have changed in the new terms imposed by the Globalization of capital in the sense that there are divisions related to the control of land and orchard properties even amongst themselves (and not just the landowner's), it seems that an economy and spirituality of Grace has prevailed. The traditional relations of economic and affective reciprocity amongst indigenous cultures in Perú have demonstrated strength and have even produced many challenges to the market system. For that, we need to reflect on the institution of economic reciprocity used at the level of peasants' interchange which is called the *Ayni* or 'tenderness'. (Fioravanti 1973). The *Ayni* is a gift economy based on a type of ritualized friendship which interrelates traditional spiritual and social issues and is manifested at the level of relations of production amongst the Peruvian peasant societies. The *Ayni* relies on rituals of friendship which include the use of special words of greeting amongst peasants, and also the exchange of food and/or presents.

How does it work? For instance, if someone needs help during the harvest season, a relative, friend or a neighbour can be asked to perform that service. The person who is soliciting the help for the harvest will, when required, reciprocate by offering her or his own services to those who have helped during the seasonal work. The only expectation is in reality, reciprocity, and following this example, it would not be necessary to retribute with helping the neighbour in the harvest, but in any other need. In fact, in this system anybody can somehow retribute, even older people, the sick or the children. They all belong to the system of tenderness of their community.

The ritual of the *Ayni* works as follows: The person who needs help for the harvest visits a relative or any member of the community to ask for help. The relatives or neighbours of the person who have been asked and have agreed to help with the harvest will accompany him or her to the field, bringing with them an offering that in Spanish can be translated as *el cariño* (love or tenderness). The 'tenderness' might consist of *aguardiente* (a traditional alcoholic drink), some cigarettes or any other present considered suitable (Fioravanti 1973: 122). The person whose service is required takes with him or her this 'love' or 'tenderness' as the beginning of the reciprocity cycle of mutual service between two people and two families. Is in interesting to notice that when the person goes to work in the harvest, other people who are not going to work, accompany him or her symbolically, to show that behind that worker there is a community happy to serve a neighbour in need. The highly ritualised cycle of reciprocity has something sacramental in it. It is a community sharing work, but not just that. There is a sense of spirituality in working in the field that belongs to the Inca cultures, and which pervades the system of the *Ayni*. In a way, the Quechua people have an authentic theology of Land in which God's grace is manifested in the harvest but also in the midst of the community work. Without reciprocity, there is no spirituality.

This is not a system which is based on debt but, as the name says, on love. The *Ayni* subverts the master/slave dialectic present in the 'debt economy' of redemption and converts it into gift and mutuality. The violence which is implicit in a doctrine of redemption is here subsumed by an understanding of a relation of a celebratory nature. That relation is remembered and celebrated in the traditional *fiestas* which signal the end of the service given to someone in need, without the expectation of an economic reward. In that way, poor peasants never lack workers for the harvest, and even when workers are paid for their services, people still tend to respect the *cariño,* by giving offerings and presents to the paid workers and celebrating the end of the work with a *fiesta.* The fact is that in any Peruvian community, the element of reciprocity organises labour because labour is part of a wider spirituality of the land.

The *Ayni* is part of the reciprocity system of many Latin American communities, but its challenges penetrate deeply into the social and economic structure of the market economy. However, the *Ayni* is also part of a Quechua spirituality. Reciprocity in community is understood as part of a process of spiritual development. Feelings and emotions such as love or tenderness are considered important to manifest the soul of a person. The *Ayni* is in itself, a path and a liturgy of spiritual and material growth in a culture where the dualism soul and body does not exist as such. Theologically we are challenged by the presence of God in the midst of a different way of conceiving labour and family relationships, as also economy and society.[5] The redemptive implications of this system set us apart from the ethos of a society where profit is present in all transactions. The *Ayni* is about giving without receiving profit, based on rituals of expenditure of the accumulated, given away with happiness, with grace, in the *fiestas* of celebration organized for the work done (Godelier 1971: 102). The economic goal of the *Ayni* is to minimize economic inequalities in the community by graceful giving, while improving people's living conditions. Redemption has all too often been reduced to a welcome to an economically based order that should be questioned. What would happen if we had a redemption narrative which does not presuppose indebtedness but gracious giving and celebration of the giving as in the *Ayni*?

### Redemption without Debts

Could we have redemption without debt? After all, to redeem is a specific action to be located in a situation of debt. In the Hebrew Scriptures, a person who has been enslaved can be set free by paying a sum of money. In the current times of external debts, the 'Jubilee

---

5.   For a more developed reflection on the theological implications of the *Ayni* see M.M. Althaus-Reid, *The Queer God* (London: Routledge, 2003), especially ch. 7.

2000'[6] campaign tried to ask for the remission of the interest of the international debt to the IMF (International Monetary Fund) for the most impoverished countries of the world.[7] Christ's redemption cancels the debt of humanity, but we are still struggling here with the ideology of debt. How we get free from debts by God's forgiveness or mutual forgiveness (as in Jesus' prayer) is not the issue, but why we assume that debts can and should be contracted. This takes us into another reflection, one of a God who does not recognize debts being rather a God of reciprocity. An '*Ayni* Messiah' who comes to the world because he is a God who needs to give and to receive love, and needs to show a different economic model of relationship. An *Ayni* Messiah who can tell us that a system of debt does not need to preclude our way of conceiving life. That perhaps there are cultures where people do not work for money, because their needs are re-distributed in different ways, and therefore challenge the inefficacy of a system based on currency. This is not a 'Master God' nor a 'Father God' of the colonial theologies but a God as a neighbour, a God truly amongst the poor and marginalized involved in a dialectical more than a master/slave relation with humanity. The *Ayni* Messiah is a God who takes the path of reciprocity in tenderness as a concrete one. We may wonder if theology can take that challenge, but if not, How can the churches claim any authority to speak on ethical debates on peace and justice? The time has come to re-position Christ outside patterns of power and authority but in community and reciprocity.

The point is that no economy of freedom and no alternative *Basileia* or Kingdom of God can happen while Christ keeps being linked to an economy of debt, as in the case of redemption, which has serious cultural and economical limitations. There is a need for a radical breakthrough in the understanding of human relationships and humanity's relationship with God, which needs to reconsider economic and theological experiences outside the Western way of thinking and living. Unfortunately, the problem with religious

6. For the Jubilee 2000 campaign see Martin J. Dent, *Jubilee 2000 and Lessons of the World Debt Tables* (Keele, Staffs: University of Keele, 1994).

7. It is curious to note that in April 2002, James Wolferson, President of the World Bank, said that the moment has come for the World Bank to act, and not to speak and to 'educate for love' (see BBC webline, HTTP://www.news.BBC.co.uk/Hi/Spanish/business/newsid.stm. April 2002). The concept of love used by Wolferson is dependent on a world view very different from that of the *Ayni* system of reciprocity.

metaphors concerning the cancellation of debts is that they do not cancel the existence of a system of debt. We may consider ourselves or our communities free from debt or redeemed, but we will still perceive others as in debt. The core of colonial theology is based on that perception which divides the world between the free from debt and those who need to be told of their 'debts' even if they did not partake of such a theology of debts in the first instance. From theological debts to economic debts, it seems difficult to conceive of a world where debts are not just abolished but where an alternative order of reciprocity, gift, expenditure without retribution and is created, in sum, an economy of Grace in which debt does not exist. In fact, it is Grace that has been cancelled by a debt ideology and not vice versa.

The challenge of the *Ayni* and other gift economies is a challenge to the assumed (and sacralized) economic universe of the Scriptures.[8] However, it is more than that for it represents a challenge to the way we conceive God, and God in Christ. A challenge to a theology which is more Roman jurisprudence than Freirean,[9] and that needs the dialectic, less hierarchical worldview of reciprocity, solidarity and tenderness as a currency of the Andean cultures. The cross at Golgotha, and the lunchtime crucifixions of the excluded people from Argentina dying under the heavy weight of the external debt and the Structural Adjustment Programmes have something in common. They denounce the system of debt as violence against humanity, and also, Christ's crucifixion as violence inflicted against God. If theology is the way of actions and reflections, there is then hope that the understanding of the inhumanity of the economies of debt in the Global Market may help us to reconsider our theological doctrines using more appropriate economic metaphors to understand the love and the constant presence of God amongst the marginalized.

8. It is obvious to say that there is more than one economic system in the Scriptures. We are referring here only to the ideology of redemption as it contributes to our understanding of Christ, but the redemption system in the biblical times needs to be studied in its different contexts too.

9. Paulo Freire, the Brazilian philosopher of education, developed a method of education for liberation based on a dialogue for conscientization. Its style of work was non-hierarchical but dialogical and egalitarian. Theology has still to learn to rethink its categories from a dialogical perspective. See P. Freire, *Pedagogy of the Oppressed* (London: Penguin, 1993).

## Conclusion

At the end of the day, a theological reflection engaged with present debt structures presents us with three distinctive challenges. First, the challenge to consider if our current Christologies (including some Liberationist approaches) should depart from cultural and economic metaphors which cannot challenge the economic structures of sin in our world. Moreover, they may have contributed to it. Should the churches repent of their contribution to systems of indebtedness in society? At least, this should be a call to be aware that there are economic alternatives. The reality of economic alternatives is what Global Capitalism does not want to accept, but the good news of the Kingdom is more than a concrete historical project, but a call to alternatives. Second, and closely related to this point, we may need to reflect in the place that culture should have in our praxis of theological action and reflection today. This would not be the case of advocating a 'Gospel and culture' approach which usually succeeds in leaving Christianity culturally intact although adapting to another culture. In this case, the demands should be higher. Culture, sadly, has been used as a way to transmit a Christian message while keeping the cultural baggage intact (or even sacralized). To think about the *Ayni*, is to think a different Christology and even ecclesiology. For instance, the churches would have a different structure if they had respected and taken seriously many of our indigenous organizational patterns. To think Christ outside the economic model present in the metaphor of redemption, while finding that same Christ in the economic system of tenderness and retribution of gifts, enlarges our understanding of the Messiah amongst us. It helps us to re-discover a bigger God and a bigger Christ, while untangling the hegemonic historical relationship between theology, ideology and culture which has contributed so much to injustice and oppression.

Thirdly, we may ask if Christianity could survive such disentangling of ideology and Christology. Obviously, this may have serious consequences in theology. The question to ask is how pivotal is a dominant cultural and economic viewpoint for our faith? Theology has never been culturally neutral, but the cultures of the countries of the Global South have been ignored or distorted. Yet, as we may see, they have more to contribute to our understanding of Christ than a hegemonic Western theology has thought. The final questions may be: Would Christ survive a postcolonial theology? Would Christ survive a non-redemption theology? If we recognize that redemption as a doctrine is dependent on a cultural and economic metaphor of limited value, yes. In this case, we will be referring to theology as *poiesis*, creation and possibility and not as a fixed, ordered corpus of divine understanding. As I have said elsewhere, in theology it is a sense of discontinuity that brings revelation, not un-revised traditions.

Some time ago, during the collapse of the Socialist Block, the Latin American theologian, Pablo Richard, was asked about the future of Liberation Theology. His answer still is valid, and it is valid also to reply to my question about a Christ without a doctrine of redemption. Richard said: 'The main question is not what will happen to Liberation Theology but what will happen to the lives of the poor'. (Richard 1994: 245). It is not the future of theologies that should be concerning us, but the future of real people. Paraphrasing Richard we say that the main question is not about the future of Christology, but of the people of Christ. In other words, if what concerns us is Christ when thinking Christology at the time of Global Capitalism and social exclusion, then we have forgotten Christ in the process. If our concerns are the lives of the poor and marginalized, the ones that Christ loved and still does, then the answer is clear. To think Christ amongst the disposed of today call us to a different understanding of the alternative Kingdom of God, as announced by a Messiah who may need to be able to transcend the limitations of the economic models which still permeate our understanding of his life and work. The magnitude of the current crisis of the world requires Christological kenosis and postcolonial suspicion, as well as courage to produce a different theological praxis amongst the excluded of Global Capitalism. The Christ of the *Ayni* (and the Christ of many cultures based on the gift economy) should give us food for thought.

# Symbolizing Our Desires

## Agnes Rafferty

This paper attempts to examine the symbols being used by the protagonists in the war in Iraq relative to traditional Christian theology, the myths on which it was built and ensuing praxis. In particular, I wish to consider the value allotted to 'the feminine' in the cultural and religious symbolic realm that underpins societal understanding of the relational climate necessary for liberty and justice to be effective.

During the Lent and Easter season of 2003 I found myself constantly distracted by the television news of the war in Iraq being played out in the corner of my living room. I found this strange as reports of wars are a constant part of everyday life that we have become accustomed to; we are war weary just as we are compassion weary, wanting to turn off when we feel that the terrible events taking place are remote from us, one step removed from our reality and we feel unable to influence change. This is a state recognized by feminist theologians like Mary Grey who believe it is the result of our communities 'being blocked from being in mutually just relations with one another...the roots of compassion...not touched because the fragile connections between us are ruptured'.[1] Maintaining the tenuous connections as individuals is impossible when war is an accepted part of the environment and the culture that gives us our support and strength and forms our way of relating, violence tearing apart empathy.

It seems that the television images of violence that disturb children the most are those seen on the news, violence that apparently we

1. Mary Grey, *The Outrageous Pursuit of Hope* (London: Darton, Longman and Todd, 2000), p. 96.

have to accommodate in order to maintain the legally sanctioned way of relating in society. The constant repetition of war as a means of working out differences gives it a legitimacy and authority that those who demand that it not be done in their name find hard to combat. I do not wish here to get into an argument about just wars or the legitimacy of pre-emptive strikes or the privilege of living in a democratic society but to ponder on why watching this war proceed has been so absorbing and disturbing for me as a feminist interested in sacramental theology. Why could I not just press the remote button and switch off?

I am using the understanding of symbol as an object, quality or relation that make present a reality and sacrament in turn as symbols and symbolic actions that make present the reality of God. The tradition of the sacramental principle in Catholicism recognises that everything within the cosmos has the capacity to make present the divine, the reality that we symbolize in religious rites being a distillation of the experience of the divine in everyday life. That reality, mediated through our bodies and psyches, is always within the context of the community, both local and global, symbols expressing deeply held cultural values reflecting the desires of the community and its understanding of humanity's relationship with the divine. Cohen points out that symbols not only express meaning but also give us the capacity to make meaning, stating:

> the community itself and everything within it, conceptual as well as material, has a symbolic dimension, and…this dimension does not exist as some kind of consensus of sentiment. Rather it exists as something for people to "think with". The symbols of community are mental constructs: they provide people with the means to make meaning. In so doing, they also provide them with the means to express the particular meaning which the community has for them.[2]

Any symbol can represent differing realities—so watching the images of the regime in Iraq being pulled down by the Coalition forces has the capacity to make real the end or the beginning of security, as it might make real the good or the evil of the power of the West. Symbols contain an ambiguity that brings a range of meanings to their interpretation reflecting the subjective experience of the individual. This does not take away the power of symbols but highlights the necessity of maintaining a critical stance to the

---

2. Anthony P. Cohen, *The Symbolic Construction of Community* (London and New York: Routledge, 2000), p. 19.

symbols being used to express and reiterate our reality, and to question whose reality is being put forward as the norm.

The overarching icon of war as theatre has perhaps taken on a new significance as television audiences give to the writers, producers and actors of the drama access to an auditorium of worldwide proportions to get across their values and the means of establishing their ideas. Both protagonists in this latest war graphically illustrate the value placed on achieving their goals in the upholding of a vast military complex, an economic investment that, as Jantzen points out, if spent elsewhere could eliminate worldwide poverty.[3] This military complex however bringing life to the script is an essential and carefully chosen element in the repeated performance of cultural values, ultimately acquiring a symbolic function. A corollary may be found in religious rites including sacramental rites making use of words and elements to convey cultural understanding of the sacred with which to celebrate and mourn the reality of living and dying.

Liberation theologies confront the status quo in calling on different experiences of 'being Church' to inform their understanding of the presence or absence of the divine in communities. Feminist liberation theologians are questioning the validity of the symbols used in traditional Christianity as they have been bound within a particular world view, any ambiguity or polyvalent potential being limited by their restriction to making real a man's world, both that of everyday life and that of the male psyche as expressed in rites, myths and images.[4] Symbols function to connect these two areas of life, some symbols being common to most cultures but when everyday life and psychic images do not correlate with the symbols used in community their power is negated.

Language is perhaps the most potent bearer of symbolic meaning, political correctness in the use of inclusive language going far beyond the use of the correct pronouns, but asking what is being made real within the social context and common usage of the cultural values it carries. Many Christian symbols laden with misogyny deny

---

3. Grace M. Jantzen, *Becoming Divine: Towards a Feminist Philosophy of Religion* (Manchester: Manchester University Press, 1998), p. 130.

4. Ronwyn Goodsir-Thomas, 'Symbols', in Lisa Isherwood and Dorothea McEwan (eds.), *An A to Z of Feminist Theology* (Sheffield: Sheffield Academic Press, 1996), p. 224.

women's ability to incarnate the divine, Eve's sinfulness, as symbolic of all women, requiring that women bear the responsibility for evil in the world necessitating the rebirth and nurturing of all children born of women into a spiritual world defined by a masculine psyche, a religious world that women were not allowed to influence.

Educating children in such a world involves telling stories, passed from generation to generation, stories that are held in the memory and shape our understanding of reality. Subconscious memories came to the fore as I heard the news reports coming from Iraq laced with names of places that recall foundational stories of Christian belief. Here places such as Mesopotamia, and the rivers of Tigris and Euphrates on which the cities of Babylon, now renamed Hillah, and Nineveh were found, and the ancient city of Ur, birthplace of Abraham, were taking on a new significance as it was here that armies were going to war in my name; here, in the place that has been claimed as the site of the birth of civilization, where the first words were written in the earth and where the ideal of the Garden of Eden was first conceived. This was the place where, I'd been told, God marvelled at creation and where humanity was born and given the responsibility of taking care of all that was good. It was here in the Garden where the rivers Tigris and Euphrates flowed that God walked in the cool of the day and where now all hell was being let loose in the name of righteousness. The child in me did not want to let go of this awesome place but the adult recalled that this story had been written and passed down to me in a culture that did not question the patriarchal mindset that created it and that another drama had been enacted here: the battle between the man and the woman that ended with the feminine relegated as subject to the masculine, legitimizing the ascendancy of the male father god while the mother goddess, with her capacity for creating life, symbolized by the serpent, was crushed. Patriarchy was established and made divine. The androcentric mindset outlined in the Genesis story has polarized the dialectical relationships of female and male laying the foundation for the application of this dualism to good and evil, nature and grace and body and soul that has provided the basis of relationships with the cosmos, nature and the sexes in both church and state in the ensuing centuries. As Starhawk[5] points out, these relationships sanctify prejudice of all kinds by

---

5. Starhawk, *Why We Need Women's Action and Feminist Voices for Peace* (Sophia Newsletter, 1.3, March 2003), pp. 2-4.

dehumanizing and devaluing the Other, the not like me, whose desires have to be negated and subject to the desires of the one who has the means of enforcing their will: legitimized by calling on the authority of an omnipotent God who can justify all the trappings of war to uphold the institutions of power that maintains the status quo.

Sjöö and Mor state:

> A global God of War, served by the global religion of money, defines the human condition today. Our various nationalities, our sectarian beliefs, our local customs, our personal opinions, may serve as individual definitions but they no longer define the condition of the world, in which global missile systems and global factory-economic systems have rendered national, sectarian, local and personal definitions merely soporific and in fact, obsolete. All humanity today lives under one global god: the God of War, who is continuously empowered and enlarged by the religion of money. The "arms race" is now the major global economy, the world economy is now a war economy, with virtually all national military systems and military budgets taking precedence over all domestic economies and domestic budgets.[6]

In this climate, compassionate relationships are of secondary importance. War is our reality; we live in a climate of war that numbs our sensitivity to the way we are manipulated and our complicity in the murder of the god of compassion and love. Creativity is subjugated to destruction and the serpent continues to be crushed.

The leaders of the Western world I presume had chosen their words with care as they proclaimed their mission to facilitate freedom and democracy by mobilizing their troops in such force. Britain's Prime Minister, in the face of mounting opposition, expounded the high moral ground for military action whilst the American President suggested that prayers should be offered for the soldiers and the people of Iraq. In response the Costa Rican theologian Elsa Tamez voiced the bewilderment and indignation of many in her letter to Christians when she asked: 'How can one bomb a people with weapons of mass destruction and at the same time pray for them?'[7] Feminists might respond: when the god prayed

---

6. Monica Sjöö and Barbara Mor, *The Great Cosmic Mother* (New York: HarperCollins, 1991), p. 394.

7. Elsa Tamez, *Letter to All Christians*, 14 March 2003, Biblical University, San Juan, Costa Rica.

to is made in the image of man, a god who reflects the patriarchal and phallocentric cultures that have trapped love and mercy within a legalistic and ritualized religious mindset that births ethical principles and praxis reflecting a basic understanding of the world as one divided into subjects and objects, into the sacred and the profane; where toughness is equated with brutality and interdependence with weakness. In such a world hierarchy and power go hand in hand, power being the domain of the dominant, the one who has control over life and death, and in traditional Christianity the one who has control over life after death. Such a god requires a saviour to rescue humanity from evil, brought about through the woman's desire to partake of the knowledge of good and evil, a redemption that could only be achieved through the sacrifice of his son, who by conquering death, was reborn into eternal life with god in heaven. The natural world and the female were relegated to the world of profanity.

Such a god gives to the male the right of conquest of the earth and the woman, paving the way for discrimination of all kinds in the name of righteousness, and the concept of complementarity in relationships, upheld to the present day in hierarchical institutional religions and maintained through history in the constant repetition of the norm of masculinity enacted symbolically in rites of culture. The Magisterium of the church is still exclusively male, persisting in excluding women from officially informing religious belief, justified by the incarnation of a male god in a male body. Emanating from this belief in the superiority of maleness is the pervasive abuse of women and children in the home that has led to the challenge of traditional theologies of atonement and ownership that underpin Christianity and Western culture, questioning if such places are safe and empowering places for women, refuting any notion that Jesus' death was necessary to placate a vengeful god for the misdemeanour of women, but the price paid to maintain the integrity of his relationship with a loving god and with his friends whom he wished to liberate from oppressive structures.

Sjöö and Mor posit that 'all religion is about the mystery of creation' and the basis of that mystery is 'woman's aw+e at her capacity to give birth',[8] claiming that 'men's original rituals were imitations of the female mysteries of menstruation and

8. Sjöö and Mor, *The Great Cosmic Mother*, p. 71.

childbirth',[9] exactly those mysteries that have excluded women from positions of leadership in the field of religion and ethics. Naomi Goldenberg and Kelly Raab argue from a psychoanalytical stance that the myths of gender and the male appropriation of the Eucharist act out the male desire to reproduce without women, signifying their envy of women's creativity, their ability to bleed without dying and to bring forth new life, women's agency and creativity being constantly displaced by the exclusive male enactment of these desires in sacrificial ritual, asserting that 'men are the primary, if not the sole, agents of creation'.[10] In their desire for transcendence the creative and nurturing power relegated to the world of women has to be subjugated. In response to the marvel of Being awe has been linked to violence.

One of the aims of religious education for young children is to draw out a sense of awe and wonder of creation, including their own bodies, using the archaic understanding of awe as respect for all that god saw that was good. Children listening to the threats of a show of military power that would cause 'shock and awe' were fed with a different connotation to that word; that connected with horror. Threats of violence creating fear and limiting agency are not unknown to children. Bullying is reported to be one of the three major concerns reported to Childline along with physical violence and family tensions. These concerns reflect the concern of the many women who are victims of violence in the home. Encouraging even the youngest children in school to find non-violent ways of resolving conflict is often met with the response from parents that it is a hard world out there and they have to be taught to be tough and how to fight. It is difficult to argue that it is not a hard world: national and international structures work in the favour of those with military and economic might. Those who resist place themselves on the margins of accepted ways of relating in cultures that glorify the strong individual, where making the grade means being the best at the expense of the rest and where compassion is equated with weakness. Not surprising after centuries of patriarchal

9. Sjöö and Mor, *The Great Cosmic Mother*, p. 72.

10. Naomi Goldenberg, 'The Divine Masquerade: A Psychoanalytic Theory about the Play of Gender in Religion', in Kathleen O'Grady, Ann L. Gilroy and Janette Patricia Gray, (eds.), *Bodies, Lives, Voices* (Sheffield: Sheffield University Press, 1998), p. 200. Kelly A. Raab, *When Women Become Priests* (New York: Columbia University Press, 2000), p. 123.

societies whose philosophy is upheld by religious dogma, patriarchy, as Starhawk points out, finding its ultimate expression in war where 'the tough can prove their toughness and the winners triumph over the losers'.[11] The vast collection of military hardware does not symbolize compassion and tenderness, and as the women worldwide who are sexually abused can witness, 'invasion and penetration are not acts of liberation'.[12] Starhawk pits feminist voices as a defence against the warmongering of patriarchy, claiming that as feminism analyses 'the constellation of values, ideas and beliefs that reinforces male control over women'[13] it has the potential to bring freedom for all to express the alternative values relegated to the private world of women and the home.

However, analysis is only the first step: giving value to the concept of the flourishing of all would entail its incorporation in the symbolic realm of the public world of our national and international institutions. Tissa Ballasuriya pointed out the potential of the institution of the church to bring about personal and global transformation, stating:

> Every week about 200 million persons meet all over the world in Christian communities. The Sunday celebration is perhaps the most numerous regular gathering of human beings around a common theme that this world knows. If it is vitalized into being truly a sacrament of communion through effective sharing, it can be the most efficacious means of bringing about the radical cultural revolution required amongst Christians.[14]

He cautioned that any transformation would require the death of consumerism, seeking of power and prestige, and organized selfishness. That transformation however is unlikely to take place in the present sacramental system that seems to be a topsy-turvy world where men enact the ultimate freedom for humans in finding the divine presence in the experience of birth, growth, nurturance, healing and the cyclical nature of life and death, while the menstruating, lactating female bodies that make present the reality of birth and nurturance have been marginalized; replaced by a spiritual expression of these realities that denies the presence of

---

11. Starhawk, *Women's Actions and Feminist Voices for Peace*, p. 2.
12. Starhawk, *Women's Actions and Feminist Voices for Peace*, p. 2.
13. Starhawk, *Women's Actions and Feminist Voices for Peace*, p. 2.
14. Tissa Ballasuriya, *The Eucharist and Human Liberation* (London: SCM Press, 1997), p. 132.

the divine in the carnal while proclaiming the incarnation of god in the world.

Some scientists are suggesting that the value of the 'feminine', with its link to the natural world and the subsequent power relations needs to be re-assessed in light of findings emphasizing the inter-relatedness of all life, as also the traditional dichotomous subject/object split[15] that has affected the development of human relationality. Rita Nakashima Brock[16] calls on psychoanalytical theories of development in maintaining that we are all subject to wrong relation through the polarization of gender identities in childhood leading to negative masculine independence and feminine over-dependence, making us all broken hearted. She argues that if relatedness of the heart, or the self was the focus of devotion the symbol of the presence of god could be the embodied interaction of right relation where justice is felt, and the lived life one open to as yet unknown possibilities. If we included in our consideration of ethics the knowledge gleaned from the heart as well as the head, if we based our moral judgements on an ethic of care and justice, would our world leaders be at the front of a line of army tanks or would the male potential for compassion, tenderness, kindness, loving co-operation and reconciliation be allowed to temper the callous toughness being shown in the battle for hearts and minds?

If the consciousness of our role as co-operators in the divine unfolding through relationality and mutuality was used as the basis of ethics and politics would a new world view emerge in which power was seen as the ability to empower, to nurture and to facilitate affective bonding, requiring in religious terms, not the intervention and sacrificial offering of a superior being to rescue humanity from the degradation of earthiness and bodiliness symbolized by woman, but the recognition and encoding of the dignity of being co-creators of the divine unfolding in which earthiness, bodiliness and relationality were essential values in the continuation of life? And if so, would we need to refer to the Geneva Convention to learn how to treat those we had taken prisoner? Or could the puzzle of how many cluster bombs equal a phial of Anthrax

15. See for instance, Maria Mies and Vandana Shiva, *Ecofeminism* (London: Fernwood Publishing, 1993), pp. 44-48.

16. Rita Nakashima Brock, 'Losing Your Innocence and Not Your Hope' in Maryanne Stevens (ed.), *Reconstructing the Christ Symbol* (New York/Mahwah: Paulist Press, 1993), pp. 30-54.

as a weapon of mass destruction become part of a history lesson for our children exemplifying the dearth of moral thinking in the 21st century that necessitated Rules of War? And would giving our children action men in the shape of Comical Ali be unthinkable?

As a young woman I was confirmed as an adult Christian in the Catholic Church. In the course of this rite of passage I was gently and symbolically struck on the side of the face by the Archbishop of Liverpool fully regaled in ecclesiastical dress to remind me that I was now agreeing to become a soldier of Christ. I often wondered what on earth that meant, as I had no desire to fight anyone. However, I cannot claim ignorance any longer: the icon of muscular Christianity, President of the USA and spokesman for the British government, Mr George Bush, has made it very clear in his victory speech to the American combatants. President Bush chose as his platform the flagship named after another American Patriarch, The USS Abraham Lincoln, returning home after its long tour of duty in liberating the people of Afghanistan and Iraq. Dressed in full military uniform as Commander-in-Chief of the armed forces, he used the words of the Prophet Isaiah to congratulate the assembled troops for their part in setting captives free and to justify and mourn the loss of those who had died in the cause of democracy, these same words of Isaiah used by another prophet, Jesus of Nazareth, at his inauguration address in the temple at the start of his public ministry, following his own struggle in the desert to discern the rightful use of power. It seems Mr Bush saw himself as continuing Christian tradition in the struggle for liberation, a soldier for Christ, Father of the Nation who was willing to sacrifice his children in the name of godliness. This, as Elsa Tamez reminds us, 'is a complete inversion of all Christian values in which we see in Jesus Christ, the Prince of Peace, and in God, the fullness of love and mercy'.[17] Jesus in confronting the oppressive structures and regimes of his time chose the way of non-violence and vulnerability.

A different interpretation of Christianity is being put forward by theologians such as Heyward and Brock, incorporating the thinking emanating from the scientific world of the relational nature of the cosmos and the interdependence of humans on the natural world and one another. These theologies refute any notion of a

---

17. Tamez, *Letter to All Christians*.

God of War but the symbol of the presence of the divine would be in right relations, that is relations that empower. Heyward states:

> Our capacity to god is the only creative, liberating response to the "patriarchal logic" of traditional Christianity (Heyward 1993). Godding we ourselves become agents of transformation in the world and church and, together, bear up the hope of the world...our sacred power to god...is the power of women to struggle, sometimes apart from men, sometimes with men, for mutual relation in and out of the church.[18]

Heyward defines wrong relations as those that disempower.

During the TV coverage of this war, time and again the reporters spoke about symbols. Perhaps the most popular reference was to the images of Saddam Hussein and his trappings of privilege being pulled down by coalition troops and the people of Iraq; the reality that those symbols made real now changed. But of the many images two in particular have stayed with me as a feminist theologian as symbols of women's bodies once again brought to prominence in the experience of two young women. The first was Private Jessica Lynch, the American soldier taken captive on 13th March at Nasariya, a nineteen year-old who, like many worldwide, had found employment in the armed forces, reportedly, in her case to earn enough to pay for her college education. At the beginning of April, she was carried from the Iraqi hospital where her broken bones and war wounds were being treated, rescued by US Special Forces in a dramatic show of the daring and might of the American war machine. The second was the sixteen year-old in the town of Basra hanged from a lamp post for waving to the Coalition forces she thought had rescued her from the oppression she had lived with all her life under the guise of a protective Iraqi regime. Two young women who became sacrificial offerings to the God of War, whose battered bodies highlight the reality of living in a world that subscribes to a masculine norm in which to be safe women must stay out of the public arena and conform to a world view in which God is made in the image of man.

In considering the future government of Iraq one reporter, commenting on the position of the Shi'ite clerics and the difficult question of the representation of women in a democratic Iraq,

---

18. Carter Heyward, 'Godding' in Lisa Isherwood and Dorothea McEwan (eds.), *An A-Z of Feminist Theology* (Sheffield: Sheffield Academic Press, 1996), p. 85.

observed: 'that sort of detail is too messy for the global leaders to cope with'. The truth of that remark could be confirmed by the women of Afghanistan who after risking death to educate their daughters during the Taliban regime were not allowed onto any public platform to influence or participate in the new government.[19]

During this Easter season I did not need to attend the church's liturgies to be immersed in the symbolic realm of the religion in which I was nurtured. From the TV in the corner of my living room I was assailed by war correspondents' reports and images of the central place in world politics of the familiar elements of the religious rites that were part of my culture: sacred texts, water, food, oil, flesh and blood. Massed armies made real who had the power of controlling these constituents of life, all used as tools of manipulation to keep the wheels of global capitalism turning for the enhancement of the few at the expense of the many. Elected leaders of democratic governments paraded as messianic figures dictating to the masses their belief that war was the only way to peace. The God of War was ensuring that his disciples were well cared for.

War enacted in the centres of civilian populations, where many of the victims are women and children trapped in their homes, destroys any illusion that society's public and private spheres can be separated and regulated from different ethical standpoints but highlights the necessity of recognizing and addressing the feminist issues related to the insidious polarization of gender values and its effect on our concept of justice.

Symbols come naturally from human experience: communal universal and enduring symbols have through history reflected and made real different realities in differing contexts. The understanding of the reality of our relationship to the divine is conveyed through sacramental symbols. Desiring to expand that understanding has led feminists to apply a hermeneutic of suspicion to many areas of traditional theology, unearthing its androcentric bias. Applying that same tool to sacramental symbols might pave the way for a symbolic that embraces and encompasses the values relegated to the feminine that are being re-assessed in face of the reality of the violence we and the earth are subjected to. Using the elements of water, food, oil, flesh and blood to symbolize a concept of the divine presence would then require an awareness of our

19. Starhawk, *Women's Actions and Feminist Voices for Peace*, p. 3.

interdependence and mutuality and a deep desire for all to have equal access to the elements that sustain life and enable all to flourish. If we desire a god of peace, our symbols will need to make real relationships rooted in justice for all people and the organic world on which we depend.

THE HIDDEN WARS: VIOLENCE AGAINST WOMEN AND
JUST WAR THEORY*

*Nicole Soleto*

It is generally acknowledged that in wartime the incidence of rape increases. Recent evidence now indicates that women also experience higher rates of domestic violence directly before, during and after war. Sadly, the evidence regarding violence against women and war seldom registers in the considerations of those who initiate and perpetrate war. The just war theory, crafted to assess the use of force in given circumstances and, where permissible, to limit violence between groups of people, does not consider the violent affects of war upon women. While men[1] wage war on the battlefields, little attention is paid to the parallel and often invisible war of violence being waged against women in homes and neighborhoods, schools and shops, surrounding land and refugee camps. Indeed, women are experiencing the hidden wars of violence.

Secular and religious scholars have developed just war theory over a long period when patriarchy was the dominant ideal. With

*   I thank Molly Gower, colleague and friend, for her assistance with library research and comments. I am also grateful to Professor David Little and Atalia Omer for their encouragement and support of this project. I dedicate this paper to my Tata, Joe Sotelo, Sr., and all my grandparents and ancestors who have known all too well the horrors of war and yet found the strength to live when so much has been destroyed.

1.   Although I use the word 'men', I am well aware that many women also participate in war and that terms 'men' and 'women' represent approximate ends of a gender spectrum as conceived by society. However, the majority of combat is still fought by 'men'. I also want to note that although I speak about violence against women, I am aware that there are women who abuse men and that abuse occurs between people of the same sex, also. All violence that arises from conflict and war should be acknowledged and assessed within the parameters of the just war theory.

the rise of feminist consciousness, and after a century of wars where documentation of violence against women has begun, there is a need to integrate the new understandings of war and women into the just war theory. Just war theory has been subject to alteration based upon the historical period in which it rests, most recently with consideration of nuclear warfare. In light of recent statistics that depict a drastic rise in domestic violence before, during and after war, I believe it is again time to reconstitute modern conceptions of just war theory to reflect the new understandings of how war affects women.[2]

## Violence against Women

In general, violence against women is nothing new within our historical consciousness. However, the concept that men should not commit violence against women is a more recent cultural development. So-called 'Western' history offers us written accounts of violence against women that originate from ancient Greece. Sadly, these ancient tales such as '[t]he abduction of Helen of Troy and the rape of the Sabine women are archetypal in Western culture, so much so that their human tragedy is obscured'.[3] Not only is the human tragedy obscured, but also the violence is often condoned based on 'patriarchal assumptions about women's subordinate status'.[4] These assumptions of women's inferiority are found prevalent in the Christian religion that developed in this Western, patriarchal culture. As the Christian feminist theologian Rosemary Radford Ruether has pointed out, 'The subordinate legal status of women was expressed in classical Christianity in an elaborate theory

2.   Although I refer to women in most of this paper, much of the hidden violence before, during and after war occurs against children, also. Unfortunately, while there is little evidence of war's affects on women, there is even less about its effects on children. Nevertheless, children are raped and subject to domestic and non-domestic violence often just as much, sometimes more so, than women. So although I call for a renewed look at just war theory and women's war-time experience, it is truly a call for integrating the concerns of all lives during war into just war theory and policy.

3.   Shana Swiss and Joan Giller, in *Journal of the American Medical Association* 270.5 (August 1993): 612-15.

4.   Rosemary Radford Ruether, 'The Western Religious Tradition and Violence Against Women in the Home' in Joanne Carlson Brown and Carole R. Bohn *et al.*, *Christianity, Patriarchy and Abuse: A Feminist Critique* (New York: The Pilgrim Press, 1989), p. 31.

of the inferiority of women's nature'.[5] The subordinate status of women in religion and society led to a culture in which violence against women was justified. This violence is not confined to ancient societies or classical Christianity, but exists around the world today. In the United States, 'a woman is beaten every 15 seconds; every six minutes a rape occurs; every day four women are killed by their batterers'.[6] In Sri Lanka, 'three-quarters of the women interviewed in an International Labour Office (ILO) study of plantation workers said they had been beaten by their husbands or estate superintendents'.[7] South African studies have concluded that 'one adult woman out of every six is assaulted regularly by her mate. In almost half of these cases, the man involved also abuses the woman's children'.[8] In Peru, statistics have shown that 'one of every four girl children will be the victim of sexual abuse before she reaches her sixteenth birthday, and a third of all adult women report that they have been forced to have sex against their will'.[9] This violence against women is reinforced in art, literature, media, politics, theology, and even just war theory and it is within the context of war that the incidents of violence against women climb to their highest levels.

## Just War Theory

Most cultures across civilizations have constructed some form of justification for, or limitation of, the use of violence. Within Western culture today, the term 'just war theory' is used to refer to a set of principles used when deciding if and how to go to war. This theory has been created and shaped over centuries by the hands of both Western religious and political forces who sought peace but knew the realism of war. Most people of antiquity held 'the myth of a one-time warless world in a lost age of gold, whose recovery was the object of desire and endeavor' within a religious context.[10] This

---

5.	Ruether, 'The Western Religious Tradition', pp. 31-32.

6.	Aruna Gnanadason, *No Longer a Secret: The Church and Violence Against Women* (Geneva: WCC Publications, 1993), p. 3.

7.	Gnanadason, *No Longer a Secret*, p. 3.

8.	Gnanadason, *No Longer a Secret*, p. 9.

9.	Gnanadason, *No Longer a Secret*, p. 3.

10.	Roland Bainton, *Christian Attitudes Toward War and Peace: A Historical Survey and Critical Re-evaluation* (Nashville: Abingdon Press, 1960), pp. 18, 20.

desire for peace prompted some to construct principles of war that
would encourage an eventual cessation of battle and a return to
this long-sought golden state. Both Hebrew and classical culture
included some notions of what we term today as 'just war theory'.
Most early Christians maintained pacifist attitudes and also
abstained from much political involvement. However, once the
Emperor Constantine legitimized Christians within the political
sphere there was a need to reconsider their formerly pacifist stance.
In addition, the early hopes for an imminent kingdom of peace had
not been realized and Christians had to reevaluate their relationship
with the world and its politics. When 'the Christian Church...came
under Constantine to the assumption of political tasks, the gap in
the New Testament ethic at the point of politics was supplied by
borrowings from Judaism and the classical world'.[11] The Christian
Augustine drew from these rich traditions and left a body of work
that later scholars would consider to be some of the primary origins
of Western Christianity's relationship with just war theory.
However, it was not until 'the compilation of canon law known as
the *Decretum*, written by the monk Gratian in the mid-twelfth
century' that one source gathered the just war notions into 'a single,
recognizable cultural consensus on the justification and limitation
of violence'.[12] Although scholars have expounded just war principles
in the centuries since the Middle Ages, the Catholic monk, Gratian,
endowed Western culture with the skeletal structure of modern
just war theory. Modern theory still adheres to this structure of *jus
ad bellum* criteria that decides if one should engage in combat whose
principles include the need for a just cause, right authority, right
intention, general proportionality, last resort and reasonable hope
for success. The structure also encompasses the *jus in bello* criteria
that limits conduct of war through 'discrimination', or distinguishing
combatants from noncombatants, and 'tactical proportionality', the
concept that a particular strategy's benefits must outweigh its harms.

11. Bainton, *Christian Attitudes Toward War and Peace*, p. 14.
12. James Turner Johnson, 'Historical Roots and Sources of the Just War Tradition
in Western Culture' in John Kelsay and James Turner Johnson *et al.*, *Just War and Jihad:
Historical and Theoretical Perspectives on War and Peace in Western and Islamic Traditions*
(New York: Greenwood Press, 1991), p. 14.

## Women's Voices Speak to Just War Theory

With the rise of feminism, it may be understood that the just war criteria were shaped in a realm where patriarchal concepts dominated and influenced all thought. To begin with, some feminists consider war, the subject of just war theory, to be an 'inherently patriarchal activity' where 'the aggressive character of the war itself...is to dominate and control another nation or people'.[13] With regard to the actual principles, some feminists critique the patriarchal political and religious influence that led to the theory's preoccupation with abstraction rather than focus on the lived experiences and consequences of war, particularly for women. For example, Augustine believed that 'the self and the body have only a relative and temporary value as parts of earthly existence' that could be given up for a 'higher' cause.[14] In light of this understanding, it is clear how the 'just cause' criterion may have been constructed in a way that was too abstract, dismissing the consequences of war on a body in support of a higher, 'just cause'. In addition to a critique of the theory's tendency for abstraction, feminists have also critiqued the theory's bent towards dichotomized thinking. A dualistic inclination creates a theory in which '[m]en were constituted as just Christian warriors, fighters, and defenders of righteous causes', finally given permission to fight after 300 years of relative pacifism.[15] However, women were left unmentioned and 'solidified into a culturally sanctioned vision of virtuous, nonviolent womanhood' under the heading 'noncombatants'.[16] This dichotomy sanctions men's actions and mutes women's agency. Many women are placed under the banner of passive noncombatants, subject to the consequences of a just war theory and practice that they had little or no part in constructing. In addition, feminists critique the religious and political influences that created a just war theory that upholds

13. Indai Lourdes Sajor *et al.*, *Common Grounds: Violence Against Women in War and Armed Conflict Situations* (Philippines: Asian Center for Women's Human Rights, 1998), p. 3.

14. Lucinda J. Peach, 'An Alternative to Pacifism? Feminism and Just-War Theory', in Karen J. Warren and Duane L. Cady *et al.*, *Bringing Peace Home: Feminism, Violence, and Nature* (Bloomington: Indiana University Press, 1996), p. 198.

15. Jean Bethke Elshtain, 'Reflection on War and Political Discourse Realism, Just War and Feminism in a Nuclear Age' in Jean Bethke Elshtain *et al.*, *Just War Theory* (New York: New York University Press, 1992), p. 266.

16. Elshtain, 'Reflection on War', p. 266.

the state's authority over individuals, particularly under the 'right authority' principle. Some feminists recognize that 'the Old Testament tradition of God's commandments that fed command-obedience conceptions of law in Judeo-Christian discourse' lingered into the final construction of just war theory that upholds state authority and mandates that citizens obey the state's decision for war.[17] This command to obedience has particularly disadvantaged women and children who often have little voice in war decisions since many nations' authority rests in the hands of men, albeit often only the elite men. Even in nations where there is a democratically elected government, sometimes economic, education, historical, religious and/or social structures hinder women from full and equal participation. This sample of critiques of just war criteria are a first step towards shifting the theory to include considerations of the violence experienced by women in war.

In light of these general feminist criticisms, one may question whether Western culture's code of war should be reconstituted or simply rejected for a new set of principles that take into account modern warfare and the way it adversely affects women. With regard to Western culture's code of war, some critics believe that the introduction of modern warfare necessitates the abolition of just war theory. From a religious standpoint, Catholic Cardinal Ottaviani proclaimed *bellum omnino interdicendum*, believing that 'war is to be entirely interdicted, by which he meant that modern war is incompatible with the just war'.[18] However, other religious voices such as the American Roman Catholic Bishops have kept the just war theory and expanded what can be considered under the existing principles to include nuclear warfare. From a feminist voice, philosopher Sara Ruddick offers to replace Western just war theory with a new concept based on 'maternal thinking'.[19] Alternatively, feminist scholar Lucinda Peach does not want to reject just war theory, but seeks to present 'how feminist perspectives and insights can provide a framework for revitalizing the application of just-war theory'.[20] Knowing that Western culture is unlikely to reject the just war theory in the near future, I agree with Peach in believing

17. Elshtain, 'Reflection on War', p. 272.
18. Bainton, *Christian Attitudes Toward War and Peace*, p. 234.
19. Sara Ruddick, *Maternal Thinking: Toward a Politics of Peace* (Boston: Beacon Press, 1989).
20. Peach, 'An Alternative to Pacifism?', p. 194.

that, like the Catholic Bishops who revitalized the just war theory in its application to nuclear warfare, Western culture must for now also integrate our new understandings about warfare and the resulting violence against women within the theory's existing structures. Nevertheless, I do believe that we, as a human community, must do everything within our power to prevent war and work towards a world in which war will never occur.

This work of integrating the new understandings of war and its affects on women into war codes has begun. During the last two centuries, the 'political and cultural hegemony exercised by Western nations led to the extension of positive international law, expressing just war concepts conceived as grounded in natural law, over much of the globe'.[21] There have been concerns about whose theories of war find credence within international bodies; nevertheless, just war thinking has extended beyond its traditional function as a national public and political discourse to become institutionalized within the codes of international laws of war. Additionally, the international community has begun to integrate some feminist concerns into its considerations of war and wartime activity. In October 2002, 'the first UN Security Council Resolution on Women and peace and security was passed unanimously'.[22] This resolution, in theory, 'makes the pursuit of gender equality relevant to every single Council action, ranging from mine clearance to elections to security sector reform'.[23] Although the long-term results of this resolution have yet to be seen, this is a hopeful step for women who experience violence during war. This step comes after a few other small but significant steps towards recognizing violence against women during war and conflict. The Tokyo War Crimes Trials after World War II were the first trials to identify rape as a war crime, among other crimes against humanity. In 1949, the Fourth Geneva Convention Relative to the Protection of Civilian Persons in Time of War declared wartime rape a human rights violation. Finally, in 1993 the United Nations Commission on Human Rights crafted a resolution that situates rape within the category of war crimes and the UN General Assembly created the Declaration on

21. Johnson, 'Historical Roots', p. 6.
22. Elizabeth Rehn and Ellen Johnson Sirleaf, 'Women, War and Peace: The Independent Experts' Assessment on the Impact of Armed Conflict on Women and Women's Role in Peace-Building' (New York: UNIFEM Headquarters, 2002), p. 3.
23. Rehn and Sirleaf, 'Women, War and Peace', p. 3.

the Elimination of Violence Against Women. These are positive, conceptual *first* steps towards ensuring women's lives during war are taken seriously by international political bodies. But I ask, are women taken seriously within just war theory?

It may seem that as long as international political bodies take note of women's lives, it is unnecessary to return to the just war theory on which the international law was often based or to integrate the concerns about violence against women during war. I strongly disagree. The just war theory refers not merely to written codes but represents a general Western, and increasingly international, cultural consensus regarding the justification for and the limitation of war. Just war theory often embodies popular sentiment towards war and is part of most Western public and political discourse when war is considered. If the world community fails to revise just war theory, then the public must rely upon international authority to dictate when war is justified and how it may be fought. This subjection to hierarchical discourse merely perpetuates the patriarchal problems already inherent in just war theory that allow 'authority' to dictate when and how wars will be battled. Instead, just war theory needs to be reconstituted to include concerns about violence against women by the voices of women and men from around the globe. It is my hope that the voices and evidence I present below will help to expand the just war theory's criteria to include the understanding of violence against women during war, much like the U.S. Catholic Bishops' *Challenge to Peace* has extended the dialogue of just war thinking to include considerations of nuclear warfare. Although the evidence of violence against women must be considered when judging the criteria of the just war theory as a whole, I believe this evidence has a particular need to speak to the principles of 'proportionality', 'discrimination', and 'reasonable hope for success'.

## Proportionality

I was at my house with my aunt and her five children when a group of Interahamwe came shouting and making noise. We tried to escape. Everywhere, people were being killed. I was caught by a group of Interahamwe on 1 April 1994, along with about twenty other women, and we were held by them in Gatare sector. Some of them decided to rape us before killing us. Others of them refused to rape us. The ones that wanted to rape us began to rape the women one by one. About ten of them would gang-rape a woman, and when they had finished, they would kill her by pushing a sharpened stick the size of a broomstick into her vagina until she was bleeding and almost dead. I saw them do this to several women. All the time, they were saying things like, 'We want to have a taste of Tutsi women'. One of them told us that they were going to chop the Tutsi women into pieces over days — one leg today, another arm tomorrow — until we died slowly. I managed to escape from them while they were raping and hid in the bushes until 2 May when the RPF [Rwanda Patriotic Front] saved us.[24]

Within the just war context, 'proportionality' refers to the idea that the benefits of going to war and the benefits of particular strategies will outweigh the harm. However, the benefits of going to war and the harm of war have not traditionally considered women's experience of violence, such as the above account. If violence against women were taken into consideration, would the U.S. and other countries have intervened sooner in the Rwandan conflict when it was determined that between 500,000 and 1 million men, women, and children were killed in four months and that 250,000 to 500,000 women and girls were raped in less than one hundred days?[25] Or, in a different pre-war context, would the magnitude of the possible harm that could be done against women in a conflict lead to a decision where war would be averted?

In light of the experience of women during war, proportionality should: 'require a more compulsive examination of the potential long-term consequences of contemplated intervention. Such considerations should highlight the impact on civilians. This includes not only their survival, but also the quality of their lives and relationships'.[26] I agree that proportionality must take into account the experience of men *and* women's 'lives and relationships' and not just what happens on the battlefields, economic fields or political fields. We must recognize that the harms of going to war include mass rapes and domestic violence against women and, if war is not stopped, the violence against women only escalates. Taking the evidence of rape and domestic violence into war deliberations may encourage some countries to increase their military power to one

24. 'Jane', Human Rights Watch.
25. Laura Flanders, 'Rwanda's Living Casualties', in Anne Lewellyn Barstow *et al.*, *War's Dirty Secret: Rape, Prostitution and Other Crimes Against Women* (Cleveland, OH: The Pilgrim Press, 2000), p. 96.
26. Peach, 'An Alternative to Pacifism?', p. 205.

particular side, change the amount or type of military support given, or refrain from using military might at all. For example, feminist scholar Peach proposes that if the rape of Bosnian Muslim women were to have been taken into consideration under proportionality there may have been 'a determination that armed intervention, or at least additional military support for the Bosnian Muslims would [have been] morally justified'.[27]

The evidence of what happens to women and children during war must be brought to light so that those who make decisions about the war's proportions, and the public who may have the ability to influence the democratic state, may make informed decisions. What *are* the proportions of violence against women and children during war? How do greater proportions of military violence correlate with greater proportions of violence against women? With regards to domestic violence and violence against women in general, the correlation is great. Recent studies have pointed to a correlation between increased levels of violence against women and the rise of war. Although violence against women may include rape, it also includes increased emotional, economic, physical and other sexual trauma. Domestic violence and/or violence against women increases significantly immediately before, during and after a war. Before a war when economic, political and social structures break down, domestic violence rates escalate. An example of the rise in domestic violence comes to us from Serbia where a women's and children's hotline received a sharp rise in calls for help when 'men became enraged after listening to and watching the nationalist propaganda [on television news] and beat women as a way to avenge their wounded national pride'.[28] The high rates of violence continue during wartime. During the United State's mission in Afghanistan, four military men murdered their wives within a short span of just six weeks. Three of the men had recently returned from the conflict in Afghanistan. In fact, a 2002 study showed that U.S. military families seem to have a domestic violence rate much higher than the general U.S. population.[29] Unfortunately, this domestic violence

27. Peach, 'An Alternative to Pacifism?', p. 205.

28. Lepa Mladjenovic and Donna M. Hughes, 'Feminist Resistance to War and Violence in Serbia', in Marguerite R. Waller and Jennifer Rycenga (eds.), Frontline Feminisms (New York: Garland Publishing Inc., 2000), p. 269.

29. Holly Prigerson, Paul K. Maciejewski and Robert A. Rossenheck, 'Population Attibutable Fractions of Psychiatric Disorders and Behavioral Outcomes Associated with Combat Exposure Among U.S. Men' in *American Journal of Public Health* 92.1 (2002).

does not stop at the conclusion of war. In Cambodia it is estimated that 75 per cent of women experienced domestic violence during and after war as men took out their frustrations upon women and social structures of support were less available.[30] It is clear that 'when the army comes back, it visits on the women at home the escalated level of assault the men were taught and practiced on women in the war zone'.[31] In fact, a study by the Veteran Affairs Medical Center and Yale University discovered that 21 per cent of current spousal abuse by U.S. veterans would not be in existence had the male partners not participated in combat.[32] The large rise in domestic violence correlated with war means that not only soldiers but also civilian women suffer on the hidden battlefields of their homes, neighborhoods and refugee camps.[33] With this new evidence regarding the proportion of violence that women experience from war, I reiterate that the just war principal of 'proportionality' needs to consider the deeper impacts of military power on civilians, particularly the violence against women and children.

## Discrimination

In the capital, Monrovia, one mother, who wanted to be identified only by her village name, Ma Voph, screamed as she recounted how her daughter, Nannu, had been raped and killed on the morning of her 10th birthday.

On that Sunday morning in July, in a quiet residential section of Monrovia, she recalled how she had sung a chorus of "Happy Birthday", fixed Nannu a bowl of oats and let her indulge in a bottle of syrupy grape-flavored Fanta.

It was not even noon when men loyal to Mr. Taylor burst into her home. Terrified, Nannu clutched the end of her mother's blouse, yelling, "Mommy!"

30. Bridget Bryne, Rachel Marcus and Tanya Powers-Stevens, 'Gender, Conflict and Development' II (Cambodia Case Study Report. Bridge: Brighton, 1995).

31. Catherine A. Mackinnon, 'Rape, Genocide and Women's Human Rights' in Stanley French, Wanda Teays and Laura Purdy *et al.*, *Violence Against Women: Philosophical Perspectives* (Ithaca, NY: Cornell University Press, 1998), p. 48.

32. Prigerson, Maciejewski and Rosenheck, 'Population Attributable Factions'.

33. Many men who suffer post-traumatic stress disorder from war inflict abuse upon their partners. Combatants suffer beyond a war's declared end, also.

One soldier, who called himself Black Dog, raped and killed Ma Voph's daughter. Another militia-man assaulted a 14-year-old girl whom the mother was raising.

Most of all, Ma Voph said, they took away her sense of herself. A stout, proud woman of 42, she described how she had pulled herself up from her village, cared for her siblings when their own mother died, opened a shop in the capital, bought a car, raised her own children and took in someone else's. Then three men with guns wrecked it all.[34]

In just war theory, the 'discrimination' criterion differentiates combatants from noncombatants, considering noncombatants to be under a banner of immunity. In theory, this discrimination clause should have protected 10 year-old Nannu and her 14 year-old friend. It did not. Nations are at fault for not enforcing the discrimination clause that should have protected these young girls and their mother.

The 'discrimination' criterion in just war theory originates from the Catholic Church's attempt 'to protect churchly persons...and lands from harm during warfare' but '[t]he broader development of the idea of noncombatant immunity [includes] all persons not capable of bearing arms...or not actually involved in bearing arms'.[35] However, this banner of immunity has simply succeeded in veiling the horrors of violence done against women during war instead of taking affirmative steps towards preventing violence against noncombatants. The discrimination clause of just war criteria needs to include not only a banner of immunity for noncombatants, but specific wording or goals to ensure political, religious and/or social support that will actively prevent violence against women in pre-conflict and conflict settings and support them if violence does occur.

What horrors of violence do these 'noncombatants' face and how many women experience this violence? Looking first at the violence, women 'noncombatants' are often victims of horror by the 'hidden' weapons of rape, domestic violence and violence in general against women.

Rape and other forms of violence are often used as weapons of war with a variety of intentions. Sometimes rape is used as a method of boosting soldiers' morale. In a *New York Times* interview with a Serbian soldier, the young man 'explained that his commanders had advised him and his companions that raping Muslim women

34. Somini Sengupta, 'All Sides in Liberation Conflict Make Women Spoils of War' (New York: *The New York Times*, 20 November 2003).
35. Johnson, 'Historical Roots', p. 15.

was "good for raising a fighter's morale", and that he had followed their advice several times at a motel used as a prison for Muslim women'.[36] Rape has also been utilized as a method of ethnic cleansing to frighten women and cause them to flee a territory. Refugees in the former Yugoslavia 'described how public raping of women by military forces was used systematically to force families to flee their villages, achieving the goal of "ethnic cleansing"'.[37] Rape as part of an ethnic cleansing strategy may also carry the intention of impregnating the women with men's sperm from a particular ethnic background to re-populate the territory with the 'proper' ethnicity. An international team of physicians, at the request of the UN, performed an investigation into forced pregnancies in the former Yugoslavia by a sampling of six hospitals and found at least 119 pregnancies that resulted from rape. This statistic tells us that at least 11,900 rapes had occurred, based on the conservative estimate that only 1 per cent of rapes result in pregnancy.[38] Despite these and other intentions, it is clear that rape is a weapon of war and that it is being used against noncombatants.

Although there exist a variety of intentions for the use of violence against women during war, the way it has been carried out in the last century ranges from pre-war propaganda to wartime trafficking. Although violence against women may be considered by some an individual act, it often occurs within a group context, or as part of a group strategy. Before the war began, State propaganda in Yugoslavia was used to incite the mass rape and abuse of women. Serbian communities watched their television screens fill with 'footage of actual rapes, with the ethnicity of the victims and perpetrators switched, to inflame Serbs against Muslims and Croatians'.[39] The government and/or military may not just promote the rape of noncombatants through propaganda, but often these institutions subtly or overtly order it as part of a conflict's strategy. Although not all militaries give orders to soldiers to engage in mass rapes, it is often encouraged through socialization. Most men would not commit rape, but in particular situations men may become socialized rapists. In fact, 'it is the socialization of men by men in

36. Gnanadason, *No Longer a Secret*, p. 16.
37. Swiss and Giller, in Journal of the American Medical Association.
38. Swiss and Giller, in Journal of the American Medical Association.
39. MacKinnon, 'Rape, Genocide', p. 52.

their bonding groups, and the view of women that is engendered, that provides the strongest cues towards rape'.[40] Unfortunately, this socialization becomes part of official strategy in some wars when the military not only subtly but also overtly directs soldiers to rape noncombatants. It has been learned that some Serbian soldiers raped Muslim and Croatian women, often by encouragement from 'groups of fellow soldiers, and even sometimes by their commanding officers' in a war where 'gang rape in concentration camps, at least at the beginning of the war, seems to have been common'.[41] The military strategy of raping women extended to the construction of 'rape camps' throughout Bosnian Serb-controlled territory, as well as a far smaller number of camps run by Croatian and Bosnian government forces.[42] Not only does conflict give rise to rape camps, but trafficking of women and girls also increases during wartime. 'Even when the military person is not involved in a sex "crime" — the mere presence of the military or even peacekeepers in an area — promotes the business of trafficking in women and prostitution as an economic means' (Women's International League for Peace and Freedom website).[43] These are just a few examples of the variety of ways in which violence against noncombatants occurs during wartime.

Although the world community is beginning to understand the horror women experience as 'noncombatants' during war, including pre- and post-conflict situations, the precise number of women affected is difficult to assess. However, if one looks beneath the blanket of immunity, one may *begin* to discover how many women 'noncombatants' are wounded or casualties in war — buried underneath the 'discrimination' clause and invisible to history books and the public eye. Rape, domestic violence and general violence against women is under-reported in peacetime, but it is even less

40. Larry May and Robert Strikwerda, 'Men in Groups: Collective Responsibility for Rape', in Karen J. Warren and Duane L. Cady *et al.*, *Bringing Peace Home: Feminism, Violence and Nature* (Bloomington: Indiana Univeristy Press, 1996), p. 182.

41. May and Strikwerda, 'Men in Groups', p. 176.

42. George Rodrigue, 'Sexual Violence: Enslavement and Forced Prostitution', in Roy Gutman and David Rieff *et al.*, *Crimes of War* (New York: W.W. Norton, 1999).

43. Women's International League for Peace and Freedom 'Militarism and HIV/ AIDS: The Deadly Consequences for Women'. Background paper for UN General Assembly Special Session on HIV/AIDS, June 2001. See http://www.wilpf.int.ch/ publications/2001hiv.htm.

likely to be reported during wartime due to 'the profound emotional pain and stigma attached to it, fear for the safety of family left behind, and lack of ordinary support systems' (Swiss and Giller).[44] Additionally, the means to measure such statistics are often absent 'in a country where everything has been destroyed'.[45] Although we have some sense of the magnitude of the crimes committed, we do not have a full understanding of how widespread violence against women becomes during war. Nevertheless, the figures we do have for noncombatant victims of violence are horrifying and we know that the actual figures can only be worse. In the former Yugoslavia, estimates for the first months of war indicate that 30,000 to 50,000 Muslim women were raped by Serbian soldiers.[46] During the Tokyo Tribunal on Japan's Military Sexual Slavery, a public hearing depicted '[t]he widely practiced epidemic of rape during war—by one state for example—claimed the physical and mental integrity of 500,000 Korean victims'.[47] In Rwanda after the 1994 genocide, it was 'concluded that nearly every female over the age of 12 who survived the genocide was raped'.[48] In Colombia, 'perhaps as many as 50,000 women are being trafficked annually out of the country' as part of the societal and economic breakdown during the civil war.[49] This violence is not limited to middle-aged women but extends to females of all ages. In Liberia, 'mothers and daughters were raped by the same men. Boys assaulted women old enough to be their mothers'.[50] The experiences and statistics exist in all corners of the globe and cut across age, economic, and social strata; they portray a world of women suffering violence at the hands of soldiers, government officials, and intimate partners during wartime. If these women were counted as combatants in the struggles they find themselves facing during war, what would the wounded and casualty totals number from wars of this last century when added to traditional battle figures? The number would be

44. Swiss and Giller.
45. Sengupta, 'All Sides', p. 22.
46. May and Strikwerda, 'Men in Groups', pp. 178-79.
47. Women's International League for Peace and Freedom.
48. www.unicef.org/protection/index_armedconflict.html.
49. Rehn and Sirleaf, 'Women, War and Peace', p. 13.
50. Sengupta, 'All Sides', p. 4.

astounding and sickening, beyond the already gruesome sum recorded in history textbooks. Also, sadly, we know that the number of women harmed is only increasing. It has been found that in the twentieth century, 'civilian fatalities in war climbed dramatically from 5 per cent at the turn of the century, to 15 per cent during World War I, to 65 per cent by the end of World War I, to more than 75 per cent in the wars of the 1990s'.[51] So although, theoretically, women may be 'protected' under the banner of immunity, the lack of its enforcement and actual protection before, during and after war must be publicly exposed and the extent to which noncombatants are harmed demands that the discrimination clause of just war theory include specific ways that noncombatants will actually be protected, not just hidden under the banner of 'immunity'.

### Reasonable Hope For Success

In the autumn of 1991 the SOS Hotline started receiving calls from women who were battered after men watched the TV news in which there were stories filled with hatred for 'the enemy'. Women said the men became enraged after listening to and watching the nationalist propaganda and beat women as a way to avenge their wounded national pride. Some women reported that they were beaten for the first time in their lives after the men watched one of the nationalist reports on Serbian victims of war. Women reported that their husbands cursed the Croats and Muslims in Croatia and Bosnia-Herzegovina while beating them. In most of these cases the ethnicity of the woman was the same as her partner. In cases where the ethnicity of the man and the woman was different, the man beat the woman, claiming 'Our five minutes has come', meaning that this was the man's opportunity to be the victor for his ethnicity for a short period of time.[52]

The just war criterion of 'reasonable hope for success' has traditionally focused on the hope of success within the perimeters of the military endeavor. However, as one may note in the above story, most women and children do not see wars as successful when they cause the men in their lives to commit violence against them—

---

51. Rehn and Sirleaf, Women, War and peace', p. 3.
52. Mladjenovic and Hughes.

sometimes even before a war officially breaks out and often leading
to a lifetime pattern of abuse and/or a lifetime of difficult healing
from the trauma.

It is vital for the lives of women, children and the warring nations
in general, that this just war criterion include a conception of 'success'
that encompasses the long-term welfare of the warring nations *and*
the individuals within those territories. For women and children
who have been victims of increased violence during war, these war
wounds last long after the last shot has been fired and raise the
question of whether a war traditionally deemed 'successful' may,
in fact, be a failure for the country as a whole.

The failure of war in this light often comes from the grave, long-
term damage that results from the increased violence done against
women. One outcome of the violence women experience during
war is long-term psychological damage. Each culture experiences
rape and domestic violence differently. The psychological effects
of rape and domestic violence on women come mainly from research
done in Western cultures during peacetime. However, it may be
possible to use this information as a starting point for understanding
what women worldwide might experience after being victims of
violence. In the short-term, women victims experience 'shock, a
fear of injury or death that can be paralyzing, and a sense of
profound loss of control over one's life'.[53] The long-term
psychological effects include 'persistent fears, avoidance of situations
that trigger memories of the violation, profound feelings of shame,
difficulty remembering events, intrusive thoughts of the abuse,
decreased ability to respond to life generally, and difficulty
reestablishing intimate relationships'.[54] Although these symptoms
have the potential to be treated, most countries lack the money and
resources to effectively care for victims of rape or domestic violence.
Sadly, even in cases where women find care, the symptoms may
persist for their entire lifetime. A Dutch woman who testified in
1992 to the UN Commission on Human Rights in Geneva said, 'the
deep and lasting psychological damage sustained can never really
be compensated for or erased'.[55] It must be noted that in non-

53. Swiss and Giller.
54. Swiss and Giller.
55. Gnanadason, *No Longer a Secret*, p. 15.

Western cultures, women may experience psychological trauma and express their symptoms differently. In Uganda, women victims of violence more often reported physical concerns including 'headaches, chest pain, and rashes' and 'vaginal discharge or pelvic pain, dating from the time of the rape… [and] persistence of perceived infection…reflect[ing] a common sequel to rape of feeling dirty and infected'.[56]

The experience of violence during war not only causes psychological trauma, but also results in physical suffering and long-term health problems that diminish a war's 'reasonable hope for success'. After becoming a victim of domestic violence or rape, women often suffer from bruises, deep wounds and broken bones. In Mexico City, a study showed that more than 'two-thirds of the visits for treatment of injuries at health care services were associated with domestic violence'.[57] One may only imagine what suffering women experience in war-torn areas where access to medical care is rare. Additionally, women who experience sexual violence may become infected with sexually transmitted diseases (STDs) that go untreated. For other women, even if they have received medical intervention, it only prolongs their lives in order to meet being overwhelmed by inevitable death if the rapist has left them with an HIV death sentence. The rapist becomes a double-murderer when the woman conceives a child who also contracts the disease. The Women's International League for Peace and Freedom reminds us 'women worldwide are contracting the virus as a result of wartime activity. Killing with weapons and killing with infected body fluids will continue as long as there is war. And women who are infected at higher rates than men, pay the deepest price' and that '[a]dequate efforts have not been made to link the role of the militarism paradigm to infection rates'.[58] It is clear that rape and domestic violence victims are left with long-term health problems for years after the actual act, many times ending in death. Success on a battlefield diminishes when you are left with a country of traumatized women who have not experienced the 'success' of war.

56. Swiss and Giller.
57. Alberto Concha–Eastman and Andres Villaveces, 'Guidelines for the Epidemiological Surveillance on Violence and Injuries' Pan American Health Organization, February 2001. www.paho.org/English/AD/SDE/RA/VIP_Guidelines.pdf.
58. Women's International League for Peace and Freedom Website.

The lasting trauma of rape and domestic violence from war extends to the children of the country. Although most of the statistics that I have presented have focused on the experience of adult women, children are often victims of rape and domestic violence, as well. A UNHCR staff member recalls:

> Nothing had prepared me for the plight of these women who came to us in the UNHCR office every day, desperate for help... One woman told us that her fourteen year-old daughter was raped, and then, because of shame and poverty, she gave her daughter to an old man in marriage as his second wife. In some cases, the girl is given to the man who rapes her.[59]

These children who experience or witness violence endure similar psychological and/or physical symptoms. A study from Canada 'reports post-traumatic stress, clinical dysfunction, behavioral and emotional disorders in children from violent homes'.[60] Again, this study comes from a Western culture that has not recently experienced war upon its own soil so it may only be imagined what must happen to children's psyches when the war rages outside the doors of their home *and* within the confines of their homes in the form of domestic violence. This and multiple other studies show that children, whether the direct victims of violence or whether witnesses to violence, suffer greatly. Just like adult women victims of violence, children's symptoms may last for their lifetimes and, subsequently, affect generations after a war. In fact, once violence begins, the cycle of violence often continues for generations within a family. Retrospectively, we see that a war is a starting point for decades of domestic violence against women and children. However, this cycle of violence may be prevented or interrupted by decreasing the amount of violent conflict on a national level, an investment that may yield 'long lasting effects on children and the future of a nation'.[61]

Finally, it is important to look at how the violence suffered by women and children during war affects the country as a whole when one ponders the category 'reasonable hope of success'. Again, if one expands the understanding of 'reasonable hope of success'

59. www.eurasianet.org/policy_forum/vand022001.shtml.

60. Roxanna Carillo, *Battered Dreams: Violence Against Women as an Obstacle to Development* (New York: UNIFEM/Women Ink, 1992), p. 10.

61. Carillo, *Battered Dreams*, p. 10.

beyond the war to encompass what the war's impact might have on the success of the development of a nation, it is fairly clear from research done by UNIFEM that war is not successful for a nation's development. UNIFEM reports that 'female focused violence undermines widely held goals for economic and social development in the Third World', in part, because 'where domestic violence keeps a woman from participating in a development project...development does not occur'.[62] Nations lose up to half of the power of their people when women are plagued by domestic violence and its lingering effects. Oftentimes, women are so traumatized by violence or fear of violence that they lose the ability to participate in development projects or abusive partners keep them from involvement. In fact, many failed or struggling development projects report that 'violence against women is often a direct obstacle to women's participation'.[63] Not only does domestic violence keep women from participating in development projects that could otherwise help the nation repair itself after a war, but domestic violence also costs the country money and other resources that could otherwise be spent on the nation's development.

Most developing countries do not have the resources to spend on domestic violence services, or chose not to do so. However, when countries do have the resources and attempt to curb the affects of violence upon its population, it costs money that could otherwise be spent on developmental success, such as education and healthcare. Since most developing nations that have recently experienced war have not been able to set up the complex care services needed for women victims of violence, the research on the costs of assistance to domestic violence victims comes from Western, industrialized cultures. Nevertheless, the Western culture's financial figures for helping domestic violence victims are astonishingly high. The Australian Committee on Violence estimates that the 'cost of refuge accommodation for victims of domestic violence for the year 1986–87 was US$27.6 million' and this figure does not include the amount of resources that go to counseling, healthcare and other services for domestic violence victims'.[64] It is difficult to imagine a

62. Carillo, *Battered Dreams*, pp. 8, 11.
63. Carillo, *Battered Dreams*, p. 12.
64. Carillo, *Battered Dreams*, p. 11.

developing nation that could even begin to help its women and children recover from the violence imposed by a war. Additionally, the financial costs are only one part of helping women to recover from violence experienced during war. Many cultural attitudes preclude recovery assistance for women. In Croatia, victims of rape and domestic violence appear to be ignored 'where predominately male, Roman Catholic, and conservative health officials are too discomforted by the subject to provide care or compassion'.[65] Indeed, there seems to be a dim 'reasonable hope of success' for the development of a country after a war when one considers a war's effects upon women and children.[66]

## Conclusion

In Liberia, women 'were raped when Mr. Taylor was a rebel leader fighting his way to the presidency. They were raped when the next band of rebels fought to oust him. They have been raped since Mr. Taylor's departure on 11 August, as his loyalists and enemies continue to fight in remote jungle outposts'.[67]

It is evident that the culture of war will continue for the foreseeable future. Knowing this, it is essential that Western, Christian-influenced societies, responsible for crafting just war theory, should continue to re-shape the theory's principles in light of on-going research and cultural progress that allows the plight of women during war to emerge so that, for the first time, women might explicitly be included within just war criteria. It is also important for other cultures and traditions to continue creating their own theories of 'just war' in light of women's experience of violence. Additionally, researchers who study the effects of war upon women must continue to carry their findings to the attention of state and international figures that decide the *jus ad bellum* and *jus in bello* of war. If the extensive statistics and stories of rape and domestic violence during war are integrated, as I have suggested, into the categories of just war theory and seriously considered in the

65. Warren and Cady *et al.*, p. 6.
66. Despite the odds against women during war, I want to note that women are not always the victims and that many women are part of solidarity and peace movements that support people before, during and after war which include being involved in local and national post-conflict development processes.
67. Sengupta, 'All Sides', p. 34.

deliberations of those going to war, wars would have to be fought differently, if at all. Realistically, I know that patriarchy and militaristic culture within an empire mindset precludes most research on women's experience of violence from having any impact upon wars in the near future. Nevertheless, it is my hope that the world community will continue to move in a direction that takes this new understanding of women's experience of war seriously. I hope that Western culture, particularly the religious voices that were some of the just war theory's most important contributors, will again re-shape the just war theory to include these new findings as they did in light of nuclear warfare. It is also essential that governments and their militaries take note of these findings when considering engagement in armed conflict. Finally, citizens of governments, including women, need to hold their national governments and world councils to an expanded just war criteria that takes women's experience of violence during war into consideration so that the worldwide destruction of lives does not continue. Indeed, a rape victim counselor in Liberia told one of her patients during the war, 'You have to be the one now to stand up'.[68] It saddens me that women who are victimized must also bear the burden of changing the system that often keeps them from standing. Nevertheless, I know that women are the ones who know most intimately the destruction that war brings and are the ones capable of revealing and stopping the hidden wars of violence against women.

68. Sengupta, 'All Sides', p. 37.

# JEWISH WOMEN IN SEARCH OF GOD AND HUMANITY IN TIMES OF ATROCITY

## Thalia Gur Klein

### Historic Perspective

Repeated history of persecution, lethal hostility and genocide have affected Jewish liturgy, literature, collective memory and socio-theological visions. In the aftermath of national disasters and atrocity, texts expressed horror, lament and protest. Historically, literature of atrocity has been grappling with the Jewish belief in the Hebrew God and His covenant with His people; and it is this belief that was put under painful strain in time of atrocity.[1] This motif inheres in the complexity and depth of Jewish literature and hagiography in time of atrocities. Harsh reality poses a dilemma between predicament and belief, and mystical search of God may arise or falter in times of predicament. Recurrently, in time of atrocity, theology generates a deep sense of atonement and self-expiating accusation before God, enhancing piety and search for righteousness. Closely related, belief in God and His covenant has produced messianic visions of a utopian era without persecution, trouble, death or toil; this messianic world will come through expiating good deeds that will rid the world of evil and redeem the righteous. Concomitant with messianic visions comes the mystic advocacy of suffering envisioned as 'pangs of messiah', whereby times of atrocity and persecution are delineated as painful labour before the birth of messianic times.[2] The Jewish people have

---

1. Raphael Patai, *The Messiah Texts* (Detroit, MI: Wayne State University Press, 1979), p. xxxi.
2. Patai, *The Messiah Texts*, pp. 95-104.

traditionally vindicated their belief in God's covenant by interpreting atrocious times as a transitional path to messianic time.

This messianic theology has epitomized victims of persecution and atrocities as holy martyrs and forerunners who pave the expiating road to messianic times. Compromising between atrocious reality and belief, sanctified martyrdom has served as consoling theology, helping the community undergo predicaments while holding to their God and in corollary be comforted by messianic promise of another world to come by piety, righteousness and expiation. Epitomizing their victims as martyrs, *kaddosh*, persons victimized and died for God and Jewish belief; such death has been sanctified as *kiddush hashen*, sanctifying the Name of God. In close proximity to the martyr, we meet the living holy person, a righteous person entitled *zaddik*. The *zaddik* shoulders the suffering of the community and the world, and promulgating goodness, unbound empathy for others, piety and self-sacrificing deeds for God, the living holy person restrains evil from immersing the world. The two types of holy people relate to suffering in times of atrocities. However, the righteous person experiences vicarious suffering with the world, while the martyr is subject to it. Both types enhance the coming of the Messiah that will end all violence, hate and persecution.

Secularization of the bulk of the Jews has irreversibly permeated Jewish life in the twentieth century. In corollary, literature of atrocity has distanced itself from mystical theology that promulgates collective disasters as pangs of Messiah paving the path to utopian times. Messianic visions have altered into Zionist hopes; and ensuing politics, which was utopian as well as defensive and militant, related the historic persecutions of Jews to their political vulnerability in the Diaspora. However, in the wake of the Holocaust era, Jewish mysticism still continued to permeate collective memory. Appropriated by both secular and religious sectors of the Jewish people in Israel and around the world, victims of the Holocaust have accumulated a degree of veneration on a par with sanctification of holy martyrs. Demonstrating precipitation of mixed mysticism in contemporary politics, the *Knesset*, the Israeli Parliament, passed a bill in 1952 granting all Jewish victims of the Holocaust a posthumous citizenship in this world and a place in heaven as *kaddosh*, a holy martyr.[3] Following the model of a *Kiddush Hashem*,

3. Zev Garber, 'Jewish Perspective on Edith Stein's Martyrdom' in Harry James Cargas, *The Unnecessary Problem of Edith Stein* (Lanham: University Press of America 1994), p. 70.

sanctified martyrdom of Jewish victims of atrocity, the Israeli State has promulgated the traditionally religious sanctification of Jewish victims *Kiddush Hashem* while enforcing secular legislation. This paradoxical veneration attests to veneration of Jewish martyrs carried out by a secular public on secular altars outside religious institutes.

### The Holocaust Artist, Texts of Atrocity

Residing in proximity with historiography, art of atrocity grapples with the dilemma of authenticity. Eventually, artists of atrocity face the fact that any experience can be authentic only at the moment of occurrence. In the aftermath, experiences may be retold or sunk into the crude silence. The moment an experience is told, horrific and degrading as it was at the moment of occurrence, it requires formal and artful means to communicate. Here we see the moot idea of texts of atrocity. What would appear to be the appropriate means to convey times of violence and extremes, direct or indirect discourse, extensive description, or minimal art? Would a direct discourse do more justice to authentic experiences or would indirect discourse sublimate them into a better vehicle of communication? Extensive description may encompass more truth in quantity, yet may fail in literary quality. But can minimal art conceive the immensity of the atrocities like the Holocaust? Eventually, art of atrocity balances between the urge to coil up into wordless forgetfulness and the pulse to re-capture every detail for the sake of truthful testimony. If an artist tries to grasp every detail, his message might be lost for excess of information, and its horrifying details could repel the listener in their accumulation. However, if an artist says nothing, he may betray his mission as an artist, victim, witness and human being.

There are various kinds of artists of atrocity. The artist who recorded his/her experiences at the time of their occurrence leaves us with a claim of authentic testimony. Creating from within a momentary context, a holocaust poet is the observer, 'the noble and tragic hero who suffers unjust predicament' and artist of atrocity.[4] The Holocaust poet is also the witness who subjectively

---

4. T.S. Dorsch (ed.), *Aristotle Horace Longinus* (Harmondworth: Penguin Classics, 1965 [1963]), pp. 38-41, 47-52.

relates his/her own suffering and that of others. Having experienced the events themselves, the artist and witness commemorates the presence for the future. When the artist and witness dies under atrocious circumstances like the Holocaust, the anonymous victim, the witness and the lamenting storyteller merge, turning art of atrocity into a posthumous lament; in memoriam, their testimony conceives of a protest and statement of existence in the face of annihilation and destruction.

In close proximity, we see the survivor, who is a witness retrospectively recording atrocities in their wake; this artist writes his/her memoirs in the aftermath, recreating past experiences in flashbacks of memory. Being settled on safe shores of the aftermath, this witness artist nonetheless feels compelled to gaze back into the past and vindicate his/her humanity in his/her testimony. In their diversity, Holocaust artists simulate being both witnesses and victims. Recording the atrocity they have experienced, these artists become the lamenting poet, tragic hero and victim. However, one artist retrospectively looks back to the past; while the other introspects authentic experiences in the making, recording atrocity of the present time and transforming authentic reality into communicative art for the future. The third type is the artist who has not undergone any of the experiences he/she describes, and yet chooses to vicariously recreate experiences from history and testimonies of other people's experiences in their wake.

Whether authentic, retrospective or vicarious, texts of atrocity turn into subjectified testimony of the individual in the face of atrocity that has dehumanized and defaced its victims. Commemorating victims of crimes and violence, artists of atrocity serve as witnesses and observers of inhumanities and thereby speak for the anonymous victims and the dead deprived of mouth to tell. Once subjectified and formulated, experiences of loss and horror are transposed into artistic expression of bereavement, mourning and tragedy.

In retelling, repeating and subjectifying experiences of atrocity, texts protest the destruction, lethal inhumanity and crimes of hate and bigotry. Retelling of atrocity is foremost a statement claiming that the event should not have occurred. In the deep idea of art of atrocity lies therefore a protest. As a form of protest, art of atrocity evokes biblical texts whose prophet both records and protests the afflictions befalling his people. Under the pretence of compliance with God's will, the prophet raises a cry of lament at the sight of his people's suffering and destruction, which repels any justification in its protest: 'behold, and see if there be any sorrow like unto my sorrow, which is done unto me, wherewith the Lord hath afflicted me in the day of his fierce anger' (Lam. 2.12). Art of atrocity thus turns the victim into a rebel who protests arbitrary predicaments, and while lamenting, searches for God and humanity in the world.

In the following case studies, I will discuss Jewish women and the search for spirituality in the shadow of the Holocaust. I will elucidate their search for God and humanity in relation to transpositions of traditional mysticism in Holocaust literature. Literature, poetry, melody, confessional texts and live interviews offer themselves as material. The first part deals with two Holocaust poets who turn to prayer and lament in the midst of the Nazi era. In the second part, I present literature in the wake of the Holocaust. These post-Holocaust texts delineate Jewish women that have vicariously adopted the suffering of victims, even though they have never been in the Camps themselves. In dividing my cases thus, I distinguish between firsthand art of atrocity created from within the context itself, and vicarious texts of atrocity created in the aftermath.

### I. In Search of God and Humanity: Jewish Poets Lament the Holocaust

If evil harbours a conspiracy to deface the other, art of atrocity finds its affect in particularity and personalization of the subject of suffering, the victim. In search of God and humanity, Jewish women transpose the horrors of mass destruction of the Holocaust into art of atrocity. Facing the destruction of their communities, poetry, melody, art, mysticism and diaries become their protest and testimony of belief in life, humanity and God. Their language is minimal; their description spare; their discourse direct. Their poems have been sung in Hebrew and Yiddish since the years of their composition during the Holocaust.

As the poems come from women's lips, the poets transcend the tragedy of womanhood. Being the bearers of humanity, women are mankind's vulnerable daughters. The greatness of women's qualities, inherent in bringing forth and caring for life embody their inability to protect their offspring, their loved ones and each other in times of violence, atrocity and war. In their poetry, minute details are magnified to represent the collective, paradoxically individualizing the anonymous victim.

*Hannah Szenes 1921–1944*

Hannah Szenes was a Hungarian born poet, play writer and Zionist activist. In an heroically doomed mission to organize a resistance in the Jewish community, she was trained with Tito's partisans in the woods of Yugoslavia and eventually infiltrated Hungary together with a group of six other Jewish partisans. She was soon caught, tortured and finally executed by the Hungarian pro-Nazi regime in November 1944. Her poetry is learnt and sung in Israel in schools, synagogues and on memorial days, serving as a paragon of a soldier poet in resistance the partisan poet, who celebrates life and dignity as a lament and protest witnessing the Jewish population of Europe from Holland to Russia, Greece to France and Romania is deported, starved in Camps, shot into their self-dug graves or gassed.

Szenes' poetry celebrates life and human dignity on the background of the genocide of European Jewry from Holland to Russia, Greece to France and Romania. Her poem and song *Eli Eli*, 'My God, My God' was written in November 1942, two years before her execution. On the background of the Holocaust, extra literary information has turned the song into a lamenting memoriam:

> My God, my God
> May all this never cease to be
> The sand and the sea
> The murmur of water
> Human praying (http://www.tocatch.info/en/Hannah_Szenes.htm)

*Eli Eli* is an imagist poem. Minimalist in its spare syllables, it elevates each word into a singled out metaphor for life and humanity, celebrating the creation in a few essential images of existence: the sea, the sand, the illuminating light over the sky, the murmur of water and human prayer. Prosaic Elements of life, heaven, sand, light and water are illuminated, whose image is the word, and the word is its image, alluding to life proper. On the background of WWII, the elements embody tertiary life lost for all war-victims in camps, shelled cities and towns, who trod on grounds between debris that had been their houses and towns, who raised their eyes to heaven not in their daily habit of hope for healing rain and morning sun, but to see bombardments descending on them.

Written in Hebrew, 'My God my God', *Eli Eli,* derives its emotive appeal from the direct discourse with God, while praying. Subjectified, the poem opens with the poet's appeal to God, and discloses with the image of a human praying to God. The first line alludes to the last, and the last line retorts the first. The poetic lines conceive of praying in the form of exalting praise. After the mode of biblical psalms, the poet dialogises the Hebrew and Jewish tradition of lament in the form of personal appeal to God, culminating in praise of creation and divinity. Following the personal dialogue with God of biblical psalmist, Szenes' poetry evokes the direct plea to divinity while bearing afflictions in time of atrocity and violence:

> The sorrows of death compassed me, and the floods of ungodly men made me afraid. The sorrows of hell compassed me about: the snares of death prevented me. In my distress I called upon the LORD, and cried unto my God: he heard my voice out of his temple, and my cry came before him, even into his ears (Ps. 18: 4-6).

In corollary, Szenes also evokes the Jewish mourning prayer *Kaddish,* recited over the grave and in services:

> *'Jitgadal ve jitkadash shemei rabba bealema di verrra kheruutah ve jamelikh malekhuutah bekhajekhon uve jommeikhun uvee khajeei de khol beet Israel be aagalah u vi zemaan kariv ve iimeru Amen'.*

Its liturgy going back to the sixth century, *Kaddish* is a Hebrew and Aramaic hymn recited over the open grave during funerals and read at every Synagogue during services. Lamenting the dead, *Kaddish* celebrates the greatness of God and creation in chanting enumeration of praises. Eventually, Szenes both revolutionizes and evokes her Jewish heritage in her poetry.

Szenes' poetry draws on the pathetic mode. The pathetic mode presents women, children and vulnerable humanity as its protagonists.[5] Communicating through 'pathetic' *dramatis personae,* the pathetic mode dichotomizes innocence with arbitrary violence. In Szenes' poem, the pathetic mode surfaces in human vulnerability in praying, while annihilation and destruction relentlessly hold them

---

5.   Northrop, Frye, Anatomy of Criticism (Princeton, NJ: Princeton University Press, 1957), pp. 38-39.

in their sway. Facing atrocities of war, the poet is armed with a mere instance of wonder in the presence of life's greatness, the vulnerability of its existence illuminating its uniqueness. In its haunting melody, the song pleads with God to preserve all that life stands for, in corollary praying that exaltation of life in human prayer to God may never cease; the last line evokes the opening and vice versa. The poem becomes a prayer within a prayer.

In the veneration of the soldier poet Hannah Szenes, we revisit the traditional holy martyr of Jewish persecution in a secular robe. Instead of a holy grave, she is extolled on national altars. Worshiped as a secular martyr, Hannah Szenes' story is taught as a sacred tale of devotion and self-sacrifice. Several monuments have been erected to her throughout Israel. She has also been the subject of several artistic works, including a play. Numerous streets, a forest, and a species of flower have been named after her. A museum, established by the Hannah Szenes Legacy Foundation, was built at her former home in Kibbutz Sdot Yam. Many of her popular poems, including 'Towards Caesarea' and 'Blessed is the Match', have been set to music and are sung like hymns and anthems. Nearly every Israeli can recite Szenes' poem 'Blessed is the Match' from memory. This her last poem was written in a Partisan camp in Yugoslavia in 1944:

> Blessed is the match that burned and kindled flames,
> Blessed is the flame that set hearts on fire.
> Blessed are the hearts that knew how to die with honor,
> Blessed is the match that burned, and kindled flames.
> (http://www.tocatch.info/en/Hannah_Szenes.htm)

Posthumously published, Hannah Szenes' diary and literary works have been adopted to the collective heritage of Israel newly born out of its Jewish aggregated sources. Ingrained in sacred tradition, her writings corroborate the values of unconditioned devotion to the Jewish values in nationalist framing. Classically, the following lines demonstrate the alocation of hagiographical context of revelation, calling and evocation into the national context, drawing on the empowerment of the sacred so as to elevate the national and yet remaining with the sacred:

> The voice called, and I went.
> I went, because the voice called
> (http://www.tocatch.info/en/Hannah_Szenes.htm)

Eventually, extolling women like Szenes like martyrs has appropriated the Holocaust as a painful path vindicating the establishment of the State of Israel, very much like the traditional idea that suffering and martyrdom enhance the coming of the Messiah like painful labour of birth. In her being both a partisan and a Holocaust victim dying for a Jewish cause, Hanna Szenes has allowed Israel to insufflate the infallibility of the Zionist idea with long tradition of Jewish messianic hagiography that sanctifies *Kiddush ha-Shem*, a sacrificial death for Jewish causes and beliefs. In corollary Hanna Szenes' life-story, diary and poetic works have served her community like hagiography, and like holy texts they have been promulgated, taught, recited and sung in schools, synagogues and Holocaust memorial days in Israel and around the world.

## Lea Rudinska 1916–1943

Lea *Rudinska* was a young teacher, a poet and editor of a literary Yiddish Journal entitled *Vilna Emes* (Vilna's Truth). A contemporary of Hanna Szenes under the Nazi occupation in the Ghetto Vilna, Lea Rudinska played an active role in the Jewish cultural committee that kept performing plays, poetry readings and lectures under the shadow of hunger, roundups and deportation. Having written numerous poems during these years, the text was lost and only a few of her poems have survived. Within the Ghetto's walls, Rudinska also became a member of the social committee in charge of the Ghetto's humanitarian organization and aid. As the Nazis rounded up Jews en mass in the ghetto streets for deportation to the Death Camps, babies, toddlers and children were left behind in the houses after raids. With other members of the social committee, Lea Rudinska would go into emptied houses in search of abandoned children and bring them to shelter. Although childless herself, Rudinska became the mother of these ghetto orphans. The poem presented here was written to one of the orphans in her care. I translate here two verses into English from the original Yiddish poem written in 1942 (music composed by Leyb Yamploski):

> Birds drowse on branches
> Sleep my precious child.
> By your cradle at your bed-side
> An unknown woman sits and chants.

This is your cradle where it stood
Wounded out of happiness;
and your mother, oh your mother
is never returning back (Rudinska 1943 [1983]: 56)

In this ghetto song Lea Rudinska rewrites a well-loved lullaby transposing it from time of peace to the era of atrocities. Sung in the ghetto, her Yiddish poem, *Dreimle Feigel*, Drowsing Birds conceives a protest and anti-war manifesto camouflaged in domestic images. Innocent details of home life become the silent witnesses of a destroyed family and community. Elements of tranquillity and domesticity are allocated and rearranged to describe the horrors of the war, neither mentioning the place, time or enemy, nor naming the child or the woman who cares for it, whereby the personal and particular touch the general. Written to one of the anonymous orphans picked up at the ghetto and cared for by Lea Rudinska, the poem reaches its human context in its minimal particularity. The poet's protest resides with anonymous domesticity and daily details that are dislocated from their habitual context and displaced into a time of mass annihilation and moral disintegration.

In search of humanity in inhuman days, Lea Rudinska employs the 'pathetic mode' proper to accommodate the most vulnerable members of society in her poetry. As a formal device, the pathetic *dramatis personae* dichotomizes the heroic, the epic and the romantic heroes. The poem thus accommodates the most vulnerable member of society, materialized in the weak, vulnerable and inarticulate protagonist, an anonymous baby robbed of its parents and home. Drawing on emotive appeal for sympathy and compassion, Rudinska finds her protagonist in an abandoned child left behind by parents who were arbitrarily rounded up on the street of the ghetto. As the poem leaves the child's name and gender unknown and sparing the circumstances and surroundings of the ghetto, the poem elevates the child to represent the anonymous murdered innocents, whereby she personalizes the feminine, helpless and infantile of all wars. Poignantly, protagonist and poet shared the very same lot. Nothing is known about the child's fate; and but little more is known about Rudinska's fate, only that she perished in the camps, either in Treblinka or Majdanik in 1943.[6]

---

6.   Eleanor Mlotek and Malke Gottlieb (eds.), *Mir Zeinen Do* [*We Are Here*], (New York: Workmen's Circle, 1983), p. 56.

God does not speak nor is spoken to in this text. However, following Lamentation and the prophetic texts, the protagonist alludes to the elevation of the victim to represent the collective suffering of the nation before God. Embodying the anonymous victim in the least and most humiliated of humanity, it is he/she who appeals for God's compassion and grace: 'He was oppressed, and he was afflicted, yet he opened not his mouth: he is brought as a lamb to the slaughter, and as a sheep before her shearers is dumb, so he openeth not his mouth…Yet it pleased the LORD to bruise him; he hath put him to grief: when thou shalt make his soul an offering for sin, he shall see his seed, he shall prolong his days, and the pleasure of the LORD shall prosper in his hand' (Isa. 53.7-10).

Lea Rudinska subjectifies the national holocaust in her domestic tragedy. In omitting the identity of both child and woman who adopts him, it is in anonymity that the protagonist rises to the level of classical tragedy, whereby the poem ironically reaches its humanistic heights. Only extra literary information gives away the ethno-historical context. It could have been written anywhere at any time, in Rwanda or Yugoslavia.

*Summary*

Holocaust poems posthumously vindicate their creators. Witnesses, observers, tragic heroes and artists of atrocity; their texts are their testimony, epitaphs, legacy of belief in life, and search for humanity and God in the face of crimes against humanity. Today, as a post-Holocaust woman, I recite and sing these poems as inspiring belief in the values that had empowered these women during the Holocaust. I know that in the future there will be wars, persecution, racism and anti-Semiticism, and that there will always be some who choose to bring destruction on individuals, families and communities in newly sinister formulas. With the realization that there will be future victims and orphans, I also believe that there always be will women and men who will offer humanitarian aid, shelter and fostering to the deprived and orphaned. Statistically, the latter may not counterbalance the former; but humanely it does. Let it be a testimony of belief that in Poland alone, which became the graveyard of three million full, half and quarter Jews, hundreds of thousands were hidden and saved at the risk of their benefactors' lives. Similar self-evidential humanity was demonstrated throughout Europe in Germany, the Netherlands, Czechoslovakia and Hungary, where my own mother had been offered a shelter as a child. Eventually, I wish to cease counting the horrors and atrocities done to my people, and instead of recounting the atrocities done to my people, remember what was done for my people. In my own search of belief in humanity and God I believe that even if there was a global conspiracy to repeat the destruction of the Jewish people, and there was merely one person who helped one single Jew, I would still hold to my belief in humanity.

## II. Vicarious Suffering in the Aftermath of the Holocaust

In the aftermath of the Holocaust, we encounter the artist of atrocity and the vicarious victim, recreating suffering of others in texts and art and/or reliving them in the mind. My following case studies elucidate texts written by post-Holocaust writers about Jewish women who vicariously adopt post-holocaust traumas without having been directly victimized themselves. On the one hand these texts represent the poet, observer and artist of atrocity, witnessing the affect of the Holocaust on its contemporary generation. On the other hand, these texts put to the fore the vicarious victim in the wake of atrocities and crime against humanity.

My primary material is drawn from semi-biographical literature written by Jewish writers in the sixties and eighties about their mothers. The first text is *Kaddish*, a poetic elegy in a romance length written by Allen Ginsberg. The other semi-biography is traced in the pages of two books for children written by a contemporary Israeli writer and actress Gila Almagor, *A Girl with a Strange Name* (1985) and *Our Tree on the Top of the Hill* (1992).[7] Two respective film productions followed the books; and personal interviews with the writer have complemented my insight into these books.

In their respective ways both American and Israeli societies were turning materialistic and militant in the fifties and sixties. The following case studies deal with two women who would not adapt to their societies or families. In corollary, they were haunted by the Holocaust, and in vicariously adopting the traumas of Holocaust victims, felt they were being persecuted, tortured, starved and victimized over and over again in their minds. Both women were

7.  Gila Almagor, *The Summer of Avya: A Girl with a Strange Name* (Tel Aviv: Am Oved 1985); *Our Tree on the Top of the Hill* (Tel Aviv: Am Oved, 1992 [1997]).

clinically diagnosed as paranoiac-schizophrenic, suffering from hallucinatory symptoms. Independently of each other, the two writers sketch a biographical youth in the shadow of a mentally ill mother. However, both writers also describe their mothers as women of extra-ordinary sensitivities and unbound empathy for the suffering of the world. In their writings, Allen Ginsberg and Gila Almagor, transform the figures of their mentally ill mothers into the righteous woman who shoulders the suffering of her community and that of the world; their ecstatic love for the suffering world being perceived as clinical insanity. Were they mad or holy? In the wake of the Holocaust, how do these Jewish women cope with their lives; how do they vindicate their vicarious adaptation of other people's suffering in search of God and humanity?

If the holocaust victim evokes the legacy of holy martyrs of persecution, the vicarious victim relates to the holy person who adopts the suffering of the world through emphatic pains and mental agony. Self-willed and voluntarily, such a person identifies with victimization and the suffering of others. Modern time however, forces a choice between psychiatry and theology — being incompatible tools of analysis; the latter discipline declares a vicarious victim to be clinically insane, whereas the former discipline simulates him/ her with a holy person.

The two writers, the American Allen Ginsberg and the Israeli Gila Almagor straddle between incompatible disciplines. Presenting their personal life-stories, they sketch the chronology of their mothers' mental illness with a harsh brush of realism. Following modern psychology, their portraits submit minute details of mental deterioration culminating in death in the mental home. Their writings however, also picture their mentally ill mothers as selfless persons who have shouldered the suffering of the community and the world. Juxtaposing psychoanalysis with theology in these texts, ecstatic adaptation of the Holocaust precipitates paranoia and Jewish mysticism side by side. Both writers interlink their mothers' psychotic illness to the realm of the Kabbala, reviving a long legacy of Jewish medieval mysticism. They conceive their mothers as a living *zaddika,* the righteous and holy woman who vicariously suffers for her community; and representing a paragon of humanity intermediates between God and humanity. How does this mystical tradition fit in these texts; and what does it entail?

*The Righteous Person: the* Zaddik

The *zaddik* is a mixture of Wisdom Literature, folklore and kabalistic mysticism. Ranging across the mimetic spectrum of mystical elevation, the living holy *zaddik* represents a righteous person and devotee, whose figuration delineates a heavenly entity and a mystical paragon on the one hand and a humble devotee on earth on the other. He or she is thus a person unreservedly dedicated to Jewish and humane causes alike. In pursuing goodness, the *zaddik* fulfils his/her idealized destination or innate task on earth, entitled *tikkun*. Accumulating goodness on earth enhances the messianic times to come, which purports the *zaddik*'s task.[8]

The redemptive function of the *zaddik* complements the kabalistic idea conceiving the *zaddik* as one of the foundations of goodness on which the world rests. Drawing on Prov. 10.25, 'A just man is the foundation of the world', legends relate that God requires at least thirty-six *zaddikim* (plural of *zaddik*) in every generation so as to retain His hope and trust in mankind; by their good deeds and virtues the thirty-six righteous persons keep the balance between good and evil in the world from overturning, lest evil gains the upperhand. For the *zaddiks*' merits, God keeps His covenant, *brit*, with humanity given to Noah (Gen. 9.17) and refrains from inflicting another apocalyptic flood on earth for humanity's sins. If the generation is proven worthy, one of the thirty-six righteous men may rise as a messiah. Materializing as an intermediary figure between the community and the God; the *zaddik* appeals to God's compassion in time of stress and may avert disaster from befalling the community by actions of marvel, miracles or in self-sacrifice. In corollary a *zaddik* of low mimesis resurfaces in domestic, humble and demure circumstances and is believed to possess a holy and pure soul. He/she may function as a humble person whose true identity remains hidden to his/her surroundings. Entitled *Hidden Zaddik*; that person may even be embodied in a *Tam*, a simpleton. Based on a Talmudic passage, *Sukkot* 45b, the idea of the *Hidden Zaddik* surfaces in folklore and Chassidic legends. Since the rise of Chassidism in the eighteenth century, the *zaddik* has featured in many illuminated folktales of wonder, devotion, boundless compassion and charity. Both mysticism and folk imagination allude to an open text of wide

8. Gershom Scholem, *Elements of the Kabbalah and its Symbolism* (Jerusalem: Daf-Khen, 1976), pp. 213-59.

range, reinforcing the idea that woman could function as a holy person. A female *zaddik, a zaddika,* thus conceives of inhering continuity of Jewish tradition rather than a deviation from it.

The following analysis elucidates the reciprocal relations between Jewish mysticism and the various manifestations of the righteous holy person, entitled *zaddik.* In his book *Kabbalah,* Moshe Idel classifies mysticism in three-mainstream typology, theosophical mysticism, ecstatic mysticism and magical mysticism (Idel 1993: 9-18).[9]

1. Theosophical mysticism is descriptive and philosophical concentrating on the divine structure and the relation of the human to it.
2. Ecstatic mysticism purports mystical union between God and human by means of ecstatic devotion delineating an ascending upward movement of the soul toward the divine.
3. Conversely, magical mysticism enhances the descent of divine powers towards the earthly by means of cultic objects and magical practice.

In corollary, the figure of *zaddik* shows interdependent relation between theory and practice, and between mysticism and human figuration. The various streams of mysticism allude to diversity of holy persons and variety of functions and practices. In the following I will set out Idel's theory and adapt it to my present analysis of the holy women; only the first two mystical streams prove relevant to my present discussion.

Theosophical mysticism delineates the divine structure, defining man's affiliation and place in the world in relation to the divine. This theosophical worldview draws on creeds promoting the perfection and infallibility of the Godhead, implying the perfection of His creation. However, reality generates a discrepancy between the existing world and the theosophical idea of a pre-designed perfect one created by an infallible divinity. To evade tarnishing God's perfect image, the discrepancy is bridged by theosophy advocating a pre-designed perfect structure that had existed on earth but was lost in the primordial time. In medieval kabbala, the imperfect state of the world is explained by a primordial cosmic break in the divine structure, epitomized as *shvirat ha-kelim,* the breaking of the cosmic vessels that happened during the Creation.[10]

9.   Moshe Idel, *Kabbalah, New Perspectives* (Tel Aviv: Schocken Books, 1993), pp. 9-18.
10. Scholem, *Elements of the Kabbalah,* pp. 94, 107-108, 110, 341, 349, 351.

In corollary, a holy person operates from a theosophical worldview promoting a divine design originally intended to be perfect. Since a cosmic crisis caused the loss of the primordial perfection, man's expiating good deeds should amend and retrieve the perfect state that had been lost in the world. Accumulating good deeds aggregates goodness in the world whereby the lost perfection will be regained, and the existing imperfect state will be redeemed from the low state into which it had sunk. Hence the kabbalistic concept of expiating amendment, *tikkun,* that would retrieve the pre-designed state that had been lost and would re-establish it on earth.[11] Righteous person therefore adopts the pain and suffering of the world that has penetrated the world since the cosmic break from the perfect state. In striving towards righteousness, the holy person works towards amending the present imperfect state with the purpose in mind to enhance goodness, in corollary enhancing the messianic future. To render oneself a vessel for God's design, one has to be a holy after the paradigm of *Imitatio Dei.* An identity of a theosophical holy person is therefore analogous to the divine design. As divinity has designed goodness as part of the originally idyllic state, so must the *zaddik,* the holy person aspire towards goodness. As God is good, compassionate, holy and emphatic, so must the *zaddik* be compassionate, holy and good so as to accumulate goodness on earth towards its pre-designed perfection clearing the road for messianic times to come.

In close proximity, ecstatic mysticism describes an upper movement towards the transcendent, ascending the human towards the metaphysical.[12] Ecstatic mysticism encompasses the idea that humans are created after the divine image, and thus contain it. Divinity is the origin of humans who are therefore pre-destined to introspectively find and reunite with the divine, whereby the imperfect reunites with its perfect. Ecstatic mysticism thus purports the union with the divine origin of the soul, which is life's pre-intended purpose. In ecstatic mysticism, the devotee strives to acquire a mystical union with an entity elevated above and outside the border of the Self. Mystical union is eventually experienced in elated feelings, unreserved devotion and love towards a highly elevated 'being', this and unbound amalgamation with the

11. Idel, *Kabbalah,* pp. 9-18, 53-91.
12. Idel, *Kabbalah,* pp. 9-18, 53-91.

transcendent. Following the model of Abraham Abolaffia, a twelfth century kabbalist from North Africa, mystical union is delineated in a symbol of two complementing halves of a circle horizontally divided, the upper half circle embodying the divine and the lower half representing the human.[13] In this symbol, ecstatic union between God and human draws on the idea of mystical love of mutually complementing entities. Abolaffia's unionist mysticism simulates earthly love with mystical love after the carnal union between the primordial man and woman; delineating the union of God and human as complementing halves, perceived as an ecstatic union between two entities of a whole.

Setting out Idel's model illuminates the role of the righteous person as an ecstatic mystic aspiring to reach mystical union with the divine. As a unionist and ecstatic mystic, a devotee reaches a transcendent union in mystical love. Requiring total self-effacement, mystic love is acquired by means of deep devotion, prayers, meditation, fasting, ecstatic trance, mystical mourning, weeping and assimilation of vicarious suffering of the world.[14] Aided by these means, a holy person erases his/her personal borders, allowing the creation to stream into the self; in an ecstatic wonder the soul ascends and unreservedly cleaves to the transcendent. Mystical union draws on the feeling that every moment of one's life is shared, observed and rewarded by the subject of devotion. Eventually, an ecstatic mystic demonstrates an identity, which is both metaphoric and analogous. Like a theosophical mystic, an ecstatic mystic draws on analogous identification with the divine after *imitatie dei*, finding an ego ideal in a transcendent entity elevated outside and above the Self. Confluent with theosophical identity, ecstatic mystic adopts a metaphoric identification with the divine; a unionist and ecstatic mystic feels holy on becoming a pertinent part of the holy, which is the goal of ecstatic mysticism. Due to the nature of mystical union, the metaphoric Self becomes transcendent as it unites with the complementing transcendental subject. Eventually mystical union bequeaths a holy person with qualities drawn from the transcended subject of devotion. Empowered thus by mystical union, the *zaddik* is endowed with the function of an intermediary who mediates between the metaphysical dimension and the human domain and God and community.

13. Idel, *Kabbalah*, pp. 80-88.
14. Idel, *Kabbalah*, pp. 9-18, 56-59.

*The Mad and Holy Mother in Allen Ginsberg's* Kaddish

My first case alludes to feminization of the *zaddik* in Allen Ginsberg's poem *Kaddish*. Written between 1959 and 1961, Allen Ginsberg composed his great elegy in memoriam of his mother, Naomi Ginsberg.[15] Commemorating his 'mentally ill' mother in a long elegiac poem of more than 300 stanzas, the poet intertextually resonates biblical and kabbalistic sources. The poem *Kaddish* draws its inspiration from the traditional mourning prayer in Aramaic and Hebrew entitled *Kaddish* recited over the dead by the closest surviving member in funerals and by the community in synagogue services. The traditional *Kaddish* accumulates exhaling praises generating rhythm of incantation:

> *Jitgadal ve jitkadash shemei rabba bealema di verrra kheruutah ve jamelikh malekhuutah bekhajekhon uve jommeikhun uvee khajeei de khol beet Israel be aagalah u vi zemaan kariv ve iimeru amen' (Jewish Prayer Book).*

Its liturgy going back to the sixth century, *Kaddish* is a Hebrew and Aramaic hymn, a prayer and praise. Evoking the archaic prayer over the dead, Ginsberg insufflates a modern elegy with atavist heritage.

Stretching over more than three hundred couplets, Ginsberg's poem delineates the tragic-life story of Naomi Ginsberg, a Russian Jewish immigrant whose mental state had deteriorated in alienation from her children and husband; leading to repeated commitments to a mental home, she was subjected to electric shocks, heavy medication, culminating in lobotomy and a lonely death in the mental ward. In focussing on a woman who responds to the period's atrocities in depression and paranoia, the poem precipitates socio-historical testimony of a period as much as a domestic tragedy:

> Looking back on the mind itself that saw an American city
> A flash away, and the great dream of Me and China, or you and a
> Phantom Russia, or a crumpled bed that never existed—
> Like a poem in the dark—escaped back to Oblivion—
> No more to say
> Sighing, screaming with it, buying and selling pieces of phantoms,
> Worshipping each other,
> Worshipping the God included in it all—longing or inevitability
> While it lasts, a Vision—anything more? (vv. 6-12).

15. Ronald Gottesman and Francis Murphy (eds.), *The Norton Anthology of American Literature*, II (New York and London: W.W. Norton, 1979), pp. 2407-425.

The individual woman amalgamates with collective, as Naomi Ginsberg mirrors her community's utopian hopes in the new world; and being an adherent of the communist belief of world revolution, she also reflects the period's disasters and disillusions. An embodiment of their desperate hopes and tragedies alike, her unguarded soul has contained the trials and crisis of the Jewish community during the first half of the twentieth century. Driven away by lethal persecution and pogroms in the end of the nineteenth century, they emigrated from Eastern Europe *en masse* to an America that substantiated a promised land of hopes and equality. Meeting poverty and hardship, they saw their families and old communities perish in the Holocaust in Europe just a few decades later. In concomitant with the disillusion of the American Dream came the atrocities of Communism juxtaposed with the persecution of intellectuals during the McCarthy period in the USA in the fifties. Disregarding distance and time, Naomi Ginsberg vicariously adopted the illness and atrocities of her period. A paranoiac-schizophrenic person or a holy one?

The modern poem *Kaddish* inserts kabalistic interpretations into contemporary socio-historical crises of the Jewish community. In describing his mother's vicarious suffering, the poet evokes the Jewish heritage embellishing Rachel Our Foremother as the archaic grieving matriarch. Drawn on Jeremiah's lamenting over Zion, Rachel's maternal grief attracts God's compassion and grace; it is for her merits that He promises messianic redemption for the afflicted nation: 'A voice is heard on the heights of Ramah, lamentation and bitter weeping, Rachel mourning for her children, refusing to be comforted, because her children are no more'. This is what the LORD says: 'Restrain your voice from weeping and your eyes from tears, for thy work shall be rewarded', declares the LORD. 'They will return from the land of the enemy. So there is hope for your future', declares the LORD. 'Your children will return to their own land (Jer. 31.15-17).

The maternal protagonist rises out of the poetic lines of *Kaddish* evoking biblical and mystical archetype of holy maternity who in her adaptation of her community's pains enhances the messianic times in her unbound love and pure soul. On the background of the period's atrocities and disillusions, Naomi simulates with a holy mother who mediates between God and the afflicted community. In the poetic vision of *Kaddish*, messianic paradise is regained and

society retrieves its primordial innocence for the merits of its holy
mother. Naomi precipitates foremother Rachel reigning on a newly
born world amidst carefree children:

> Oh Russian faced, woman on the grass, your long black
> Hair is crowned with flowers, the mandolin is on your knees —
> Communist Beauty, sit here married in the summer among
> daisies, promised happiness at hand —
> holy mother, now you smile on your love, your world is
> born anew, children run naked in the field spotted with
> dandelions,
> they eat in the plum tree grove at the end of the meadow
> and find a cabin where a white-haired negro teaches the mystery of
> his rainbarrel — (204-209).

Soaring towards mysticism, the poet resorts to kabalistic
theosophy in the aftermath of the greatest destruction ever to have
befallen contemporary Jewry. Messianic visions undergird the
mystical layers of the poem. Naomi Ginsberg embodies a holy
mother, a righteous woman and mystical *zaddika* domesticated within
the walls of her family, household and the mental home. Analogous
to the domestic *zaddika*, divinity is incarnated on the domestic realm
of low mimesis. The domesticated God appears as a lonely old
'unmarried' man living in a tree house in the wood. The maternal
*zaddika* climbs up a ladder to cook Jewish soup for Him. Empowered
by her ecstatic ascent, Naomi becomes a holy intermediary who
mediates between the community and God. Classically, as a mystical
intermediary, she acts as humanity's advocate before God; and thus
petitions for His intervention begging Him to stop the atrocities on
earth. Hallucination or a revelation?

> Naomi: 'And when we die we become an onion, a Cabbage, a carrot,
> or a squash, a vegetable'.
> She reads the Bible, thinks beautiful thoughts all day.
> 'Yesterday I saw God. What did he look like ? Well, in the afternoon I
> climbed a ladder — he has a cheap cabin in the country, like Monroe,
> NY the chicken farms in the wood. He was a lonely old man with a
> white beard.
> 'I cooked him a nice supper —
> lentil soup, vegetable, bread & butter — mitlz — he sat down
> at the table and ate, he was sad.
> 'I told him, Look at all those fighting and killing down
> there. What's the matter? Why don't you put a stop to it ?
> 'I try, he said — That's all he could do, he looked tired.
> He's a bachelor so long, and he likes lentil soup'. (vv. 137–153)

The ladder in Naomi's revelation/hallucination evokes Jacob's ladder whose head was reaching heaven and its foot resting on the earth, while angels descend and ascend on it in up and down: 'And he dreamed, and behold a ladder set up on the earth, and the top of it reached to heaven: and behold the angels of God ascending and descending on it. And, behold, the LORD stood above it, and said, I am the LORD God of Abraham thy father, and the God of Isaac: the land whereon thou liest, to thee will I give it, and to thy seed' (Gen. 28.12-13). Evolved from the biblical revelation, medieval kabbala has simulated the image of Jacob's ladder with the metaphysical spheres of the Tree of Life, which substantiates God's qualities in embodiment perceivable for human perception.

Like a classical mystic of ecstatic union, Naomi is endowed with ecstatic elation prior to her mystical revelation; a state of mystical ecstasy amalgamates her personal self in the most humble phenomenon of creation, a vegetable:

> Naomi: 'And when we die we become an onion, a
> Cabbage, a carrot, or a squash, a vegetable...

The revelation transcends Naomi's hallucinations to the ecstatic experience of mystical union with nature and God. Acting as a pure soul who enhances goodness in the world, mystical experiences empower her to act as a holy intermediary between God and community. Her revelation interlinks her to a *zaddika*'s evocation whose soul embraces the suffering and horrors of her generation. Bringing their plight before God, He endows His grace upon them for her merits.

Naomi pays with mental anguish for her vicarious suffering for the sake of her community and mankind. In psychotherapeutic terms, her unbound mental suffering with the world has materialized in the form of disassociated behaviour and paranoia. The phenomenon of unbound identification with the suffering of the outbound world becomes a mystical and ecstatic union between a holy soul and God and between the holy righteous person and humanity's pain and affliction.

Following his mother, Allen Ginsberg the poet inherited a capacity for ecstatic devotion, transforming her holy passion in his own life's vision, art and political activity. She became his guiding voice, his link to Jewish heritage, mysticism and passion for justice and social reform. Allen Ginsberg became the prophet and bard of the sixties and seventies, which have irreversibly changed the values of American society. As an influential leader of the Beat Generation and Flower Movement, he became one of the forerunners of the anti-Vietnam flank that brought the American soldiers home, and was a pioneering advocate of tolerance for the gay community. It is for these reasons perhaps that the last part of Ginsberg's *Kaddish* promulgates an incantation of praises, sanctifying life to its lowest and most banished manifestation:

> In the world which He has created according to his will Blessed
> Praised
> Magnified Lauded Excited the Name of the Holy One Blessed
> Is He!
> In the house of Newark Blessed is He! In the madhouse Blessed
> Is He! In the house of Death Blessed is He!
> Blessed be He in homosexuality! Blessed be He in Paranoia!
> Blessed be He in the city! Blessed He be in the book!
> Blessed be He who dwells in the shadow! Blessed be He!
> Blessed be He! (vss. 1-5)

### *Vicarious Suffering; the Secular Zaddika in Israeli Literature*

Earlier introduced, the phenomenon of secular martyrdom is attested in the veneration of Holocaust victims like Anne Frank and Hannah Szenes. Venerated as innocent victims, victims of the Holocaust seem to be elevated as paragons of courage and belief in humanity and/or God. Their veneration has been carried outside religious institutions into newly public alters in the form of art, museums and memorial days.

In the following case study I introduce the confluent concept of a secular *zaddik,* a secular righteous (holy) person. Here I challenge my readers and myself with the idea of secular righteousness, precipitating secular modern Judaism. A secular *zaddik* accommodates the qualifying phenomena of traditional *zaddik,* the holy living righteous person; adopted to secular conceptualization we see a person devotionally functioning as a righteous and devotee, yet without divinity, Messiah, or the prophet Elijah. In this phenomenon, modern society replenishes its veneration of holy women with secular worship in new forms, outside sacred shrines, synagogues and without religious rituals. In corollary to the concept of secular martyrdom, a secular *zaddika* shows a capacity to devote the Self to expiating and amending causes without forthright metaphysics proper. For their part, these women empower themselves by ideals for the general good, uncompromisingly devoting themselves to the suffering of their community with passion and zeal on a par with ecstatic mysticism or atoning martyrdom. Becoming both devotees of general causes and unbound receptors of suffering, their evocation transcends their passion to ecstatic devotion. In their self-effacing devotion, they act like ecstatic mystics who find the other half of soul in a transcending power source, and though without mysticism, which typologically qualifies them as 'secular' *zaddika*, holy women of secular stadium.

In the following case study, I present contemporary Israeli literature grappling with the aftermath of the Holocaust. The study presents a Jewish mother whose mental history resembles that of Naomi Ginsberg in *Kaddish*. My material has been composed of various modes of presentations: literary texts, film productions and live interviews. The writer, actress and film producer Gila Almagor, memorializes her mother's life in the semi-biographical children's books, *A Girl with a Strange Name* (1985) and *Our Tree on the Top of the Hill* (1992). Two film productions respectively followed: *The Summer of Avya*, and *Children of Udim*. In both films, the writer Gila Almagor plays the maternal role. Gila Almagor remarkably also played the role of Naomi Ginsberg in Allen Ginsberg's play *Kaddish* adapted to Hebrew and performed by ha-Bimah, the national theatre company throughout 2000 and 2001 in Israel. In the summers of 2000 and 2001, I contacted the writer and completed my findings with personal interviews.

In Almagor's series of children's books and their complementing films, we follow a woman's mental agony through a daughter's eyes during her childhood and adolescence. Like my former case studies, biographical facts, history and literary imagination propel into a highly emotive portrait, collapsing demarcation between collective history and personal chronology. As the collective and personal interlock, a woman's portrait permeates the contemporary history, being retrospectively viewed from the domestic sphere and personal experiences. In these texts, the reader re-encounters a Jewish mother who takes upon herself the suffering of her community and like a classical *zaddik* adopts the turmoil of the period in her boundless soul.

The first book, *A Girl with a Strange Name*, takes us to Israel of the fifties, finding itself in the wake of the Holocaust on the one hand,

and emerging out of the 1948 War that ensued shortly afterwards on the other. Early Israel is flooded with Holocaust refugees and dislocated families from West and East. Barely grappling with the traumatized survivors of the Holocaust, the 1948 War had deprived its already afflicted volatile population of thousands of sons and fathers. Eventually however, the 1948 War was epitomized as a War of Independence. Promising permanent and secure homes for all Jews, the victims of this war were venerated as national heroes; their death considered a sacrifice paving the way to a birth of a nation. Their posthumous veneration has resonated the sanctified martyrdom of Jewish victims of previous persecutions, their death echoing the sanctified suffering of holy martyrs. We see that the casualties of the 1948 War were venerated as national sacrifices paving the way to the new state, in conjunction with the sanctified death of Jewish martyrdom that has been conceived as metaphysical labour of messianic times to be born and replace the old world of terror, toil and victimization. Perceiving the Diaspora as the old world of suffering and persecution inflicted on toothless Jewry unable to protect itself, the young State sees Israel as its replacement; the new national martyrs were vindicating the wrongs of the Diaspora and mass graves of the Extermination Camps. Eventually though the Holocaust and the War of Independence occurred with but a few years apart, waged against Jews by comparable lethal politics, the genocide of European Jewry was believed to be incompatible with the spirit of the War of Independence. The victims of the War of Independence died fighting for a cause, attesting to heroism promulgated by the insufflating messianic visions of national homeland, it was felt. Conversely, the Holocaust victims died without a cause, without dignity, bravery or resistance, it was believed, being historically untrue. Until recently, homes like the one described in the book, and the one I grew up in, have dichotomized the War of Independence with the Holocaust. By extolling the resisting Jews of the uprising in Ghetto Warsaw and Zionist and partisans poets like Hanna Szenes side by side with the casualties of the 1948 War; the victims of the Holocaust received a secondary if not undermined place in the collective memory of Israel.

Accordingly, while describing a chronology of mental instability of a post-Holocaust survivor, the book imbues the dissociated behaviour of the maternal figure with idealism and courage fitting the resilient spirit of young Israel. Through her daughter's eyes it is alluded that Henya, her mother, fought the Nazis with the partisans in Polish woods. An aunt relates that her beauty misled the soldiers; she infiltrated their lines and blew up a train loaded with ammunition. Eventually caught, she was sent to the concentration camp; Avya, her daughter recalls the blue number of camp survivors on her mother's arm. According to the book, she came to Israel with the great wave of Jewish refugees in the wake of the WWII; she married another refugee but while expecting his child, her husband was killed by an Arab sniper. The girl receives the name Avya, meaning 'her father' in Hebrew, which being a strange name gives the book its title *A Girl with a Strange Name*. Mental breakdowns govern the sequences of the book; the traumatized mother is repeatedly admitted to a mental home, and the girl is sent to 'a children farm' for orphans and children from broken and dysfunctional homes. However, through the child's eyes, idealism precipitates a domestic tragedy. Her holocaust experiences remain alluded, yet untold, which nonetheless elucidates her traumas.[16] She emerges from the past, a proud and courageous Jew, not a passive victim, vindicating her dissociated behaviour by heroic resistance. Henya's suffering receives an elevating cause; personal courage redeems her from the anonymous victimization of the Holocaust. In corollary, the unbearable absence of a father is compensated by a sense of glory endowed to fallen soldiers who had sacrificed their lives so that others could live, although Avya's father had been arbitrarily shot by a sniper away from the battlefield. Brought up on Israel's young spirit, the child's eyes colour her family history with tragic heroism interwoven with a sense of nationalistic martyrdom.

Resembling *Kaddish,* the mentally ill and malfunctioning mother reflects the contemporary ailments of the Israeli society of the fifties and sixties. Denying the traumas of the Holocaust and its traumatic survivors in its midst, the Holocaust arose like untreated infection in unconscious relapses. The Holocaust thus seems to surface in the collective psyche in dissociated symptoms and self-compensating dreams of false grandeur that border on self-destruction. Dichotomizing the Holocaust with its new political independence, while finding itself surrounded by lethal hostility and renewed threats of genocide, young Israel over-exerts itself as a highly

16. *The Summer of Avya*, pp. 33-34.

militant society. Remaining resilient but volatile, the traumatic past that had never been properly reconciled has been manifesting itself in intolerance to diversity within and without its borders.

The second semi-biographical book *Our Tree on the Top of the Hill* (1992 [1997]) and the film *Children of Udim* that follows, both conceive of a more sophisticated portrait. Henya's portrait mingles a daughter's devotion with doubts and abjection of an adolescent daughter. Henya is described as the only Holocaust survivor of her family who would not cease punishing herself for guilt known to haunt Holocaust survivors for outliving their families who had perished.[17] Her partisan past in the War as well as camp experiences are omitted; the number on her arm is never mentioned either.[18] In corollary, the film made after the second book unfolds a revealing detail. Visiting her mother in the mental home, Avya finds her mother Henya catatonically cooped up in her inner world. Trying to draw her back to reality, the girl confronts her mother uttering: 'You have never really been in the concentration camp, Mom'.

However, it is in the second book that the reader also receives a glimpse of another aspect of the mother's portrait. This book brings to the fore her unbound devotion to charity and ardent empathy with the needy. This text delineates a woman who walks through the streets dragging bags, collecting clothes, leftovers and utilities from here and there for her protégées: the poor, the old, the lonely and the orphaned. When the girl comes home from her boarding school, her mother is always receiving one suppliant or another whom she feeds and clothes. Among the frequent visitors she would fearlessly receive the misfit of the town who would give little girls a scare by flashing in dark corners.

Live interviews in the summers between 2000 and 2001 with the writer have completed her mother's portrait. The biographical mother was called Chaia, meaning she who lives. Her history is rooted in orthodox family-life in Poland. As the Nazis invade Poland in 1939, Chaia is a young woman of barely twenty. On their approaching the town, Chaia flees Poland with her older brother. One night after everyone had fallen asleep, he shut himself in the bathroom and shaved his ear-logs and beard. He then woke up his younger sister Chaia and told her to follow him. Of his large family,

17. Almagor, *Our Tree*, p. 15.
18. Almagor, *Our Tree*, [7th edn], pp. 42-45.

he could take only one person with him on his escape route; he chose her. Without a word of farewell to their parents and siblings, the two stealthily fled the house at night and smuggled through the borders; eventually, reaching Palestine. While the War is waging in Europe, in Palestine of the early forties, Chaia marries another Jewish refugee and expecting her first child she hopes to build a family in the new land. However, while still carrying her first child, the author Gila, an Arab sniper shoots her husband in the street, killing him on the spot. In the wake of WWII, comes the realization that only her brother and herself have escaped the carnage of the Holocaust while their family and community perished behind. Henya is widowed, left with none in the world but her brother who had saved her, and a young child to raise on her own.

As the years pass, Chaia gradually develops psychotic behaviour. She would evoke concentration camp memories that never happened to her, feel traumatized by atrocious events she had never experienced herself. Claiming to be a Holocaust victim, she would scratch a number on her arm with a blue pen screaming that she was there; going into fits she would try to hurt herself. Another time her daughter was peeling potatoes, and threw the peels away. Chaia broke down and seized her yelling, 'this is our food you are throwing away, we shall starve'. She would accumulate sleeping tablets, hide them in odd corners of the house, and morbidly drop hints to her daughter about their possible location, taunting her with her suicide threats. Dissociated symptoms would mark the onset of mental deterioration; suicide attempts followed, and eventually psychotic relapses would lead to commitments to mental institutions.

Eventually, my interviews with the writer also illuminated the mystical aspect of her mother's dissociated behaviour, promulgated in her writing. On my introductory phone call before the interviews, the writer, Gila Almagor, related to me that her mother was a *zaddika* in the truest sense and that she 'could attest' to it. As a child, she would observe bags bursting with clothes and utilities in the corner of the living room; people were coming to collect them while others always came to deliver more. Compatible with the literary description, Henya was in the habit of dragging a large jute sack through the streets, recruiting donations of all kinds from shops and private homes, while children followed her mockingly calling her names. During the years of the writer's youth, she supported herself by running a home-based launderette. And yet, after washing her clients' clothes, she would aggregate renewed zeal to wash, hang to dry, starch and iron clothes of charity and allot them according to age, sex and size of her suppliants. Renowned for her activity, Chaia became an undeclared *zaddika* of her town. Her community of adherents conceived of the homeless, the misfits and the mentally ill. Becoming a spearhead of charity, both needy suppliants and charitable organizations would find their way to her door, the former coming to be supported while the latter approaching her to distribute her unpaid toil further. Chaia consistently kept up her altruistic activity through her most troubled years in which her state was not much better than that of her needy protégées. Some years later, she enjoyed a few years of mental and economical stability when she remarried. However, her charitable work never ceased. By word of mouth, the hungry, the lonely, the socially disadvantaged and mentally alienated would find their way to her home, be served a meal at her table and be clothed. The town's abject and mentally ill would sit at her table, shy, demur and pacified. They would not leave empty-handed; Chaia would provide them with a little parcel containing biscuits and oranges. In the last phase of Chaia's life in the mental home, Chaia prolonged her gift of boundless compassion. A mental patient herself, she adopted another mental inmate, an irreversibly catatonic patient, forgotten by all and forlorn within her own world. Chaia fed, washed and cared for her as though she were her last destination on earth.

What voices dictated her path we will never know. She had been leading a secular life since she and her brother had left their ultra-orthodox family in Poland. However, on her final period in the mental home which would be her last home on earth, she asked for a prayer book and returned to the familiar scriptures of her childhood and youth. In the mental home, she would pray, on her own, outside congregation and synagogue; perhaps petitioning God to descend onto the unwanted realm of the mental home. With brightness on her face, says her daughter, Chaia died like a *zaddika* on New Year's Eve, a sacred day on which holy souls are summoned to re-join their pure source. A week later, the catatonic patient whom she had cared for, who seemed to notice nothing and nobody, died too.

Most revealing, Chaia had been preparing her daughter to follow her footsteps. Her testament had been transferred by example and promulgation. It covered every moment of life. 'You will feel a weight on your shoulder', she would say to her daughter since childhood, 'I will sit there and watch to see if you perform charity'. A piece of bread, taught her mother, is not eaten as if one is alone in the world, 'one piece, you cut off and put aside in case a hungry person knocks on your door; another piece you spare for the birds and put on the windowsill. The rest you may eat. And never ignore a hand stretched out for help'.

Today the writer Gila Almagor lives like a modern secular woman; she has earned her fame as an actress and writer in Israel, where she has found her voice and profession. However, she finds her mystical union in the spirit of her dead mother, the heritage of whom she devotionally follows the way a religious *zaddika* would follow a calling and revelation. Her hidden passion has been invested in charitable work. Never paid, away from the public and limelight, her work is carried out without God or synagogue, like her mother. Only her means have been modernized. She is head of a charity network and runs a registered charity fund to her name for which she won a presidential award. Modern means and finances allow her to be a patron for the poor, the needy and the sick. Like a busy bee of good deeds, she organizes trips to gravely ill children and supports an orphanage in Mombassa, Kenya, for whose benefit she raises and sends boxes of domestic utilities and clothes. Meanwhile by hearsay, constant petitions for charity find their way to her office at the municipality, where she appears at 8.30am outside her work at the national theatre. If she hears of sisters wanting or a single mother on TV she mobilizes her means and she never dares to pass a beggar in the street without a gift of alms. In her words, a woman who is considered the Diva of the Israeli theatre says, 'lest I disappoint my mother; my mother will see it. Everything I do, I do together with my mother' (Unpublished interviews; August 2000 and August 2001).

## Conclusion

I believe that Jewish women inhere the capacity for holy and ecstatic passion which is neither exclusive nor feminine proper; I am also convinced that feminine mysticism is philosophically, mystically and emotively rooted in the heritage of the Jewish people. As a cultural tradition, it has survived into the modern era through a new generation of *zaddika*, the holy woman carried forward by mothers to daughters and sons, to which Allen Ginsberg and Gila Almagor attest.

In the summer of 2001, I talked to my Israeli sister, a modern secular Jew, saying: 'in the secular sector, we would normally be satisfied by paying our income tax, by which we feel we have taken care of the welfare of the poor and needy, don't we?' To this she retorted, 'What do you think those bags in the corner are for'. In the corner of her living room bags were bursting with toys for children of foreign workers. My sister and I grew up on our grandmother's stories, one of which was the following. When a *zaddik*'s soul enters heaven, the holy soul is so paralysed and frozen with the suffering of the world that has accumulated in the *zaddik*'s sensitive soul, that God takes that soul between the palms of His hands and warms it up with His breath for one thousand years.

Clinically, both Naomi Ginsberg and Chaia were diagnosed as paranoiac schizophrenic, having been haunted by violent events they had never actually experienced themselves. According to psychotherapeutic definition, a person who vicariously adopts the suffering of others as his own, without having been victimized himself, is defined as a pseudo-path. While their contemporaries engaged in militant expansionism and material prosperity, the two mothers were persistently accommodating the Holocaust victims in their minds, relocating into their home-life the horrors that had happened to others miles away from the place of atrocity and years after the events had happened, re-living them in their enclosed homes in America and Israel. In portraying their mothers' mental illness, both Allen Ginsberg and Gila Almagor, amalgamate a people's history a domestic tragedy.

The motif of tragedy connects the two women to *dramatis personae* driven by a trait of character that disrupts their mental balance and drives them to miscalculated action ensuing their isolation and self-inflicting fall and ruin. Nonetheless, as tragic heroes, the two mothers are associated with noble humanity, which elevates their character and makes their suffering undeserving.[19] The Holocaust appears as a factor of mimetic elevation in the lives of both maternal characters.

19. T.S. Dorsch (ed.), *Aristotle Horace Longinus*, pp. 48-52.

Vicarious suffering becomes their tragedy and their noble *raison d'être* as human beings at the same time.

Translated into Jewish mysticism, vicarious suffering ensues the highest ideal of humanity in pursuit of the divine image in oneself. The *zaddik's* homologous empathy reaches its highest mimesis in adopting another man's agony as his/her own. In theological terms, such a woman reaches the ideal model of holiness. While their identification with the Holocaust victims is defined as mental illness, their agonizing souls conceive of ecstatic experiences recalling unbound devotion. Perceiving their paranoiac hallucinations as mystical union with the suffering of their community, the victims become their metaphysical partner of soul, empowering them as *zaddika*. Metaphysically and emotively uniting with the victims, their vicarious suffering mystically authorizes them to act as righteous and holy women.

Were they driven by mental psychosis or a spiritual choice? Are these terms compatible? I do not know? Divinity and ecstatic mysticism are domesticated in *Kaddish* and yet diminish in Almagor's texts. While emphatic humanity is revealed in mystical visions in Naomi's life, Chaia turns empathy into a practice, operating as a *zaddika* stationed in her home launderette and kitchen. Naomi Ginsberg has turned away from the American way of life and the world and has chosen mystical union with the Holocaust victims, God and Creation. All of this has empowered her to act as a mediator who pleads with God on behalf of the Jewish community and mankind. Eventually she pities and takes care of God Himself like a good Jewish mother. This image invokes the kabbalistic idea that man's deeds empower divine presence on earth; and it is human responsibility that determines either the presence or the reduction of divine flow in the world.[20] However, also Chaia walks the path of search for God and humanity; and in their different ways, both women valorize the kabalist concept advocating that human actions can either empower or diminish God's eminence in the world in His feminized embodiment, the *Shekhina*. The cosmic power of good deeds promotes the kabalistic idea that good deeds empower the *Shekhina's* divine presence both above in the upper spheres and below on earth; while evil weakens her divine energy.[21]

20. Scholem, *Elements of the Kabbalah*, p. 301.
21. Scholem, *Elements of the Kabbalah*, p. 301.

Intertextuality, mystical Judaism imbues the descriptions of both maternal figures with spiritual conceptualization. At the core, both mothers enfold the expiating belief in accumulating good deeds so as to enhance a better world inspite of, or even because of, existing cruelty and wrongdoing. On the background of their mental turmoil, their spiritual devotion is perceived without religious title, community or synagogue. In mimetic terms, their holiness is domesticated, materializing in low mimesis of family life and domestic tragedy. These motifs may associate the two mothers with the *Hidden Zaddik* whose identity remains unknown to his/her environment, and even to the person herself, which makes her even holier.

The women in my case studies evoke theosophical ideas of expiating amendment and messianic redemption. In their search for God and humanity, these women find elevation of the Self in both conventional and unconventional means. Although their choices differ, their experiences follow the pattern of mystical devotion and ecstatic union. Operating from the sphere of their domestic home life, these women demonstrate unbound empathy with the agony of the world, conceiving a righteous person in feminized visage. Naomi Ginsberg follows the model of a *zaddika* in her ecstatic domestication of her evocation and God. While she ascends, she draws divinity down to earth to the low mimetic level of home cooking in a tree house in the wood. The ladder complements the revelation after Jacob's dream, having its foot standing on the ground while its head reaching to the tree house embodying an ascending movement upward. Like Naomi Ginsberg, Chaia classically finds her ecstatic pains of soul in identification with the Holocaust victims. However, unlike Naomi, she actualizes her empathy in humanistic activity, virtually acting her role as a *zaddika* in her community. Religious activity proper enters her life only in her last years when she is confined to a mental home, and her visions and voices have remained unaccounted and untold.

These women share a capacity for empathy on the strata of ecstatic devotion, resembling *Agape* spiritual love, and *Philo*, love of mankind. Has ecstatic devotion been a vocation or a flight away from harsh reality for these women? Eventually, humanistic activity directs itself towards the suffering of others, not away from it. Love in all its manifestations legitimizes transcending identification with the Other. Were these women driven by unrequited frustrations, sexual or emotional deprivation? Perhaps. Naomi Ginsberg became an alienated wife, and Chaia lost her husband; but both knew love in their personal lives. Moreover, Gila Almagor, Chaia's daughter, ardently follows her mother's path while her career as a writer and actress and her married life have been exceedingly successful. All women discussed here are perceived as righteous women who take the suffering of their community upon their shoulders and embrace unbound compassion and love for humanity not merely as affable mood, but as a way of life if not an evocation.

# The Power of Male Violence as Evil: Uses and Abuses of Power in the Shoah and the Silent Genocide of Abused Women

*Victoria Rollins*

Hear my cry, O God,
listen to my prayer.
From the ends of the earth I call
to you,
I call as my heart grows faint.
(Ps. 61.1-2).

In this article I wish to deal with male violence to women in many of its forms, I hope to show that there are links between the violence of the battlefield, political genocides and the daily abuse and death of wives, daughters and girlfriends at the hands of the men they love. It is also my claim that the churches have not done enough in speaking out against these abuses or in creating environments of theological as well as physical safety for women. I insist that the Church must raise its voice against women shamed and silenced still used as 'comfort stations'[1] in armed

1. That women have been given the role of 'comforters', a word symbolically interpreted as the Holy Spirit in Christian biblical terms, is best illustrated with the occurrence of women in Asian 'comfort' stations designed during World War II and the Korean War to provide 'refreshment' in company-keeping and sexual 'favours' for military men. Although interned women were given at times a painful 'choice' of this option for survival and the hope of 'better treatment', creating a hierarchical status within imprisoned women and judgments between women, most women were never given a choice but were 'selected', imprisoned, and sexually assaulted. The raping of women as 'conquests' for invading armies and now even 'peacekeepers' has been documented by many, recently presented in BBC reports, as example, Isabel Mathison of BBC News 24 broadcast on 16/07/04. Please see works of Gnanadason, Santos and Sancho.

conflict,[2] name women and children instead of civilian war victims injured, killed and labelled 'collateral damage',[3] and name abused wives as household prisoners devoid of choice as wives forced and even drugged into 'service' in matrimonial 'duty' and sexual 'favours' as actual rapes by husbands. These exploitive practices culminate in the vast trafficking of women and girls for pornography and prostitution around the globe[4] as dangerous, demeaning, injurious and lethal abuses of power through male violences, and the Church must name all these as crimes against women.[5] The silence is as shameful as the silence over the Holocaust. In order to illustrate what I believe is the connection between public, international, political acts of violence and those carried out in private I am using the Holocaust as a partner in my argument.

2.   After the Serb army took most of the territory, 'in...1992 the mass killings changed into steady, individualized killings and rapes... In...1994 the ICRC made an extraordinary appeal to world leaders to stop the atrocities. The appeal was ignored'. International Committee of the Red Cross, as referenced by Michael A. Sells, *The Bridge Betrayed: Religion and Genocide in Bosnia* (Berkeley, CA, and London, UK: University of California Press, 1998), p. 20 (p. 171 n. 28). From the testimony given by a survivor at the International war crimes tribunal, 'They started selecting young women... I knew them all...then they started yelling: "We want the Muslims to see what our seed is". The women were never seen again'. Also, '...a rape center was set up... Muslim girls and women were held there, underwent continual rape and other physical violence, and also were sent out to apartments where they were held several days... Militiamen boasted about their gang rapes of women... Human rights reports also show rapes of Christian women'. Sells, *The Bridge Betrayed*, pp. 20–27.

3.   Writing of the similarities between present day sexual assaults and those of war histories: 'Women were part of the whole territory of invasion and conquest, their bodies and their entire being colonized by the wars for new territories and male victories'. Aida F. Santos, *Violence Against Women in Times of War and Peace* (Gender, Reproductive Health, and Development Monograph Series; Quezon City, Philippines: University of the Philippines Centre for Women's Studies & Ford Foundation, 2001), pp. 2–6.

4.   Phil Chamberlain, 'Thousands Dying for Bid for Refuge', *The Big Issue*, 28 June–4 July 2004, p. 20, Jamie Doward, 'Homeless Crisis Fuelled by Domestic Violence', *The Observer*, 17 August 2003, p. 11, Editor's Feature Article, 'Violence on the Homefront', 29 September–5 October 2003, and Santos, *Violence Against Women*.

5.   'A beating is a punishment for not fixing a man's world...wives are supposed to "make the world right". Power, control and self-esteem have been reported as rewards for beating up women...it is simply that it works...all too often men get away with it'. Loren Broadus, 'Sexuality and Violence in the Family and the Church', in Elizabeth Stuart and Adrian Thatcher, *Christian Perspectives on Sexuality and Gender* (Herefordshire, UK: Gracewing, 1996), pp. 404–405.

*The Right to Live Common for Victims and Survivors of Genocides*
*and all Abused Women and Children*

As a Christian I cannot write as one knowledgeable of the inhuman
suffering endured by the victims and survivors of human atrocities
as the Shoah and recognized genocides, but support Raphael's
search beyond women's exclusion from religious language to
gesture[6] to establish women's experiences within such suffering as
unique and valuable for remembrance and for future resistance to
evil, as I am placing the experiences, both individually unique and
collective, of battered wives in suffering from the evils of violences
inflicted by men, especially as husbands.

As voiced, 'the experience of staying alive in the camps cannot
be separated from the experience of dying in the camps', suggesting
these traumatic experiences of being violated by violence, once
encountered, meld death with life. Close to being murdered,
survivors recalling and expressing life-changing encounters having
our existence and mortality placed in another's control which,
although no longer repressed or submerged, creates the blurring
of life and death boundaries and changes the world in a way that
memory cannot forget although people inexperienced with surviving
violence including many professionals fail to understand. This is
present often but not always in a more positive viewpoint of those
divulging medical near-death experiences, perhaps in ways reaching
mystical revelation of the divine. As for genocidal and near-death
survivors, the suppression, discounting and silencing of battered
wives attempting to express these experiences creates further
isolation and separation for us to bear. Hearn writes it is necessary
to understand a social formulation of prevailing male violences
systemic to hierarchical societies creating oppressions of male
domination and violences against women and genocides in order
to counteract isolating effects upon women from societies' reluctance
to inhibit liberal individualism:

6. 'But it may also be that the gesture is all that Auschwitz leaves to us. A
substantial and cautionary literature attends to the holocaustal rupture of language',
Raphael, *The Female Face of God in Auschwitz: A Jewish Feminist Theology of the Holocaust*
(London: Routledge, 2003), p. 11. In respecting Judaism as a religion of words, although as Raphael states, not inclusive of women's, I offer Raphael's point that the
pain in the experiences of Auschwitz were 'too loud to hear' (p. 11). And I respectfully
submit the pain of battered wives is also 'too loud' to be heard.

> Despite the importance and complexity of individual responsibility, it is important to understand men's violence as much more than a collection of individual actions.[7]

The effects on battered wives of surviving near-death experiences from male abuses combined with re-victimizations and lack of support from many instances of leaving an abusive husband create a chasm in need of repair similar to those surviving camp and genocidal imprisonments such as the Shoah. Statements such as 'Everything has been wrenched from me? What's left? Nothing. Death' by Shoah survivors reverberate with the unheard cries of many battered wives. Battered wives brought close to death through repeated beatings and rapes[8] develop a shift in experiential awareness, a collapsing of time[9] and a breaking of the ordinary from the violation of trust as in the Shoah, bringing discomfort and pain to the encounter of enduring and struggling to survive without empowerment, recognition, and effective aid.[10] Perhaps best expressed in the words: 'because I know the difference between before and after',[11] battered wives similar to Shoah survivors express an experiential knowledge gleaned by surviving violations of devalued personhood assaulting awareness and expectation from surviving evil as well as upon our human bodies, minds, hearts, and souls.[12]

7. Hearn, *The Violences of Men*, p. 212.

8. *Rape Survivor Interviewed: 'The man that raped me killed the person I was'*, Sky News, 04/03/04.

9. Raphael, *The Female Face of God in Auschwitz*, p. 61.

10. 'For countless women intimacy with a man becomes a devastating encounter with betrayal, humiliation, shame, degradation and fear. For some the abuse extends to include physical violence. In the UK, it is estimated that one woman is killed every three days by a violent partner or ex-partner (Criminal Statistics, The Home Office, 1995). Since 1981, the largest increase in violent crimes has been in incidents of domestic violence' (British Crime Survey, Home Office, 1996), as cited by Goetting, *Getting Out*, p. 1.

11. Gerd Langer, 'Gendered Suffering? Women in Holocaust Studies', in Ofer and Weitzman (eds.), *Women in the Holocaust* (New York: Binghampton, 1998), p. 352.

12. Hopkins writes: 'For a woman to speak with her own voice, to name the world through her own experience and to forge her own historical subjectivity, is the beginning of a new anthropology' (the science of the nature of the human being). Julie Hopkins, 'Radical Passion', in Daphne Hampson (ed.), *Swallowing a Fishbone?* (London: SPCK, 1996), p. 69.

The power to be is a sacred right of life-giving awe; it can be dammed and constricted and extinguished from the lives of battered women and holocaust victims but it's movement towards survivorship and justice will bubble up in remembrance and from one victim to another, rise and carry more energy in gathering relationship as water bursting human structures carries possibilities of both life-giving irrigation and flourishing or devastating destruction to human lives, animals and the earth. Power to be and do in gentleness and non-violent, shared mutuality of love in marriage yet also as prophetic voice, action, and righteous anger in response to injustices[13] negated through the abuse of power by husbands in the use of domination and terror against wives indeed is serious human experience for husbands to do as choice; for battered wives to endure and perhaps survive, and for communities to tend. As in the Shoah, neither hope nor praying to change the suffering of battered wives and danger from a husband's male violence is enough. Seeking to understand God requires taking human experience seriously,[14] which bears great significance to the ways in which power used and abused through male violence causing the plight of battered wives simultaneously inform and are informed by Christian theologies. God defined as 'relational power' is God defined as 'our' relational power.[15] In its power is mutuality and plurality — it is not 'my power', or 'power over' but power in relation born anew within each of us and strengthened and expanded when shared. Power of life named as Sacred power arises in human capacities to bear God's authority in co-operation and potent together as divine and human willingness to effect justice[16] to enable life itself in resistance to the power of both individual and social

---

13. Marie M. Fortune, 'The Transformation of Suffering: A Biblical and Theological Perspective', in Carol J. Adams and Marie M. Fortune (eds.), *Violence Against Women and Children* (New York: Continuum, 1996), pp. 86–87. Please refer also to works of Harrison, Ruether, Isherwood, Heyward, Fortune, Bussert, Thistlethwaite, Engel, NiCarthy and Cooper-White.

14. Isabel C. Heyward, *The Redemption of God: A Theology of Mutual Relation* (Lanham, MD: University Press of America, 1982), p. xix, as referenced by Lisa Isherwood, *Liberating Christ* (Cleveland, OH: The Pilgrim Press, 1999), p. 93 (p. 156 n. 4).

15. 'God is our relational power. God is born in this relational power', in Isabel C. Heyward, *Touching Our Strength* (San Francisco, CA: Harper and Row, 1989), p. 24.

16. Heyward, *The Redemption of God*, p. 40.

evil. Named as a theological problem[17] is the limiting and blocking of the creative, Sacred energy of God in life-giving forms by patriarchal uses of power exerted in relationship as control, force, domination, aggression and violence. As a man is safest in his home, whilst a woman is least safe there,[18] especially if she is married,[19] the use and abuses of power as acceptable men's violences[20] permeating our cultures in hierarchical dualisms of glorified dominant/submissive, male/female, win/lose practices under-girding oppressions of women as partners and wives destroys ironically for both men and women our desires, capacities for compassion, and our need for intimacy and love.

The epidemic of violence against women and the battering of wives is as significant to our cultures in all its forms as and within human and civil rights movements rooted in private/public dichotomies as in the Shoah and all genocides beyond personal issues of domestic terror reaching wide dimensions of human rights violations destroying the marital vows and ultimately the marriage, the family, and most often, the diminishment or destruction of the woman's life itself. As in the Shoah, the prevalence of male crimes against women worldwide comprises crises of theological magnitude of deep anguish and destruction for women's lives, relationship and the world formed as its own genocide — placing even the doing of theology without regard for this suffering as insult in the face of this magnitude of evil from men's violence world-wide as

17. James N. Poling, *The Abuse of Power: A Theological Problem* (Nashville, TN: Abingdon Press, 1991, 1993), p. 32. 'Evil is proportionate to power, the treatment of other people as objects, both the agent and the effects are necessary in defining evil…the pattern of destroying persons by rejecting their basic human needs'. Elizabeth Bettenhausen, 'Evil', in Russell and Clarkson (eds.), *Dictionary of Feminist Theologies* (London: Mowbray, 1996), pp. 93–94.

18. Despite the acculturated role of men as 'protectors', this predominance of choosing to do male violences leaves women most unprotected and vulnerable at home: Dobash and Dobash, *Violence Against Wives*, pp. 20–21.

19. 'Edwards, 1989, p. 214, as cited by Hearn, *The Violences of Men* (London: Sage Publications, 1998), pp. 4–5.

20. Referencing K. Pringle, *Men, Masculinities, and Social Welfare* (London: University College London, 1995), p. 100, Hearn states: 'Drawing particularly on the work of Tifft (L. Tifft, *Battering of Women: The Failure of Intervention and the Case for Prevention* [Boulder, CO: Westview, 1993]) and Kirkwood (Catherine Kirkwood, *Leaving Abusive Partners: From the Scars of Survival to the Wisdom for Change* [London: Sage Publications, 1993), he stresses that such violence is behaviour *chosen* by men, and is the product of choice within a *structural* context of hierarchical power arrangements', Hearn, *The Violences of Men*, p. 35.

incalculable, worldwide loss. Atrocities of domination, humiliation, beatings, rapes and restricted freedoms for battered wives by husbands as against Shoah victims rendered defenceless[21] within the supposed sanctity of marriage against the evil of stereotypical prejudices held against women as evil in need of control and conquering, manifest within 'ordinary' marriages, witch-hunts, rape camps, practices of genital mutilation, pornographic practices, stonings, gang rapes, suti, foot-binding, 'honour' killings, and female infanticide — radiating from individual to gang and group repeated assaults from homes to p.o.w and refugee camps. Too little improvement has been made towards safety by the amounts of miscarriages and birth injuries at present linked to wives with direct male violences against pregnant women causing injuries and damage to the immune system of the wife from being beaten, increasing risks of life-threatening diseases.

The link between the violated bodies of abused women and the questioning of what creates for humanity its meaning is found in the common pain of the degraded body and the meaning gleaned of its degradation. According to Raphael, the holiness of Auschwitz is to be recognized not in the place but in the space created by the reactions and responses to the horrors done to its victims for themselves and each other named as a 'service of the heart'[22] in holiness as openness, risk, gesture, and invitation with the divine as for battered wives despite being controlled, beaten and raped to the point of near-death:

> There is no doubt that, as in other camps, 'solitude alternated with frustration or despair, as the challenge of staying alive under brutal conditions tested human resources beyond the limits of decency.[23]

21. Battered wives often become too abused and too terrified to defend themselves, or despite all coping efforts and skills developed, unable to avoid worse beatings or being killed if they try, Dobash and Dobash, *Violence Against Wives*, p. 109.

22. 'The sheer scale and quantity of impurity beneath which the victims struggled and died is not to be dismissed if because to underestimate the power of the demonic profane is also to underestimate the power of the Holy to resist and therefore transform it;' Raphael, *The Female Face of God in Auschwitz*, p. 80.

23. Langer, Lawrence, 'Gendered Suffering? in Ofer and Weitzman, *Women in the Holocaust*, p. 362, as cited by Raphael, *The Female Face of God in Auschwitz*, p. 9 (p. 169 n. 27).

### Women's Experience of Challenging Oppression and Societal Apathy Common for Shoah Survivors and Battered Wives

Gospel praxis can only be justly undertaken I am arguing through examining experienced oppressions and working towards the liberation of the oppressed. To connect Scripture with experience is a task of the theologian, as Cone relates,[24] as well as to highlight the Church's role in God's liberating work positing life's struggles within embodied empowerment in the life, death and resurrection of Jesus. Yet the predominant use of power over others through male violence inflicts pain rather than creating and making space for spiritual and emotional joy. Todorov believes power over others can produce either joy or pain, but believes greatest proof of such power is achieved by inflicting pain.[25] Battered wives learn through the assaults and the pain that there is no safe place or haven of refuge even as refugees, but there comes a wisdom from the struggle in attempting to survive male violence as for some Holocaust victims becoming anchored within our own integrity as power in a suffering God despite the apathy and cruelty of others. To enact one's faith beyond understanding, questioning, or rejecting a God of omnipotence and perfect goodness and justice providing earthly protection is to recognize the divine in the human resistance and responses to evil wherever encountered—to resist defiling the face of God by compromising one's personal integrity by choosing retaliation, vengeance, and hatred is to choose life despite evil and death, including our own murder or suicide.[26]

Crimes against wives are reflected in the prevalence of what is termed 'broken homes', family separations, divorce statistics, spiralling costs of medical care, loss of work productivity, increased government costs for crisis work, law enforcement and legal proceedings, and most of all, the cost of actual human lives

---

24. James Cone, *A Theology of the Oppressed* (New York: Seabury Press, 1975), p. 9.
25. Todorov, *Facing the Extreme*, p. 181.
26. Recognizing the probable inability to assess how important concepts of divine omnipotence or omniscience to women's roles in the Holocaust, Raphael nevertheless notes: 'But by far the most prevalent response to suffering in the women survivors' memoirs is not one of a sustained call for deliverance upon the God of Israel, but upon the assistance of Israel itself in the bodily form of the women around them... Women survivors' accounts are not preoccupied by theology but with conveying the immediate struggle to survive as an individual or as part of a family or group of friends', Raphael, *The Female Face of God in Auschwitz*, p. 39.

diminished, damaged, and extinguished due to male abuse. These crimes done to women comprising a genocide demonstrate the pervasively damaging effects of dominant/submissive relationality and personal and positional power used over women and the devaluation of women as were Jews of the Shoah within Christian tradition, teaching, theology and praxis. Added to the Jewish role of spiritual leader within the home was the reported women's ability to endure the suffering of hunger and the discipline required to ration and apportion daily food for others, maintaining family support in the struggle for survival:

> In many cases, the family structure and support did much to sustain the member's morale and struggle for survival. And in most cases, the living spirit in this struggle was the mother.[27]

As Soelle, Cargas and Roth among others rightfully call Christian theology in repentance (metanoia) or *teshuvah*[28] to an integrity of praxis in solidarity with respect for the human dignity, faith, and flourishing of all Jews and to root out all 'latent anti-Judaism' and anti-Semitism from Christian tradition and practice, it must also come into a Christian integrity of solidarity with all abused women to dismantle male domination, address and prevent all male violence against women, especially against wives being abused and working ceaselessly without bitterness,[29] in Christian tradition and practice

27. Unger, 'The Status and Plight of Women in the Lodz Ghetto', in Ofer and Weitzman, *Women in the Holocaust*, p. 136. Similar disruptions over food apportionment are noted in current refugee situations fueling husbands' anger escalating into violences against wives, as reported by Human Rights Watch Division.

28. '*teshuvah*': an act of repentance... Cardinal Cassidy noted the need for the whole Church to make an act of repentance for its role in preparing the way for and in perpetrating, through so many of its members, the Shoah'. Cassidy, Cardinal Edward, as cited by Eugene J. Fisher, 'How Have the Churches Responded to the Holocaust?', in Carol Rittner, Stephen D. Smith and Irena Steinfeldt (eds.), *The Holocaust and the Christian World Reflections on the Past, Challenges for the Future* (Yehuda Bauer, consulting editor; New York: Continuum, 2000, 1995), statement upon the 50th anniversary of Auschwitz, p. 181.

29. 'King of his castle...he had the best of everything...he picked up the plate and let it fly...mother never said a word...she cleaned it all up and went to bed', Frank Dash, as cited by Angela Holdsworth, *Out of the Doll's House: The Story of Women in the Twentieth Century* (London: BBC Books, BBC Enterprises Ltd., 1988), pp. 16–17. Mrs Dash's epitaph states: 'Here lies a poor woman who always was tired/She lived in a house where help was not hired./Her last words on earth were: 'Dear friends, I am going/Where washing ain't done, nor sweeping, nor sewing/But everything there is exact to my wishes./For where they don't eat there's no washing of dishes./I will be where loud

to enable the humanity and flourishing of all women as well as all men. Among relevant ambiguities commonly held in tension by battered women and victims of the Shoah: the 'necessary' and damaging stereotyping[30] and labelling as victims and the appropriate importance of body and validation of embodiment as experience, as the initial and perhaps lasting site of being victimized, holding possibilities and realities of both immense joy and suffering. Here I am arguing for an important re-embodiment of human bodies in divine experience within Christian theologies as Isherwood, Stuart and Nelson[31] but, borrowing insights from disability theories, offering such remembrance as not always positive, comforting, or comfortable for survivors- bodies being a source of immense suffering from violence done by men to women and limitation as well as immense joy. The symbolism of water as a powerful source of life including women's tears from many nations of the earth shared by those assembled as Church representatives pooled into a large earthenware pot in solidarity as resistance to violence against women came from:

> those who survived and those who didn't…victims of sexual slavery and trafficking…beaten wives whose bruises are ignored by the church…women whose talents have been stifled and dreams suffocated…who cry for their children lost…whose theological voices are undermined…of young women who recognize the commonality of our concerns.[32]

anthems will always be ringing./But having no voice I'll be clear of the singing./Don't mourn for me now; don't mourn for me ever./I'm going to do nothing forever and ever'. Mrs Dash, as cited by Arnold Silcock, 'Verse or Worse', in Angela Holdsworth, *Out of the Dollhouse*, p. 17.

30. Regarding acculturated stereotyping of women, held by men and some women, please refer to Cooper-White (women as evil, inferior, crazy, temptress, bearer of sin in need of being controlled and/or eliminated, gateway to death, as mother (all-nurturing, all-devouring,) in Cooper-White, *The Cry of Tamar: Domestic Violence and the Church's Response*, pp. 45–46.

31. 'Man is the norm of creation and woman never quite measures up; all that is unique about her is seen as somehow defective and suspect. She is taught to mistrust herself, particularly the knowledge that she gains through her 'guts', her body knowing. Man will define who woman is', Isherwood and Stuart, *Introducing Body Theology*, p. 15.

32. World Council of Churches Publication, *Decade Festival and Assembly, Churches in Solidarity with Women*, (Harare, Zimbabwe: World Council of Churches, 1998), p. 45.

Issues of human value and worth undergirding hierarchical domination as in Nazi eugenic experimentation and extinction[33] of Jews with women as the weakest link still exist in less strident form as women, seen merely as extensions and/or possessions of our husbands, become no longer useful or desirable—abandoned when life gets tough or discarded when women's functions of work, servanthood, beauty/status and/or childrearing success and/or failure are achieved—even culminating for some wives as burned with the bodies of husbands upon their death. While today's societal control of women has become more subtle, inherent still in marital vows are male coercion and the power of husbands to do violence to their wives:

> "Love, honor, and obey" is the lot for women in marriage. Care for him, look up to him and do as he wishes—or else. Implied in that vow is the threat of rightful control over those who fail to obey; control may take the form of coercion. Thus, foundations of wife battering are written into the marriage contract. The church as well as the state are complicitous in this.[34]

33. That women were/are to be controlled and dominated as opposed to complete extinction as of the Jews in the Shoah is perhaps the most compelling important possible difference in comparing the genocide of women to the Shoah, although the international statistics of women's deaths and murders suggest that such elimination is also prevalent, dangerous, and systemic. Please see NiCarthy, Gnanadason, etc. Darwin's theories of competitive selection, natural and sexual, included the higher status of men over women as 'man attaining to a higher eminence'. Lucy Bland, and Laura Doan, 'Introduction', *Sexology Uncensored: The Documents of Sexual Science* (Cambridge: Polity Press, 1998), p. 11. This collection of Bland's reveals the developing science of eugenics active and accepted before the Nazi programs horrific Final Solution. Unger writes of the deportations in Poland: 'The reason for the preponderance of women was that women were, to some extent, the weakest link in the ghetto. The persons selected for deportation in the first place were welfare recipients, the unemployed, and families whose male breadwinners worked outside the ghetto. Women outnumbered men in these groups'. As example, of phase one: 'Women between the ages of twenty and forty were deported in numbers double and sometimes more than triple to those of men'. Unger, 'The Status and Plight of Women in the Lodz Ghetto', in Ofer and Weitzman (eds.), *Women in the Holocaust*, pp. 126–27. Yet as the years passed, writes Unger, the disparity between numbers by gender in the ghetto'…was the higher mortality of men. By inference, women were better able than men to tolerate the ghetto conditions'. Unger, 'The Status and Plight of Women in the Lodz Ghetto', in Ofer and Weitzman (eds.), *Women in the Holocaust*, p. 127.

34. Dobash and Dobash, 'Wives: the "Appropriate" Victims of Marital Abuse', *Victimology* 2.3–4 (1992), pp. 426–42, and 'Wife-beating: the Victims Speak', pp. 608–22, 1977, as referenced in Jean Giles-Sims, *Wife-Battering: A Systems Theory Approach* (New York: Guilford Press, 1983), p. 30.

### Public/Private, State and Church Complicity in Genocides and Violence against Women

Important also in similarity between battered wives and the Shoah victim/survivors is being chosen as different from the norm or the desired (temporary and permanent) by the powerful doing male violences -seen as inferior, deficient, polluting, or threatening as women's power was perceived by men and the Church to corrupt. The issue of power intermingled with duty and religious ideology given as human commandments illustrates the intention to take away any power and influence which remained for Jewish citizens named, shamed and blamed during the Holocaust as women are named, shamed, blamed, commanded and treated by abusing husbands who rip and strip us of our clothes and our empowerment— underpinned by Christian doctrines of 'atonement' for wives as inferior human beings.[35] Identified by Power as the greatest challenge to passive indifference regarding nationally recognized genocides are the voices of those refusing to remain silent. As for male violence against women, stating what is required, I am arguing in both interrelated arenas what is needed is to honour the existing good but challenge a system and a system's use of power that works all too well in negative ways. Wistrich's placing of the Sinai Covenant for God's chosen people found not in domination and conquering but in the revelation of a divine spark uniting all for mission and justice-making as embodied in Holocaust victim, Sonya, in the face of subjugation to the heinous power of male violence resonates with battered wives as upholding the sacrality of life through the ethic of honouring one another in just and non-violent relating.

While I am not arguing competitive rank with the incalculable sin of evil compared to the Shoah, I am arguing violence against women worldwide is an abuse, an enormous sin and misuse of power comprising a genocide of crimes in its own right within and beyond research within past and present genocidal histories, as an

---

35. *The Christus Victor* atonement theory of Auslen *et al.* posits Jesus' death in the struggle against evil brings transformaton into community of the oppressed if embodied in Church praxis rather than as relief from personal sin and guilt. Feminist liberation theologians reject suffering for sufferings' sake as women's lot and divine cross but do understand self-giving can indeed bring suffering and sacrifice. See Kerry Ramsey, 'Losing One's Life for Others: Self-Sacrifice Revisited' in Susan F. Parsons, *Challenging Women's Orthodoxies in the Context of Faith* (Aldershot, Hampshire: Ashgate Publishing Ltd., 2000).

integral, real and pervasive occurrence of such horrific events against women existing in many ways ignored, unrecognized, and silenced prisoners of 'regular' and daily war throughout most societies requiring in theological terms recognition and response to women's oppressions as injustice and systemic sin.

The Church has been unwilling and unable to address the extraordinary occurrence and frequency of male violence against women because it has failed to establish theologies which promote equal and just, non-violent relationality especially for marriage.[36] The 'private' aspect of male violence inflicted upon wives by husbands similar to the more 'privatized' setting of concentration and refugee camps cordoned off from obvious public matters fuel people's ability to choose apathy and indifference to the suffering of its victims. Awareness of and attention needs to be given to the diverse and damaging particularities of these women's oppressions done by men through violence, domination and control especially for wives within myriad forms of abuses:

> Broadly defined, "women's oppression refers to dynamic forces, both personal and social, that diminish or deny the flourishing of women".[37]

Despite recognizing differences of suffering concerning genocides and the category of abused women, nevertheless the five categories of women's oppressions distinguished by Serena Jones[38] also are

36. Joy M.K. Bussert, *Battered Women: From a Theology of Suffering to an Ethic of Empowerment* (New York, NY: Division for Mission in Northern America/Lutheran Church in America, 1986), as referenced by Mitzi N. Eilts, 'Saving the Family: When is a Covenant Broken?', in Adams and Fortune (eds.), *Violence Against Women*, pp. 447 (p. 450 n. 4).

37. Serena Jones, *Cartographies of Grace* (Minneapolis, MN: Fortress Press, 2000), p. 71.

38. Serena Jones categorizes these oppressions of women to include exploitation, marginalization, powerlessness, cultural imperialism, and actual violence comprising physical, sexual, emotional, spiritual, and economic male abuses done to wives including humiliation, degradation, harassment, shame, intimidation, terror, and ridicule. Dobash and Dobash, *Violence Against Wives*, Hoff, *Battered Women as Survivors*, Kirkwood, *Leaving Abusive Partners*, Goetting, *Getting Out: Life Stories of Women who Left Abusive Men*, Isherwood, 'Marriage: Heaven or Hell? Twin Souls and Broken Bones', *Feminist Theology* 11.2 (January, 2003), pp. 203–15, Helen, Hood, 'Speaking Out and Doing Justice: It's No Longer a Secret but What are the Churches Doing About Overcoming Violence?', *Feminist Theology* 11.2 (January, 2003), pp. 216–25, Marilyn French, *The War Against Women*, and Val Binney, Gina Harkell and Judy Nixon, *Leaving Violent Men: A Study of Refuges and Housing for Abused Women* (Bristol, England: Women's Aid Federation, 1981, 1988).

expressed in aspects of the horrific sufferings of the Jews[39] in the Shoah. Pulpits, lecterns, parish and community priorities and Church pastoral care need to be purged from sanctioning husbands' male domination and violences in intimate relationships to enable stronger, healthier and safe relationships, work ethics and most of all marriages based on tenderness and trust by teaching relational living in a mutual, non-dominant ethics of caring not exclusive to wives based on non-violence, pastoral care of compassion, empowerment for battered women and community-building as justice-making.[40] Prayers of 'the people' and 'deliver us from evil' need to include the naming of the majority of crime victims as women and the vast majority of violence perpetrated by men, emphasizing most often upon wives battered and raped by husbands and intimate partners in homes most often than but including streets. Parish and community priorities need to speak again and again of women as a group of valuable and capable human beings enduring the:

> special targeting in every society of women as being, along with children…the most vulnerable ones who bear the brunt of the world's injustice.[41]

The use of power over others through male violence destroys the dignity of personhood of men as well as women, as Ellison sees the enculturated macho masculinity making male violence to women acceptable as compensatory to the powerlessness men experience against other men within the very social, patriarchal system that devalues them.[42] Many men who do not conform to male, heterosexual, macho norms but relate with enculturated, traditionally assigned feminine qualities such as shyness and gentleness become marginalized by men in power and are also treated with contempt and even victimized by the use of male violence through assigned values used against women such as age,

39. Whilst the vast majority of Shoah victims and survivors were/are Jews, this author recognizes the Final Solution selected by the Nazis also included gypsies, homosexuals, those labelled handicapped, political resisters, and Jehovah's Witnesses.

40. 'Over 90% of the women who had contact with the Criminal Justice System said that they did not receive an adequate response', Jeanine Bossy and Stephen Coleman, *Womenspeak: Parliamentary Domestic Violence Internet Consultation* (Bristol, England: Women's Aid Federation, 1999), p. 20.

41. Gnanadason, Aruna, *No Longer A Secret: The Church and Violence Against Women* (Geneva, Switzerland: Risk Book Series, World Council of Churches, 1997), p. 5.

42. Marvin M. Ellison, *Erotic Justice* (Louisville: WJK, 1996), p. 99.

physique, abilitites/disabities, and sexual orientation.[43] This acculturated misuse of power often destroys faith, diminishes cultural values and the formation of healthy, productive and just societies, and eliminates decision-making choices let alone opportunities for women in refugee and war-torn conditions including camps, ghettos, and internments as for battered women 'at home' in partnerships and marriages worldwide. Battered wives experience the psychological effects of a soldier in active combat, also feeling shame and humiliation from disempowerment as for Holocaust survivors. As for prisoners of war, today's psychologists may present a woman experiencing battering from her abusive husband with the label of 'battered women's syndrome',[44] yet better than condemnation this label again blames women by shifting the emphasis of pathology from the abusive husband onto the battered wife and rape victim. Choices of power used through physical and sexual violences upon wives perpetrated by abusive husbands create a powerful betrayal of trust from intentional psychological and physical torture, pornographic use, sleep and food deprivation, and threats and attempts to kill us, especially for women with children and their vulnerability to potential and actual experiences of receiving a husband's violences themselves compounding the terrorizing upon wives. This has left untold millions of silent children and women in unmarked graves as in many violent territories including Kosovo[45] representing part of this silent genocide directly or indirectly caused by women trapped or 'choosing' to remain as with abusive husbands and men doing male violence such as 'war'.

43. Ryan, in Devlin and Ryan (eds.), *Sinews of the Heart*, p. 152. Men countering malestream expectations suffer also from male violences from other men who find their presence threatening to their enculturated masculinities, evidenced in the extreme but regular homophobia. Please see also Ellison, *Erotic Justice*, p. 99.

44. 'Battered women's syndrome:' post-traumatic stress disorder named for battered wives attributed to the work of Judith L. Herman, *Trauma and Recovery* (New York: Basic Books, 1992).

45. 'For ethnic Albanian women who were detained or chose to remain in Kosovo, rape was a miserable reality of war. Refugee accounts described the organized and systematic nature of attacks against women by Serbian forces in Djakovica and Pec. Albanian women were reportedly separated from their families and sent to an army camp…where Serbian soldiers repeatedly raped them. In Pec, refugees alleged that Serbian forced rounded up young Albanian women and raped them repeatedly at the Hotel Karagac. Gang rapes in village homes and alongside the roads were also reported'. Vance, 'Kosovo War' (1998–1999), *Encyclopedia of Prisoners of War and Internment*, pp. 162–63.

Women suffering daily and dying either slow or quick deaths at the hands of our abusive husbands in an apathetic and woman-blaming world experience the desecration of the divine imaged within us and our loved ones as the murdered right to be human and to live:

> Being created in the image of God is the basis of the right of human beings to their future and their responsibility for those who come after them.[46]

### Power in Symbols, Images, and Language Common for Genocides and Violence against Women

Laska illustrates her research witnessing to the atrocities done by oppression and violence within the Shoah by a lithograph depicting a woman crucified on a swastika,[47] whose courage practiced resistance to evil by voice and action. Raphael defines finding the Holy in caring moments of experienced history as sacred space and time 'from the afflictions of physical and spiritual defilement…to a world defaced by the demonic exercise of patriarchal power'.[48] We must respond respectfully to the evil against women who are assaulted by male violence with no lesser cleansing of defilement to the image of God in the battered bodies, ripped clothes and hearts of battered wives as the women's cleaning the bodies – theirs and others – as restoring the face of God within the exiled Shekhinah and the 'torn garments of the exiled Shekhinah'[49] in bruised faces then as now restored once again for ourselves and one another in the divine by those who do not turn away from us. In the Christian tradition, the biblical parables of the Good Samaritan, the woman

46. Jürgen, Moltmann, *On Human Dignity: Political Theology and Ethics* (Philadelphia: Fortress Press, 1984), p. 28.

47. Lithograph, frontpiece illustration, Colin, Paul, Courtesy of the Library of Congress, 1983, as referenced by Laska. Laska writes: 'I can no longer be silent', Vera Laska, *Women of the Resistance and in the Holocaust: Voices of Eyewitness* (Westport, CT: Greenwood Press, 1983), p. 241. Please refer also to depictions of women on crosses as Christas, including Bosnian (representing women's victimizations from physical and sexual assaults by men in the Bosnian genocide) and the sculpture in bronze of a crucified woman done in 1984 by Sandys now part of Christological images and as 'Christa/community' (Brock) for many feminist liberation scholars. Please refer to Carter Heyward, 'Christa', in Russell and Clarkson (eds.), *Dictionary of Feminist Theologies*, pp. 39–40 and also Isherwood, Ruether, Brock and Grey.

48. Raphael, *The Female Face of God in Auschwitz*, p. 78.

49. Raphael, *The Female Face of God in Auschwitz*, p. 42.

with the alabaster jar, and the women of Gospel tradition both witnessing the crucifixion and preparing to anoint and bury Christ's executed body take on new meaning of personal, social and political vulnerabilities and resistance to evil through care being the embodiment of the divine.

The power of religious symbolism, especially Christian, influenced both the Shoah and still the ongoing genocide of women to sanction, promote and ignore violence done to the oppressed, calling for women's remembrance and expression as prophetic action, justice-seeking and societal transformation as required for Holocaust remembrance. The steadfast and courageous witness of faith given by many Jehovah's Witnesses to the God of creation whose resistance to allegiance to anyone above God brought torture, camp imprisonment, separation from loved ones and often death seems rarely valued by Christian historians perhaps because of their marginalized status among denominations but should serve as a benchmark to those hoping to prevent genocide and a benchmark to the Church—I am stating in a less dramatic but no less important way paralleling what battered wives embody, face, witness to and transform beyond the torture by abusive husbands and the societal disease of apathetic or judgmental response. Battered wives facing abusive husbands with steadfast faith and Jehovah's Witnesses keeping steadfast facing Nazi persecution are linked by the use of power over the oppressed in the prevailing norm interactive with culture to define, marginalize, and oppress. We need to symbolically pledge ourselves to embody in thought, word and deed the emblem of the Witnesses' purple triangle to enable God's kingdom on earth through mutual, non-violent and just-relating, responsibility, and accountability to eliminate women or wives' subservience to men and abusing husbands and no longer tolerate the price battered wives pay of losing safety, community, and custody of children as well as our lives through the power of male violences and a defective 'family' court:

> The moral significance of the purple triangle is that it symbolizes a resounding No to human arrogance and a life-respecting Yes to the conviction that all human thought and action should be subservient to and judged by principles of justice, peace, love and understanding that come to mind when we reflect sensitively on the idea of the kingdom of God.[50]

50. John Roth, *Holocaust Politics* (Louisville: WJK, 2001), p. 242.

Any theological pondering of the existence of evil cannot be studied for long without awareness of its relationship to the concept of suffering, with volumes of both theological and secular writings devoted to this subject. Biblical scriptures themselves as well as most other sacred writings in many world religions and faith systems have much to say about the existence, origin of, nature of, and human response required to evil and suffering, in particular within Christianity related to human sin. Sometimes presented as a code for living, sacred writings attempt to grasp suffering's part in the lives of humanity and its relationship to a greater power, a spirit, Spirit, deity or deities, which some call God. How this becomes interpreted has been expressed through many symbols and images, and is at times identified in worship as religion — but manifests as informal as well as formal recognition often describing a Power greater than oneself, inviting relationship, communication, expression, and, for some, submission and obedience. Such ponderings at times can be linked with superstitions as well as institutional doctrines or tenants evolving in time and informing and becoming informed by other disciplines in humanity's efforts to find explanation, guidance, and meaning to life and the cosmos.

Shoah survivor Laska speaks of naming the Holocaust as 'the greatest challenge to Christianity', as Roth gives a Church mandate to eliminate from its faith beliefs all which counters the sanctity of life in the face of evil in creed and praxis. In parallel to this mandate, the Church's responsibility and opportunity to promote the sanctity of life challenging all in its creed and praxis colluding with both the destructive, pervasive, defining and prevailing criteria for maleness today and this active 'unknowing' and denial of the extent of violence against women, the plight of battered women, and male crimes done by husbands as heinous as terror abuses in the midst of all community groups including worshippers. I urge the Church to use its transformative power against the evil of male violence to eradicate the same active denial of those refusing to believe and help battered wives as to stand up to those still proclaiming the Holocaust never existed.

Roth concludes that for Lewental and for millions of Holocaust victims, choices given were essentially un-chosen- void of choice, grace, life itself- manifested as death by suicide, resistance, or hopeless attempts towards safety and freedom.[51] Societal judgment

51. Roth, *Holocaust Politics*, pp. 213–14.

upon battered wives often resulting in separation, loss of custody, loss of home, and loss of community with little to no legal protection causes the agonizing death of relationship and bond between mothers and children under the power wielded by the court based upon economic viability and earning power of mothers instead of safety for children as well as women as for Jewish mothers and for Jehovah's Witnesses during the Holocaust:

> Thus the women did not intentionally choose to die with their children. It was the Nazis who sentenced these women to death because they were mothers.[52]

Lack of choice or positive choices offering life and safety for victims of the Shoah under the power of cultural, ethnic, religious, economic, political and social conditions of Nazi control, limitations, regulations, and exclusions parallel the patriarchal control of women resulting in lack of choice and opportunities for battered wives seeking safety from abusive husbands. As expressed by Holocaust victim Lewental, one simply 'wants to live'.[53] Elizabeth Johnson places male violence done to women upon the body of God, recognizing a caring Shekinah who suffers with us:

> When a woman is raped and murdered, what does the Shekinah say? "She says, my body is heavy with violation".[54]

*Battered Women as Refugees as in the Shoah and all Genocides*

Battered wives as refugees and genocide survivors experience the loss of history, place, connection, and rootedness as the loss of

52. 'One group of women knowingly chose to die in order to be with their children until the end. When the women of Theresienstadt were sent to the family camp in Auschwitz-Birkenau, they were allowed to live with their children... As Ruth Bondy observed, all but two women of the six hundred who were given the choice decided that they could not abandon their children. They were at their side to the end'. Ofer and Weitzman, 'Introduction', in Ofer and Weitzman (eds.), *Women in the Holocaust*, pp. 11–13.

53. Salmen Lewental, Auschwitz notebook, as referenced by Roth, *Holocaust Politics*, p. 213.

54. Elizabeth Johnson, *She Who Is: The Mystery of God in Feminist Discourse* (New York: Crossroad, 1994), p. 264. This author recognizes and honours the use of God imaged as the Shekinah by Jewish scholars from the traditions of Judaism as written in works by Jewish Feminist Liberation Theologians such as Raphael and Plaskow.

Westhelle's 'being placed in God's *is* of creation',[55] jarring and disrupting tradition, belonging, actual links within family membership with extra hardships for single mothers, and the archetypal and spiritual sense of 'home' destroyed by our husbands' violence. Indeed this upheaval includes painful, forced separations from beloved family and friends including, for mothers, especially as single mothers, our children as well as further trauma in witnessing their abuse and even murder; at times sacrificial.[56] Yet unlike refugees, the migration of battered wives is rendered even more invisible— ignored, minimized, and/or forgotten due to the crucial need for safety. While often unrecognized, many women including mothers and children of the refugee, migrant, and homeless populations worldwide are indeed trying to survive personal violence from intimates, most often husbands, compounded with further stranger and acquaintance male violence arising from ethnic, political, and/or religious strife and displacement.[57] Levinas, remembered by Raphael, stated:

> God himself is a refugee in the world.[58]

Battered wives embody refugee status 'previously overlooked by both government and charitable organizations'[59] often without

55. Vitor Westhelle, 'Creation Motifs in the Search for Vital Space', in Susan B. Thistlethwaite and Mary P. Engel (eds.), *Lift Every Voice: Constructing Christian Theologies from the Underside* (Maryknoll, NY: Orbis Books, 1998), p. 151.

56. Whilst mothers are cited in numerous texts as sacrificing themselves for children, husbands, parents, and siblings, the cruelty of the regime according to Ofer and Weitzman also created mothers being forced to give up their children to save their own lives and perhaps their husbands and other relatives. Ofer states: 'Nazi cruelty and brutality toward women were mentioned in many diaries as a symbol of ultimate barbarity... When the deportations started, the abuse of mothers and children left speechless even the long-time witnesses of Nazi cruelty'. Ofer, 'Gender in Ghetto Diaries and Testimonies', in Ofer and Weitzman (eds.), *Women in the Holocaust*, pp. 162–63.

57. Santos, *Violence Against Women in Times of War and Peace*, pp. 2–3, Human Rights Watch, *Seeking Protection*, p. 93, and NiCarthy, 'War Against Women', in Ashworth, *A Diplomacy of the Oppressed*, p. 56, 67 (n. 16.).

58. Emmanuel Levinas, in Raol Mortley, *French Philosophers in Conversation: Levinas, Schneider, Serres, Irigaray, Le Doeuff, Derrida*, (London: Routledge, 1991), p. 21, as cited by Raphael, *The Female Face of God in Auschwitz*, p. 155, in Raphael (p. 203 n. 105).

59. Johnson states battered wives are refugees: 'Their needs had previously been overlooked by both government and charitable organizations which only conceived of homelessness in terms of actual destitution'. Vivien Johnson, *The Last Resort: A Woman's Refuge* (London: Penguin Books, 1991), pp. 98–99.

adequate societal recognition and support despite escalating male violences with similar techniques of control and torture as in the Holocaust. Imploring awareness and response from the gruesome news portrayals of refugee hardships dehumanized into, as example, 'a flood' to counter fears of swelling immigration into countries greater than the knowledge of mass murder,[60] Salgado highlights by photographic essay the vast migrations and cultural mixing of this past century representing:

> populations in flux and the dissolution of traditionally circumscribed borders. As the world weighs the availability of human resources for the twenty-first century, Salgado's project speaks for those who are displaced and the people and places that receive them... Salgado puts forth the idea that a truly global family can only be built on the foundations of solidarity and sharing.[61]

Robinson writes regarding recent genocides of the plight of women caught in war whose terror and own violent victimizations is layered with trauma of family members injured, maimed and killed; where rape is now used for torture and intended impregnation in an ironic and chilling reminder to the elimination of women most at risk for becoming or being pregnant in the Nazi final solution.[62] Author Virginia Wolf expresses a feminist view of

60. According to Chamberlain, responsibility becomes absolved in imaging thousands of dying refugees as 'a flood', a disaster beyond their responsibility. As for the battering of wives, their deaths are not just individual matters: 'These deaths are not isolated events. They are symptomatic of policies that no longer see the humanity of those fleeing their homeland, but prefer to see them as numbers, or worse, a natural disaster, 'a flood'. By making legal immigration and asylum nearly impossible, these policies lead to the death of refugees who fled because of war, persecution, despaired poverty or natural disasters'. Phil Chamberlain, News/Asylum, 'Thousands Dying for Bid For Refuge', *The Big Issue*, June 28–July 4, 2004, p. 20.

61. Sebastian Salgado, 'Migrants and Refugees: The Survival Instinct', from *Migrations: Humanity in Transition*, 30 June–2 September, City of Edinburgh Council, Edinburgh, Scotland, 2001 (New York: Aperture, 2000), unmarked pamphlet page, exhibited by The City of Edinburgh Council, Department of Recreation, Edinburgh, Scotland, 2001. Such a recent vision of 'a global family community' might indeed be seen as The Kingdom of God, as presented by feminist liberation theologians, as example, 'the royal stewardship given to all humans (Matthew Fox, based on *The Holy Bible*: Gen. 1.28, creating 'shalom' [*The Holy Bible*: Ps.72, 89]), webs, circles. Jenny Dines, 'Kingdom', in Isherwood and McEwan (eds.), *An A to Z of Feminist Theologies*, pp. 116–17.

62. Mary Robinson, speaking as the UN Commissioner for Human Rights in Santos, *Violence Against Women in Times of War and Peace*, p. 1.

one country, worldwide, a country I hope might be wide enough to embrace diversity of humanity in nonviolent just-relating and high enough to celebrate and honour the unique gifts of each human being.[63] Despite differing cultures, the international experiences of women's one 'global village' emerging from the broken silences, hearts, bodies, families, homes and lives from similar realities caused by male violence against women have revealed unifying reactions in a world of women's destroyed lives:

> The commonality of our reactions — first shame and denial, then sorrow and sometimes guilt, followed by anger and action — made some of us begin to believe that women live in one "country"...While we soaked up each other's gashes, sat in emergency rooms, listened and talked, we learned that women needed jobs, lawyers, medical care, child care, money to pay for all these services, group support from peers and a host of other goods and services typically required for people coming out of war zones. Out of our awareness of those needs we began to organize to stop the war against us.

Beyond recognizing the prevalence of battered wives within all migrant populations, unlike 'identified refugees', the migration of battered wives is as significant yet rendered even more invisible — ignored, minimized, and/or forgotten due to the nature of the very need for invisibility for safety sake at the time of fleeing and beyond where fleeing itself as even for some in the Shoah is described as salvation. Whilst often unidentified, many women including mothers and children of the refugee, migrant, and homeless populations worldwide are indeed trying to survive male violence from intimates, often husbands, compounded with stranger violences from ordinary, ethnic and political identities. After being forced to leave her home after a severe life-threatening beating, Stella found herself just able to cover her underwear with a garment from the laundry line, hitched a ride in the freezing night without a coat,

---

63. Virginia Wolf expressed a common vision for women when she wrote, as noted in NiCarthy: ' "As a woman I have no country. As a woman I want no country. As a woman my country is my whole world". Virginia Wolf was not alone. Other women would like our country to be the world — a world without man-made barriers to our autonomy and peace'. Virginia Woolf, *Three Guineas* (London: The Hogarth Press, 1938), cited in 'Off Our Backs, Country of Women', column, as referenced by NiCarthy, 'War Against Women', in Ashworth (ed.), *Diplomacy of the Oppressed*, p. 52 (p. 66 n. 1). This is not to say that women do not take pride in our homelands or countries of citizenships. Please refer also to Virginia Woolf, *A Room of One's Own and Three Guineas* (Oxford: Oxford University Press, 1992).

shoes or socks and became stranded in a strange town, but this Stella was living in a community in 'peacetime' USA:

> I was absolutely freezing...I was in such agony and such pain I just wanted the ground to open up and die.[64]

Many of these women, like Moses, never reach a Promised Land; like Abel, they are killed by a jealous and competitive family member; like Jeremiah, they are cast from their communities for speaking the truth like Hagar, sent as exiled to die after being used, abused, and dominated by the victimizations of both men and women; like Dinah, Tamar, and Sarah, unprotected and defiled by loved ones and strangers; like Rachel, many inconsolable mothers weep for children (and even like Jesus that are no more through forced separations as well as death and murder; more still, like Joseph are stripped and beaten by loved ones, first left for dead and then enslaved; some, like Jeptha's daughter and Queen Vashti, lose status, community, and life for their integrity and honour in the face of male domination and pride; like the Mary's and John witness the brutal murder of their child(ren) and friend, risking their own lives to speak the truth; and still more women, like the unnamed concubine, are betrayed, beaten, raped, dismembered, and forgotten; and, like Jesus, some women are ridiculed, labeled crazy and/or heretical, betrayed, threatened, silenced in their own communities, rendered homeless, spat at, whipped, tortured, put on trial, and crucified; and some, because of the power of the divine, are even remembered. Heise's question seeking the worst problem endured, as a Worldwatch researcher, uncovered an unexpected crucial answer from women living in harrowing circumstances with daily risks to their survival: 'my husband beats me!'[65]

---

64. Stella, battered wife interviewed regarding the last time she left after being beaten by her husband, in Pahl (ed.), *Private Violence*, p. 168.

65. Heise asked these women what their worst problem was: 'They are the poorest of the poor, yet they were worried about violence in their lives. "Battering, mutilation, and murder (are) still pervasive against many women" around the world', says Heise. Lori Heise 'The War on Women', *INA VAW News*, Summer, 1989, p. 2, reporting on an article of the same title from *The Washington Post*; also *Worldwatch Papers*, March-April, 1989. As NiCarthy asks: 'Is it assumed that hunger and malnutrition give immunity to the pain of a beating?' NiCarthy, 'War Against Women', in *A Diplomacy of the Oppressed*, p. 62 (p. 68 n. 33).

### Breaking Silence of Suffering as Resistance to Evil Common for Shoah Victims and Battered Women

A woman's decisive actions to break silence about an abusive husband or partner and seek safety for herself and protection for her children carry the same elements of fear, terror, determination, and hope comprising a prisoner of war's decision to join a resistance group within an imprisoned community and at times may reach an isolation and re-victimization within her community similar to war circumstances with people assigning blame, taking sides, ending friendships, gossiping and even betrayal. And they must be seen as decisive actions against male criminal behaviours, not turned by society and some professionals into a launching pad for fishing expeditions for women's qualities and competencies let alone sexual histories as re-victimized in courtrooms, psychiatric offices, casualty wards and emergency rooms.

Isherwood and Stuart locate the body as site of resistance to patriarchal order and control, reacting against a fixed image of womanhood defined in minimal visibility as well as silenced personhood.[66] As Holocaust survivors relate the frequent deaths of those who chose to commit suicide or fight back, sadly statistics of suicide, murders, murdering, and longer prison sentences for women than for men even done in self-defence[67] all speak to a gender-bias reflected in societies based upon unequal power.

The creative, embodied resistance necessitated by mothers of the Shoah as for battered wives in the soothing and attempted protection of our children, in upholding life despite torture and death beyond breaking silence about abusive husbands requires moving beyond the same elements of fear, terror, and conventional gender roles as a similar commitment required of a prisoner of war breaking silence to join or lead a resistance group through a power

---

66. Isherwood and Stuart, *Introducing Body Theology*, pp. 84–85. Please see also Raphael, *Thealogy and Embodiment: The Post-Patriarchal Reconstruction of Female Sexuality* (Sheffeld: Sheffield Academic Press , 1996).

67. As for Shoah and genocide victims, Legal aid for battered women is often difficult to obtain or retain. Also, the legacy of women as non-persons under the law lives on, despite significant strides and the dedicated work of many, reflecting: '…how deeply the thinking of lawyers and legislators have been conditioned by religious and biblical beliefs about the inferiority of women'. Jean Mayland, *et al.* (eds.), *Breaking the Chains: Of the Past, Of the Silence, Of Church Teaching…on Violence against Women*, p. 18.

of just relating in gathered determination and hope.[68] Women's efforts to resist the power of evil suffering through the active, courageous, and hard decision-making work done during the Nazi pogroms struggling to pack under strict orders, complete and collect required lists and documents, and suffering through encounters with officials including the Gestapo in order to help their families stay put, relocate, flee or even rescue their husbands from camp deportation to avoid the pain of being separated forever from loved ones[69] are resistance efforts similar to work required of battered wives dodging abusive husbands. As today, resistance given against the oppressors in varied hues of prayer and even uttered in a curse of one's tormentors during the Shoal in similar ways expresses the experiences, frustrations and varying gyrations expected of battered wives in resistance to abusive husbands risking further assaults and re-victimizations.

As aid for battered wives embodying refugee status—as groups of humanity facing challenges most often without adequate societal recognition or support—has begun from the grassroots, so also did compassion and sanctuary for some of the Jews and persecuted minorities during the Holocaust often come from within the grassroots resistance movement embodied by individuals such as Slaschta and lay and religious women. These courageous people crossed social, political and cultural boundaries at personal risk by moving against the established, hierarchies prevailing in order to honour and practice the sanctity of life. POW Survivors of Buchenwald, most now bearing physical and emotional scars, found indifference and disbelief of their devastating ordeals:

> And the cruel thing is that nobody has ever wanted to know, nor even really believed our story when we attempted to retell some of the more dramatic events. Such indifference I am certain has only made us all the more bitter and frustrated, and somewhat bitter of authority who should have taken our welfare to heart.[70]

68. Bauer, referencing Fleischmann's leadership, writes: 'It was in the unofficial and rebellious circles that feminine leadership became possible'. Yehuda Bauer, 'Gisi Fleischmann', in Ofer and Weitzman (eds.), *Women in the Holocaust*, pp. 6, 254.

69. Marion Kaplan, 'Jewish Women in Nazi Germany', Ofer and Weitzman (eds.), *Women in the Holocaust*, pp. 46–48.

70. Letter, Park Chapman, POW survivor, Buchenwald, Hull to Gunther, 1 December 1941, FRUS, 1941, II, pp. 876–77, as cited by Bard, *Forgotten Victims: The Abandonment of Americans in Hitler's Camps* (Boulder, CO: HarperCollins, 1994); pp. 109–10 (p. 144 n. 19).

Remaining in or seeking divorces after years of violent physical, sexual, psychological, verbal, and spiritual assaults and torture from husbands comprise a similar shattering of life as for Shoah victims in the loss of cultural placement and identity within the desecrated sacred bonds of marriage—sacred space of what had been hoped to be safe home space of mutual and abundant life now desecrated of personhood and of being human literally to our breath, bones, blood, and fibre as well as souls. This shattering of our lives comprises not only a violation and death of the present but also of the future, of self and of self-in-relation with and in the divine. The failure to eradicate the evil in the power of male violences erodes a potential equality and opportunity for just-relating between individual and group women and men over time like the corrosive drips of an acid upon humanity enabling the perpetuation of hierarchical injustices deeming women as 'problematic' as in the devaluation of Jews and designated 'inferiors' selected for the Nazi 'final solution'. Victims of such crimes as battered women on a private and personal level, spoken or unspoken, often ponder the same questions theologians ask regarding life, its meaning, of human worth and dignity, of opportunity or its lack, of suffering, pain, death, slavery,[71] and of a God regarding the presence or absence of a divine force in the midst of perpetrated and accepted male violence named and experienced as evil:

> For the victims and those who support them, domestic violence…is a pernicious, evil force which has seemingly destroyed the potential of their lives.[72]

For many, the Shoah and Holocaust theologies have become the epitome for theological reflection on the origins of evil with its incalculable sufferings requiring attention and a new world vision beyond domination and violence. Soelle states Christians dare not assign God to the privatized sanctuary of our spiritualities. In Engel's terms, I would name this as another corroding Christian sin, 'the

71. Ruether states wives of today can indeed be slaves left unprotected from abuse as in earlier centuries due to patriarchal practices. Rosemary R. Ruether, 'Patriarchy', in Russell and Clarkson (eds.), *Dictionary of Feminist Theologies*, p. 205.

72. Helen Conway, *Domestic Violence and the Church* (Carlisle: Paternoster Press, 1998), pp. 14, 189. Isherwood states: 'The lives of those who are abused can never be the same again'. 'Marriage: Heaven or Hell: Twin Souls, Broken Bones', *Feminist Theology* 11.2 (January, 2003), p. 215.

corrosion of sacred opportunities'[73] included with the apathetic and women-blaming individual and community responses battered wives and all rape victims endure.

The incalculable sufferings from the pernicious evils of male domination and violences against women need to be placed firmly in the centre of theological discourse and hermeneutics from its victims and survivors if theology is to be redeemable. I am arguing that sacrificial violence can never be redemptive, was not embodied or taught in the life Jesus lived rejecting the use of violence,[74] and can redeem neither humanity nor culture when societies are steeped in the glorification of male practices and abuses of violence as power.[75] Moltman locates theology and belief in and of God in the midst of the response and witness from its victims to the evils and sufferings of the Holocaust, asking:

> Can one still talk of God "after Auschwitz"? Is theology still possible after Auschwitz? We replied, "Yes", but only because there had been a theology in Auschwitz. Only in making present the prayers which were prayed in the gas chambers, the Shema Israel and the Lord's Prayer, can we again pray to God today. Only in thinking of the victims do we find courage for life and hope for the futur'.[76]

73. Engel states those who choose to turn away from abused women in disbelief, judgment, blame or apathy are: '…collaborators contributing to the desecration of the lives of the vulnerable… Christianity and North American Culture have both chosen, through their indifference and participation in the 'conspiracy of silence' to be passive and active accomplices in these crimes against the vulnerable'. Engel, 'Evil, Sin, and Violation of the Vulnerable', in Susan B. Thistlewaithe and Mary P. Engel (eds.), *Lift Every Voice* (San Francisco, CA: Harper, 1990), p. 160.

74. Giles Fraser, *Christianity and Violence: Girard, Nietzche and Tutu* (London: Darton, Longman and Todd, 2001), p. 30. Frazer, referencing Girard states: 'The world is characterized by, and founded on, violence'. *The Holy Bible*: Jn. 8.44. Please refer also to works of Gorringe, Ruether, Isherwood.

75. 'Men may use the range of forms of power and control available to those who are members of dominant categories. Sometimes this includes violence'. Hearn, *The Violences of Men*, p. 36, also pp. 3–4. 'If we define as masochistic the woman who cannot find a job or provide another home for herself and her children or resolve her mixed feelings about remaining married, then once again we make the error of blaming the woman for being beaten. In so doing we not only fail to grasp the nature of the problem; we also commit a grave injustice'. Dobash and Dobash, *Violence Against Wives*, p. 160.

76. Jürgen Moltmann, *Creating a Just Future* (London: SCM Press, 1989), p. 25. Moltmann, Roth, Soelle and Vardy and Arliss also emphasize the significance of the Holocaust as paradigm shift for theology and for discussions of the power of evil.

## Tradition's Excluded, Holy Women

Aspects of human distance from Holiness including theological doctrines of the breech by Adam and Eve with God relating a transcendent God of terror as recorded in the writings of P— suggesting separation through degrees of impurity vs. holiness root suffering and evil as part of the human condition and separate gender in differing holiness through the shedding of blood. Yet scriptural tradition is located also in sufferings within the experiential trauma of the times including the exile and the forming identities of those seeking understanding of the nature of and closeness to God as faith. Those whose experience of exile included sufferings of oppression and displacement may have had to develop a strong individual identity and faith differing from a distant God whose own Holiness emanated from hierarchical priestly castes and differing worship practices between Temple and synagogue limiting human interaction and inclusion. Perhaps the purification laws even then, while hierarchical and separating, provided an active way for the traumatized to find explanation and purpose for the suffering they endured through a connection to a God of compassion and care beyond a remote Temple worship interpreted and enacted solely through priests. The quest for holiness despite active suffering for the exiled may indeed have contributed to the historical development of human rights and the sanctity of human life within a faith belief based on inner spirituality and above all, compassion.

The Christian Church tradition, by currently deleting the perceived 'other' as abused women from pastoral mention and recognition during liturgies of regular services, deletes abused women from value to share 'Christian' care and love as were the Jews and all designated as sub-humans by Nazi devaluation and abuse, then absented from most prevailing Church liturgies including prayers. A woman's bodily sanctity as a man's prerogative to so violate understood in the desecration of temples and mosques and in prevailing male privilege and domination by authority and marital rule does little justice for women in the Church and beyond left vulnerable, injured, and without a voice. This exclusion from pastoral prayer reflects the continuing unstated acceptance of women's inferior status within the Church, within the home and beyond in similar expression as Arad speaking out against the Church's failure to protect the Jews, stating condemnation of such violence would have lessened people's willingness among the church faithful to remain apathetic or to kill:

> in the Soviet territories the extermination of the Jews by the Nazis was a known fact and was witnessed by the local population... It should be stressed that by remaining passive the population actually helped the Germans, because at that time the rescue of the Jews demanded active help.[77]

As identities and relational strengths of battered wives irritate and threaten abusing and jealous husbands belittling and objecting to kindnesses and nurturing directed to others including children,[78] Vardy and Arliss suggest the ability as strength of the Jews to maintain a strong and unique identity may be seen as a factor contributing to their being made scapegoats by the Nazis. Kindness named by Frank and Hillesum during the Shoah was seen as essential for the creation of a new order through the divinely-sparked purposes discerned by each of us through the calling within our own hearts in responsive actions of non-violent and just-relating. Battered wives who survive, even temporarily, the attempts of their husbands to annihilate and extinguish the divine spark within us re-consecrate violated bodies and desecrated homes as sacred space through an embodied resistance to the demonic profane violating our hearts, minds, souls, and bodies through such encountered male violence.[79]

77. Yizhak Arad, 'The Christian Churches and the Persecution of Jews in the Occupied Territories of the Soviet Union', in Rittner, Smith and Steinfeldt (eds.), *The Holocaust and the Christian World*, pp. 110–11.

78. Chodorow claim(s) that while women often romanticise and idealize their relationship with men, they are nevertheless more rational and sensible in their love relationships than are men are with women, as illustrated by the frequent irrational jealousy of men... Ironically, the success of women in the 'reproduction of mothering' in male dominated capitalist society apparently leaves men—as well as women and children—at a disadvantage *vis-a-vis* emotional resources and the ability to sever themselves from mother-like attention during marriage. This psycho-dynamic process supports the...analysis of battering pregnant women'. Nancy Chodorow, *The Reproduction of Mothering: Psychoanalysis and the Sociology of Gender* (Berkeley, CA: University of California Press, 1978), p. 198, as referenced by Hoff, *Battered Women as Survivors*, pp. 59–60. Please refer also to Women's Aid, *Breaking Through: Women Surviving Male Violences* (Bristol, England: Women's Aid Federation, 1989), pp. 5–6.

79. Raphael writes of the reconsecration of the sanctuary of the women whose presence to others in relationality resisted the profanation of the divine despite its intended human evil, not giving Auschwitz resolution in time but offering 'as tikkun all the more powerful in being that of a people who had nothing more to give'. Raphael, *The Female Face of God*, p. 148. ('*tikkun atzmi*: the redemptive healing of the self; *tikkun olam*: the redemptive healing of the world'. *Select Glossary*, p. 206.)

Today's defining and prevailing criteria for maleness in most societies worldwide resembles Todorov's naming of the prison guards as 'the cult of toughness—of virility'[80] as "women being battered is rooted in an international acceptance of the subordination of women'.[81] Today's prevailing assumption of male privilege and entitlement by presence, terror and next by force through male violences especially by husbands in marriage has the same effect as Hitler's policies, defined by Todorov quoting Goring's Nuremburg Trial testimony as a woman's role in keeping with tradition and 'softness' with religion in opposition to the masculine norm still operative today:

> Goring scorns the humanitarian values as "womanly" and holds heroism to be a strictly masculine affair; the role of women, if any is to admire the heroes and reward them with feminine favours for their great deeds.[82]

### Heartaches from Hierarchies: Sacred Power to Endure

While some Churches during the Nazi regime actively blessed and encouraged the killing of Jews, others chose indifference in the form of silence embodying and practicing the sins of omission to the mass executions and individual atrocities. For example, reports Arad, a pastoral letter of the Ukrainian Autonomous Church entitled *Thou Shalt Not Kill* covering this commandment, the sanctity of life,

---

80. Todorov, *Facing the Extreme*, p. 165.

81. Susan Schecter, *Women and Male Violence* (Boston, MA: South End Press, 1982), as cited by NiCarthy, 'War Against Women', p. 56, in Ashworth (ed.), *A Diplomacy of the Oppressed* (p. 67 n. 16) Please see also Perdita Huston, *Third World Women Speak Out* (New York: Praeger, 1979).

82. Goring, cited by Gilbert (Nuremburg #216), as referenced in Todorov, *Facing the Extreme*, p. 164. Of Hitler and Speer, Todorov states: 'Hitler himself was neither attracted to the world of ordinary everyday life nor particularly concerned with the valorization of feminine virtues: "A highly intelligent man should take a primative and stupid woman… I could never marry. Think of the problems if I had children" ' (Albert Speer, *Inside the Third Reich* [New York: Collier-Macmillan, 1970], p. 92). Eicke, whose responsibility it was to establish the camps, tolerated no softness: '…in our ranks there is no room for "softies"; they are better off entering a monastery. We need men who are tough and committed'. Theodore Eicke, as referenced in Hoss, Rudolph, *Le commandant d'Auschwitz*, Maspero, Paris, France, 1979, as referenced in Todorov, *Facing the Extreme*, p. 164.

and 'the basic Christian duties to love'[83] published in 1942 by the head of its church failed to mention Jews. Survivors of the Nazi regime make considerable reference to hierarchical naming and commands given to them by those in power within a cultured, civilized society committed to evil by linking the systematic annihilation of 'othered' humanity immediately upon selection and capture and/or once the usefulness of free labor was extracted from them.[84] Husbands abusing their power through male violence forbidding wives to seek medical care after being assaulted, locking wives in or out in isolating or dangerous environments, controlling conditions for wives similar to a 'house arrest', depriving the woman of water, food, or heat as well as making threats and doing assaults of bodily harm and death occur for battered wives just as for prisoners of war.[85]

A determination to live labelled as 'survival instinct' some believe rooted in biology and psychology and demonstrated both in political migration and in fleeing individual violent men often entails planned strategies towards safety for family with friends, neighbours, school and community local authorities, and may even necessitate new identities through name changes and disguised physical and historical personal attributes with sustained endangerment from being traced not dissimilar to those fleeing Nazi and other persecutions. Some holding Judeo-Christian beliefs find comfort in the Exodus narratives of the Hebrew Scriptures as in liberation theologies; others like those ancients of the desert question God as Job and offer complaint for circumstances of upheaval and terror. Of women's worldwide plight from being abused and for struggling to survive through the resulting cruelty of male violences and societal indifferences, as many Irish migrants, it could be said:

> I had heard enough of the cruelty that had, for years and years, been
> done to Ireland, to know that her people were leaving her not from

83. Yitzhak Arad, 'The Christian Churches and the Persecution of Jews in the Occupied Territories of the USSR', in Rittner, Smith and Steinfeldt (eds.), *The Holocaust and the Christian World*, p. 111. Sins of omission and commission, refer to Holy Eucharist, *The Book of Common Prayer* (New York: Church Publishing Company, Seabury Press, 1979), p. 360.

84. Laska, *Women of the Resistance*, p. 169.

85. Dobash and Dobash, *Violence Against Wives*, Hoff, *Battered Women as Survivors* and Ofer and Weitzman (eds.), *Women in the Holocaust*.

choice but from compulsion; that it was not the sterility of the soil, or any other unfavourable dispensation of nature, but the malignant hostility of laws and practices.[86]

The witness many battered wives as survivors make paralleling that of Shoal survivors would seem to reveal an affirmation of being, of existence and personhood in a struggle for life and a healing of the spirit that is universally bound up in telling, hearing, and sharing of humanity's experiences and realities and the witnessing thereof; a vital component to an effective role of the Church as community emanating from the early Church onwards.[87] The power of remembrance within the enormity of historicity is the very telling of sacrifice and heartache, endangerment and destruction of individual lives and lives most often 'loving and loved by somebody' found of the oppressed and silenced in competitive and conquering, hierarchical history by those wielding evil through violent power.

Raphael's feminist questioning of hierarchical necessities places the creation of the Holocaust within the patriarchal imaging of a male, all-powerful God as a male projection of men's desire to attain virtues related to a divine omnipotence in response to the existence of evil.[88] Whilst this writing cannot focus upon questions of the limitations of a 'good' power[89] as powerless in the presence of evil, I would reject a suggestion of gendering this power as feminized in the same way that feminist theologies reject a hierarchical structure dominated by women. Suggesting that a redemptive God of feminist theologies regards vulnerability of creation and relationship beyond coercive power, Raphael views the transcendent moment in invitation and hospitality of relationship and gesture rather than in the grand

86. Meagher, Thomas Francis, as cited in Thomas Keneally, *The Great Shame: A Story of the Irish in the Old World and the New* (London: Chatto and Windus, 1998), cover-quote.

87. Please refer to Ruether, *Women and Redemption: A Theological History* and Albrecht, *The Character of Our Communities* (Minneapolis, MN: Fortress Press, 1998).

88. Melissa Raphael, *The Female Face of God in Auschwitz*, pp. 40–42.

89. Marshal Walther von Reichenau ordered: 'The main objective of this campaign against the Jewish-Bolshevik system is to totally destroy the potential for power...' Marshal Walther von Reichenau, as cited by Leni Yahii, *The Holocaust: The Fate of European Jewry* (New York: Oxford University Press, 1990), pp. 255–58, issued as 'The Impact of National Socialism', in Neil Gregor (ed.), *Nazism* (Oxford: Oxford University Press, 2000), pp. 317–20.

events[90] of faith traditions offering an embodied power of humanity with and in the divine. In the common pain of the degraded body and the meaning gleaned of its degradation are linked the violated bodies of abused women. I am arguing with the questioning of what creates for humanity its meaning. According to Raphael, the holiness of Auschwitz, in order to avoid blasphemy or perversity, is to be recognized not in the place but in the space created by the reactions and responses to the horrors done to its victims for themselves and each other; thus in the space opened up for safety and empowerment for battered wives through appropriate societal responses as determined by the battered woman according to her needs—not by others' assessments.

Although Hearn's specific work does not consider aspects of faith, religion or spirituality upon men's violences, these interviewed, abusing men named violent actions experienced as powerlessness, a powerlessness 'relative to their expectations of entitled more power or as their 'all-powerfulness'.'[91] This has chilling implications for the way men may see themselves in relation to an omnipotent God and to the teachings of the Church sanctioning male domination and abuse of women in marriage and beyond. Whilst attributing the qualities of caring to both 'the male and female of Israel', Raphael nevertheless also in questioning the presence of God in the Holocaust counters theologies of absence with the immanent divine found in both witness and acts of caring during the Shoah linking feminine, maternal attributes of God found in Hebrew Scripture.[92] Researched male expectations of husbands doing violences, as in the Shoah, as intended and chosen power of evil over another human being block the luminous on earth but can destroy neither its power found in battered women's non-violent responses and testimony to such evil nor block its power of those risking a compassionate and caring response as witness to such crimes. To choose as a battered wife to resist in non-violent agency, to find strength and determination despite hopeless circumstances parallels Tichauer's choice among so few allowed her in Auschwitz-Birkenau:

90. Raphael, *The Female Face of God in Auschwitz*, p. 42.Vardy and Arliss state once God is rejected then there is no reference for good and evil beyond what is acceptable to the prevailing group in power. Vardy and Arliss, *A Thinker's Guide to Evil*, pp. 80–95.

91. Hearn, *The Violences of Men*, p. 215.

92. Raphael, *The Female Face of God in Auschwitz*, p. 10.

> To fight and be beaten with batons is part of the program designed for
> our annihilation. I decide that day that I will never fight to eat, that I
> will never lift a hand to beat anyone.[93]

Thus, to conclude that violence by men is rooted in the unequal,
enculturated power of human choice is not to disregard the insights
of physiology, psychology, genetics and neurobiology regarding
difference within and between both female and male, but rather
understanding that social constructions and conditioning including
formal teachings of the Church and informal enculturated
conditioning perpetrate and maintain inequities of power
distributions between men and women through them. Atrocities
committed under the guise of genetic purification in worldwide
eugenics, the Shoah, and the 'defective gene' fueling extreme
Christoslavic superiority activating ethnic cleansing against the
Bosnian Muslims along with social control accessing designated
sacred sites[94] should make us ever wary and resistant to social
'transformation' in genetic and socio-political dominance of power
from one group over another. Research of brain difference, hormonal
input, and genetic difference can inform and direct along a
continuum of varied, re-constructed and expanding potentialities,
and are being re-constructed beyond damaging limitations moving
towards freedom from gendered values of human worth skewed
in patriarchal glory by domination, discrimination, and
marginalization.

### Creating a Space for Just and Non-Violent Power-Sharing

Articulating the presence and compassionate agency of women to
God and humanity as holiness despite invisibility of women from
both the image of the human and the divine of traditional sacred
celebration, Raphael integrates the divine mystery of the sacred
with the restoration of presence of relationship and caring between
God, humanity, and each other as embodied in acts of seeing the
suffering of others and in washing, caring touch, and covering of
embodied selves and others while maintaining family traditions in

93. Eva Tichauer, *I Was # 20832 At Auschwitz* (trans. Colette Levy, and Nicki
Rensten; London: Vallentine Mitchell, 2000), p. 29.
94. Michael Sells, 'Kosvo Mythology and the Bosnian Genocide', in Omer Bartov
and Phyllis Mack (eds.), *In God's Name: Genocide and Religion in the Twentieth Century*
(New York and Oxford, UK: Berghahn Books, 2001), pp. 183–84, 191.

Auschwitz—sanctification as best possible to counteract the evil actions designed to destroy and obliterate.[95] I dare to suggest that even for Hagar's return from the desert to her dominating and abusing owners in obedience to God, the encounter of being known by God illustrates the priority of relationships of care and purpose from God—not as a superhero fixer but as one who gives power in acknowledging personhood, worth, and power as sustainer of life through the gift-giving of care, acknowledgement, and water despite human cruelties of domination, abuse and abandonment.[96] As Leddy relates, this is not suggesting a feminine theology of goodness as powerlessness but rather a recognition of power through goodness in spite of and in opposing evil, a power finding redemption in non-coercive relationship, endurance, and creativity. Leddy places the Holocaust women still birthing and caring throughout the atrocities as affirming:

> creation is always the answer to destruction.[97]

For post-Holocaust Christians, Roth places 'a hunger and thirst for righteousness', a justice, as a power stronger than the despair resulting from the Holocaust bringing 'light, the light of every human life', love, and life beyond history and within history 'as sources of hope that set people free to resist injustice and to show

95. '…too much has been conceded to the numinous horror and abyssal mystery of Auschwitz and not enough to the holiness of what it sought to destroy', Raphael, *The Female Face of God in Auschwitz*, p. 7.

96. For a discussion of Hagar, see Phyllis Trible, *Texts of Terror: Literary-Feminist Readings of Biblical Narratives* (Minneapolis, MN: Fortress Press, 1984), and the works of Delores Williams, as well as Hagar (Gen. 21.9–21; Tamar (2 Sam. 13.1–22); the un-named concubine (Judges 11.29–40); and Jepthah's daughter (Judges 11.29–40.) See also Mayland, *et al.* (eds.), *Breaking the Chains*, p. 15. It is not how God saves as protector and rescuer, but how God saves through the transformation of suffering through the receiving and giving in relationships and actions of divine, authentic love in resistance to the power of evil, as in male violences.

97. '…a powerful God, but one whose redemptive power is vested in non-coercive relation and therefore vulnerable as well as creative and enduring'. Mary Jo Leddy, 'A Different Power', in Carol Rittner and John K. Roth (eds.), *Different Voices: Women and the Holocaust* (New York: Paragon Press, 1993), pp. 359–62, as cited by Raphael, *The Female Face of God in Auschwitz*, pp. 40–41 (p. 176 n. 94) Citing Farley, Raphael includes a Christian theological perspective placing compassionate love within creation: 'Evil is a resistance to God, but love is a deathless, resilient power which will finally overcome it'. Wendy Farley, *Tragic Vision and Divine Compassion: A Contemporary Theodicy* (Louisville, KY: Westminster/John Knox Press, 1990), pp. 32, 62, 65, as cited by Raphael (p. 176 n. 94).

compassion'.[98] It is the un-chosen, un-consented, unwanted, and unpreventable rupture of one's personhood as physical, intellectual, emotional, spiritual awareness in spatiality and time by male violences in violation and assaults as dirt which long imprints a sense of personal uncleanness from the specific, individual beatings and rapes within the political, collective subordination of women. As for women of the Holocaust, I am arguing that voiced experiences of battered wives must not be viewed as 'background noise' to those of Christian calling defining and practicing Gospel mandates to dismantle oppressions and work for justice as well as peace, understanding 'love is justice'.[99] Quoting Berkovits' theological placement of the Holocaust, Raphael emphasizes the image of God revealed in the ethical responses required for our humanity. I suggest the saving event of Jesus is to be found not only in the crucifixion and resurrection but in the incarnational embodiment as God on earth in our own actions and responses to God, others, and self:

> The image of God is "the secret of (man's) humanity. To guard that image, to live in a manner worthy of it, is his responsibility on earth" '.[100]

98. Roth, *Holocaust Politics*, p. 210–11, citing *The Holy Bible*, Jn. 1: 'The Word became flesh and dwelt among us'. Many gospel accounts tell of transformative power through radical dimensions of Christ's presence, teachings, and actions as individual transformations achieved through a restoration of equal relationship and justice-making rippling beyond the momentary encounter with power in changing community as history, found as Rodriguez writes today: 'When a refugee told his or her story, it was not psychoanalysis, it was testimonio: story as warning, facts assembled to change not the self but the times'. Demetria Martinez, as quoted in Chapter 26, 'Between Two Worlds', in J. Rodriguez Luis, *Hearts and Hands: Creating Community in Violent Times* (New York: Seven Stories Press, 2001). Scripture offers many examples of individual encounters with God/Jesus moving beyond into community; for instance, Moses, Elijah, Abraham, Esther, the Samaritan woman at the well, the encounters of resurrection on the road to Emmaus, the Upper Room, the conversion of Saul.
99. Isabel C. Heyward, *The Redemption of God: A Theology of Mutual Relation* (Lanham, MD: University Press of America, 1982), p. 219.
100.    Eliezer Berkovits, *With God in Hell: Judaism in the Ghettos and Deathcamps* (New York and London, UK: Sanhedrin, 1979), p. 33. Iwakuma remarks: 'Merleau-Ponty suggests that the body "takes possession of time; it brings into existence a past and a future for a present; it... Therefore, without the body, there would be no time or space — the body sets its own position in history and it gives an identity, "who I am". It is known that the body embodies time'. Merleau-Ponty, *Phenomenology of Perception* (New York: Routledge, 1962), as cited by Miho Iwakuma, 'The Body of Embodiment', in Marian Corker and Tom Shakespeare, *Disability/postmodernity: Embodying Disability Theory* (New York: Continuum, 2002), p. 84. Please refer also to pp. 78–84.

Raphael places the numinousof God found in the human love holding greater power than death despite a humanly-created Auschwitz of hatred and evil and not the absence of God to the world but the rejection of the divine by it. Expanding on Wyschgrod, she writes of God's presence and divine, beneficent power through the habitation of God's people, manifest in the kindness and embodied love within the gathering.[101] No more crucial is the understanding of incarnation, death and resurrection in the gifting of oneself at risk in non-violent acts of facing and defying the evil of male violences as individuals for one another and those who stand with battered wives refusing embitterment one instant and heartbeat at a time. The sacrificial gift of life given by an anonymous German woman in the simple gesture of providing bread to Basch in an act of resistance to evil attempting to save his life as he was forced along the death march to Dachau is offered as explanation for Basch's unwillingness to condemn the world or the Germans.[102] This remembrance as for battered wives is described as 'seeing her now;' an indelible imprint upon his life of the gift of love given by her beyond the bounds of ordinary time and place that has become a core part of him, his survival, and his becoming who he is.

Taking the growth of authentic individual faiths beyond spiritual isolation and privatization into a praxis of care liberating the oppressed posits theological meaning central to the development of humanity, a responsibility as well as a right, as Taylor's theology describing a coming to life 'in our complete humanity' found also with the re-creation and renewal of the Jews as community of the returned exile from Babylon.[103] The failure by societies and many individuals to see salvation as individual acts of life-giving risk and the giving of tender care and attention in providing protection for the Jews of the Shoah and victims of past genocide, and the failure of the Church and beyond to see salvation as protection, empowerment and new life for battered wives and therefore for all community members in responsibility to one another by the Church is indeed a matter of life and death. As for the exiled people of Hebrew Scriptures, battered women cry: 'Our bones are dry,

---

101.  Raphael, *The Female Face of God in Auschwitz*, p. 39.

102.  Basch, *The Last Days*, p. 118.

103.  Stated by Taylor, an individual's faith needs to be found beyond private devotion as a life-giving spirit in community, John V. Taylor, *A Matter of Life and Death* (London: SCM Press, 1986), pp. 59–60, 62–65.

our thread of life is snapped, our web is severed from the loom'.[104]
Taylor writes:

> In that passage, (Ezek. 37.11-14), and in the preceding chapter of Ezekiel,
> moral cleansing, spiritual renewal, political liberation and economic
> security are given equal weight as elements of the full salvation of
> Israel which is going to bring honour to the name of their Saviour-
> God.[105]

Common to Shoah victims and battered wives I am arguing found
in the seeming presence/absence of God in the plunging of God's
presence, as the Shekinah, from the depths of the evil within
placement into 'the broken heart of Auschwitz'[106] as within the
broken hearts of battered women. Raphael places the numinous of
God found in the human love holding greater power than death
despite a humanly-created Auschwitz of hatred and evil and not
the absence of God to the world but the rejection of the divine by
it. Expanding on Wyschgrod, Raphael writes of God's presence and
divine, beneficent power through the habitation of God's people,
manifest in the kindness, inter/face and embodied love within the
gathering 'wherever personhood is honoured'.[107] In similar ways,
such gatherings manifest the absent or present numinous in the

---

104.  *The Holy Bible,* Ezek: 37.11–14: In opposition to the images of Israel as a
violated and rejected woman as punishment for the sins of Israel (See Lam. 1.9: 'Her
uncleanness clings to her skirts, no one to comfort her;' Jer. 13.22: 'It is because of your
great iniquity that your skirts are lifted up, Your limbs exposed', as well as Ezekiel and
Hosea), Raphael states the divine is found in the caring for the violated, abused,
desecrated bodies instead. Raphael, *The Female Face of God in Auschwitz,* p. 141, quoting
Ezek. 16.4–10. For objection to scriptural images of women as evil, please see Trible,
*Texts of Terror,* and Renita Weems, *Battered Love: Marriage, Sex and Violence in the Hebrew
Scriptures* (Minneapolis: Fortress Press, 1995).

105.  'Life is received through the habitual laying down of life. 'In truth, in very
truth', says Jesus Christ, 'I tell you a grain of wheat remains a solitary grain, unless it
falls into the ground and dies; but if it dies it bears a rich harvest'. (Jn. 12.24.) 'Whoso-
ever wishes to hold on to life is lost. But if any will let themselves be lost, for my sake
and the sake of the gospel's, that one is safe. What does a person gain by winning the
whole world at the cost of his true self?' (Mk 8.35–36.) Death followed by resurrection,
life through dying, this is the way things are. It is not a truth limited to the one event of
Christ's death and resurrection, nor does it affect us only when we approach the end of
our lives. It is a principle of all existence. The pattern of real aliveness is set before us in
the dying and rising of Jesus'. John V. Taylor, *A Matter of Life and Death* (London: SCM
Press, 1986), pp. 59, 61.

106.  Raphael, *The Female Face of God in Auschwitz,* p. 54.

107.  Raphael, *The Female Face of God in Auschwitz,* p. 88.

community response of the Church and beyond for abused women, choosing to create a space for or casting out as Hagar's expulsion to the desert, of the divine from the world once again. These actions parallel the image and embodiment of battered wives being cast out, or cast aside, by the power of their husbands' violences in a way similar to Hagar's expulsion to the desert, and in God's divine power within us[108] to enable human endurance and kindness.

As for the inscribed voices of Holocaust victims and expressed Holocaust survivors, the voices of international genocide refugees as battered wives and all abused women speak out of our own abused bodies, hearts, minds, and souls of pain, violations, sufferings, betrayals, losses, hope and for some, surival, and for some, finding 'God with us'.[109] Still we lament the incalculable destruction of lives, talents, and compassions sacrificed in inestimable numbers of women annihilated throughout the centuries in diminished, devalued, choice-less and terrifying existences[110] needing to be 'heard into being felt' as in speech. To be enabled to move from victim to co-liberators of one another[111] requires the courage to 'hear one another into speech',[112] and to understand the redemptive, Sacred power of mutual affirmation into wholeness and justice-making. The witness many battered wives as survivors make paralleling that of Shoal survivors would seem to reveal an affirmation of being, of existence and personhood in a struggle for life and a healing of the spirit not always with 'happy' outcomes that is nevertheless universally bound up in telling, hearing, and sharing of humanity's experiences and realities and the witnessing

108.   '...God's enduring Word comes to us face to face, in a personal form, in a particular life so that God does not identify with human life abstractly but in its utter particularity. God is with us', Roth, *Holocaust Politics*, p. 210.

109.   'Emmanuel: God with us: Feminist Christology encourages us to become more intimately involved in a circular dance of co-creation and co-redemption, one that is less concerned with the destiny than with the journey itself, a journey that involves all of one's being', Isherwood, *Liberating Christ*, p. 87.

110.   '...how frequent is the experience of women that are never listened to, never heard, and if heard, never given validity'. Mary F. Belensky, Blythe M. Clinchy, Nancy R. Goldberger and Jill M. Tarule, *Women's Ways of Knowing* (New York: Basic Books, 1986), as referenced by Mary Grey, *Redeeming the Dream: Feminism, Redemption and the Christian Tradition* (London: SPCK, 1999), p. 158 (p. 202 n. 10).

111.   Grey, *Redeeming the Dream*, p. 157.

112.   Nelle Morton, 'The Rising Woman Consciousness in a Male Language Structure', in Nelle Morton, *The Journey is Home* (Boston: Beacon Press, 1985), p. 17, as referenced by Grey, *Redeeming the Dream*, pp. 157–58 (p. 202 nn. 9, 11).

thereof; a vital component to an effective role of the Church as community emanating from the early Church onwards. The power of remembrance within the enormity of historicity is the very telling of sacrifice and heartache, endangerment and destruction of individual lives and lives most often 'loving and loved by somebody' found of the oppressed and silenced in competitive and conquering history by those wielding evil through violent power.

It is my argument that one choice to do violence, as one too many, joins another among millions within genocides as a 'massacre' requiring remembrance to eliminate the perpetration of more male violence against those with power held over them as for each and every abused woman which become genocides throughout history. Bound in liturgical Eucharist and salvation history resisting the power of oppressors, the Church requires honouring re-membrance, re-membrance for women as victims seeking survivorship of broken love and from the betrayal of covenantal marriage vows from male violence[113] within the power of words holding emotional and physical responses to experiences held in the body.[114] As the Body of Christ, the Church as community needs to teach the wider communities that authentic love, salvation, saving the family and the power of justice-making and life in abundance[115] are neither just abstract virtues as theological words nor finite commodities in need of being hoarded, controlled, separated out, and possessed for those in powerful status. They are generated by, through and within a power of an infinite Love which increases by being given away, shared and passed on in passionate, non-violent and

113.   'Victims/survivors often stay on in an abusive relationship for years because of the idea that marriage is permanent. For some women separation or divorce from their partner will also mean separation from their religious community. The first decision is tough enough in itself; feelings of failure are strong. For those women for whom separation or divorce from their partner also means the censure or expulsion from their faith community, the decision is excruciatingly painful. The victim who seeks safety, or eventually decides to seek separation or divorce, is acknowledging that the covenant which she had established with another no longer exists, *but she is not the one breaking the covenant*'. Mitzi N. Eilts, 'Saving the Family: When is Covenant Broken?', in Adams and Fortune (eds.), *Violence Against Women*, p. 449.

114.   Mayland *et al.* (eds.), *Time for Action: Sexual Abuse, the Churches and a New Dawn for Survivors*, pp. 108–109.

115.   'In families afflicted with domestic violence, the only way to save the family is to allow the victim the opportunity to rededicate herself to life abundant in an environment free of the abuse'. Eilts, 'Saving the Family, in Adams and Fortune, *Violence Against Women*, p. 450.

compassionate caring and enablement for just-relating and as justice-making for God, self, and one another as expressed within the individual and collective experiences voiced by survivors.[116] Guillebaud writes:

> They often used to say at the foot of the cross there is level ground, with no room for anything that divides.[117]

When Holocaust victims, refugees, genocide survivors, battered wives and all women victimized by the myriad forms of women's oppression reveal our experiential truths and are heard, validated and empowered, relationships then become bridges of humanity linking the power of authentic love to witness, strengthen and heal, inviting the Church to become indeed a biblical sanctuary for world shelter, advocacy, justice-making and empowerment. In loving the world and in loving ourselves and each other as God first loved us, we can share the gifts of life radiating as loving God in non-violent mutuality and in an embrace of just-relating wide enough to circle the globe, making as Hillesum suggests, a 'home for God'[118] within human hearts of authentic love:

116.  Of the Ravensbruck women who survived, Ronowicz states: 'One-quarter are crippled for life', *Beyond Human Endurance: The Ravensbruck Women Tell Their Story* (trans. Doris Ronowicz; Warsaw, Poland: Interprosp publishers, 1970 [front jacket quotation]). They write: 'We who returned from those depths of hell, we the survivors, are trying to stand guard that history shall not repeat itself. But there are too few of us. You, the present and future generations have to be the sentinels of human decency and democracy… Of the handful of us who returned to life, some are broken in body and spirit. A few others are luckier. I know what is thirst and hunger, cold and fear. I know what life is all about for I have tasted death. The experience did not break me, but made me stronger'. Ravensbruck survivor, in Ronowicz, pp. 300–301.

117.  Meg Guillebaud, *Rwanda: The Land God Forgot: Revival, Genocide and Hope* (London: Monarch Books, 2002), p. 71.

118.  Andrea Dworkin, 'The Bruise That Didn't Heal', *Mother Jones*, July 1978 (altered), paraphrased by Marie M. Fortune, 'Violence Against Women', in James B. Nelson and Sandra Longfellow, *Sexuality and the Sacred: Sources for Theological Reflection* (London: Mowbray, 1994), p. 334. Despite the warring image and the fact that women in numbers are disappearing, the words of Dworkin speak to the power to be, to relate, to care, to celebrate, to transform, to survive, and to remember those women who did not survive: 'In our hearts, we are mourners for all of those have not survived. In our souls, we are warriors for those who are now as we were then'. The reference, 'a home for God', as written: 'I shall try to help you, God, to stop the strength ebbing away, though I cannot vouch for it in advance. But one thing is becoming increasingly clear to me: that you cannot help us, that we must help You to help ourselves. And that is all we can manage these days and that also is all that really matters; that we safeguard that little piece of you, God, in ourselves. And perhaps in others as well… I

Every heart
to love will come
but like a refugee.[119]

bring you not only my tears and my forebodings on this stormy, grey Sunday morning.
I even bring you scented jasmine. And I shall bring you all the flowers I shall meet on
my way, and truly there are many of those. I shall try to make You at home always.
Even if I should be locked up in a narrow cell and a cloud should drift past my small
barred window, then I shall bring you that cloud, oh God, while there is still strength in
me to do so'. Etty Hillesum, as referenced in Vardy and Arlis, *A Thinker's Guide to Evil*,
p. 103.
    119.   Leonard Cohen, cited by Bono, in Pippa Haywood (ed.), *Poems for Refugees*
(London: Vintage, 2002), p. 179.

DARING TO DREAM:
FAITH AND FEMINICIDE IN LATIN AMERICA

*Monica A. Mahler*

Feminicide, the pandemic of women-killing, is a current crisis in Latin America. Statistics are alarming: in Ciudad Juarez, Mexico, about 300 women have been killed since 1994;[1] in Guatemala, 250 women were killed in just the first six months of 2004[2] and over 2000 since 2000.[3] Though concentrated in these two locations, feminicide is not contained here. The violence is present and escalating throughout the continent, including the Dominican Republic, El Salvador, Honduras, Costa Rica, Peru, Chile and Argentina.[4]

1. 'Informe Campaña 2003 Contra el Femicidio', http://www.isis.cl, accessed 14 July 2004. In February 2004 the National Commission of Human Rights in Mexico recognized 263 women assassinated and 4,500 disappeared in Ciudad Juarez and Chihuahua, while Amnesty International recognized 370, according to Marcela Lagarde y de los Rios, 'Por la vida y la libertad de las mujeres: Fin al feminicidio' Dia V-Juárez, February 2004, http://www.isis.cl/Feminicidio/Juarez/pag/quessfem.htm, 1, accessed 8 January 2005.

2. 'Género: Autoridades sin datos reales de Feminicidios', Centro de Reportes Informativos sobre Guatemala (CERIGUA), enviado a ISIS el 2 agosto 2004, http://www.isis.cl, accessed 24 September 2004. According to official statistics, 1,049 women were assassinated in Guatemala between 2001 and 2004, more than 300 per year; 'Unifem alerta sobre aumento del feminicidio en Latinoamérica', http://www.mujereshoy.com/secciones/2677.shtml, accessed 8 January 2005.

3. Official statistics report 2,273 cases of femicide in the five-year period from 2000 to 2005. Giovana Lemus, 'Femicidio en Guatemala', presentation at the panel on 'Crossing Boundaries: the Politics of 'Femicides' in the Americas', International Forum of the Association of Women's Rights in Development (AWID), Bangkok, Thailand, 27 October 2005.

4. Isis International of Chile maintains a data base with the most current statistics available: http://www.isis.cl

The term, feminicide, was first coined by Mexican anthropologist and parliamentarian, Marcela Lagarde. Lagarde modified the term 'femicide', first used by Canadians Jill Radford and Diana E.H. Russell as 'the misogynist killing of women by men',[5] in order to underscore the systemic nature of the crimes and distinguish it from homicide. Feminicide is not random but reflects a social phenomenon akin to genocide,[6] 'any of a series of acts whose...objective is the total or partial destruction of certain groups of persons'.[7] It is made possible by political, cultural and legal structures which support the violence and assure the impunity of perpetrators within a 'social and ideological environment of machismo and misogyny, of *normalized* violence against women'. Lagarde points to the 'silence, omission, negligence and collusion' of official authorities who are in charge of violence prevention and eradication, describing feminicide as a 'crime of the State'.[8]

Feminicide takes a variety of forms, serial and individual, committed in private as well as public, by intimate partners, acquaintances and strangers, by persons and groups.[9] What the crimes have in common, besides lack of attention by authorities, is great cruelty and serious intent to harm. Women are often tortured through rape and other forms of sexual violence as well as repeated shooting, stabbing, strangling and burning. In addition, after being killed, their bodies are often mutilated further through continued wounding and sometimes dismemberment. Thus, these crimes are marked by intense hatred, defined by Lagarde as 'hate crimes' against women.[10] Still, not only is gender a risk factor but also race, class and age; feminicide is most prevalent among women of color, young women and women living in poverty.[11]

5.   Jill Radford and Diana E.H. Russell (eds.), *Femicide: The Politics of Woman Killing* (New York: Twayne Publishers, 1992), authors' preface, xi.
6.   Marcela Lagarde, 'Por la vida y la libertad de las mujeres: Fin al feminicidio', p. 7. Translation, Monica Maher.
7.   Lagarde, 'Por la vida y la libertad, de las mujeres', p. 12. Lagarde cites this definition from international law (1948): Artículo II de la Convención para la Prevención y Sanción del Delito de Genocidio.
8.   Lagarde, 'Por la vida y la libertad, de las mujeres', p. 8.
9.   Lagarde, 'Por la vida y la libertad, de las mujeres', p. 7, 8.
10.  Lagarde, 'Por la vida y la libertad, de las mujeres', p. 8.
11.  Indeed, the description of the panel on femicide at the 2005 International AWID Forum asserted that 'the violence is racialized, sexualized and discriminates on the bases of socio-economic status and age'.

Besides being fed by a political environment which has not recognized such extreme violence as seriously criminal and an urgent call to investigation, prosecution and prevention, feminicide has occurred within a trans/national context of neo-liberal globalization marked by great social transition, pressure and dislocation. This includes urbanization, im/migration, the trafficking of persons, forced prostitution, narco-trafficking, organized crime, and internal armed conflict. The inability to address feminicide, and such a range of social phenomenom which fuel it, has created a crisis of legitimacy for many Latin American democracies, seemingly crippled in their capacity to exercise justice and provide security for women.[12] The transnational situation of civil unrest and insecurity has produced a second pandemic alongside feminicide: fear and terror among the population, especially women.

Still, in the face of state inaction, women's groups have mobilized and fought for justice at the national and international levels, growing in numbers, strength and influence. In 2001, a group of non-governmental organizations of the Latin American and Caribbean Feminist Network Against Domestic and Sexual Violence created a campaign to address feminicide, '*Por La Vida de las Mujeres, Ni una Muerte*+' ['For the Life of Women, Not one More Death'] coordinated by Isis International/Chile. A larger network of women's and human rights groups are currently pressing for recognition and reform at the international level, including a special hearing on feminicide with the Inter American Commission on Human Rights at the 124th period of sessions of the Organization of American States in March 2006.[13]

12. Ana María Portugal, 'El feminicidio a la OEA', *MujeresHoy*, 26 January 2006, http://www.mujereshoy.com/secciones/3523.shtml, accessed 31 January 2006. Portugal also states that in 2005 the data base on feminicide added a special section on armed conflict to address the increase in feminicide in Colombia and Chiapas, Mexico.

13. Portugal, 'El feminicidio'. The special hearing included representatives of: el Centro por la Justicia y el Derecho Internacional, la Comisión Mexicana de Defensa y Promoción de los Derechos Humanos, A.C., el Comité de América Latina y el Caribe para la Defensa de los Derechos de la Mujer, la Federación Internacional de Derechos Humanos, Kuña Aty (Paraguay), DEMUS (Perú), Católicas por el Derecho a Decir México, el Centro de Promoción de la Mujer, Grergoria Apaza (Bolivia), la Red Nacional de Trabajadoras/es de la Información y Comunicación, RED ADA (Bolivia), el Centro para la Acción Legal en Derechos Humanos (Guatemala), Sisma Mujer (Colombia), la Red de la No Violencia contra las Mujeres de Guatemala, Washington Office on Latin America and PATH, as identified in, 'Organizaciones de mujeres informaron a la CIDH sobre la creciente violencia y asesinato de mujeres en América Latina', Washington, D.C., 3 de marzo de 2006, www.isis.cl/feminicidio/doc/doc/cejil.doc, accessed 13 March 2006.

While Lagarde and other feminist rights activists have addressed the legal and juridical structures of feminicide as a crime of the State, this chapter explores the symbolic and religious structures which have allowed and encouraged a culture of violence towards women. For symbolic structures, including hegemonic religion, affect if not determine mainstream social norms, values and perceptions. The realm of the symbolic, of cultural imagination, delineates the possibilities for the formulation and exercise of power and authority. Indeed, symbolic structures ground political and legal structures.[14] Questioning hegemonic religious symbols, stories and myths is thus imperative for establishing the political, cultural and psychological conditions to eliminate violence against women. In fact, feminists of faith in Latin America are increasingly working to uproot the stories and myths deeply embedded in individual and collective psyches which underlie gender inequity and violence.

The first part of this chapter begins by asking in what ways feminicide can be understood as a crime of Christianity, as rooted in mainstream Christian religious teachings and practices, and then focuses on religious responses, specifically the efforts of faith-based feminists to identify and transform symbols, stories and myths which underlie gender-based violence. Both the religious roots of and resources to resist gender-based violence are presented through the lens of Latin American feminist theology as expressed by Ivone Gebara and by the praxis of grassroots women's groups. The second part of the chapter places the discussion within the context of a case study, describing the Mercy Weaver of Dreams Program in San Pedro Sula, Honduras.

14. For discussion of the social role of symbols and symbolic structures, see Paul Ricoeur, 'Introductory Lecture', in George H. Taylor (ed.), *Lectures on Ideology and Utopia* (New York: Columbia University Press, 1986), esp. pp. 8–11; and Clifford Geertz, 'Ideology as a Cultural System', *The Interpretation of Cultures* (New York: Basic Books, 1973), pp. 208–20. Geertz asserts symbol-systems to be 'extrinsic sources of information in terms of which human life can be patterned — extrapersonal mechanisms for perception, understanding, judgment, and manipulation of the world. Culture patterns — religious, philosophical, aesthetic, scientific, ideological — are 'programs'; they provide a template or blueprint for the organization of social and psychological processes, much as genetic systems provide such a template for the organization of organic processes', p. 216. I am grateful to Ivone Gebara for introducing me to these intellectual resources while a Visiting Professor at Union Theological Seminary in New York City in the spring of 2005.

*Religious Roots and Resources*

In what ways can feminicide be understood as a crime of Christianity, as rooted in mainstream Christian religious teachings and practices? Some might say such a question is outrageous. The core teachings of Christianity support the fundamental dignity of the human person. The foundation of the Bible, Genesis 1, states that all human beings, male and female, are made in the image and likeness of God from the beginning of time. Such teachings could never serve to justify the genocide of women!

Others might say this question is rhetorical, the answer obvious. The issue of a relationship between Christianity and feminicide — the systematic targeting of women for their elimination — is centuries-old, as the 'witch' burnings of the Middle Ages clearly attest. Christianity since its institutional unfolding has served as the cultural underpinning for the subordination of women, provided the ideological foundation for gender inequity which is the root of violence against women, of which feminicide is the most extreme form.

In describing feminicide as a crime of the State, Lagarde points to the silence, omission, negligence and collusion of authorities charged with the prevention and eradication of violence against women. With few exceptions, official Churches have committed the sins of silence and omission in the face of such violence as well, rarely taking an active and vocal public stand against this extreme form of gender-based violence. Furthermore, Church officials are often negligent in reporting crimes of sexual abuse and violence to State authorities; rather they traditionally encourage women victims to return to the perpetrators in the name of family unity and spiritual sacrifice. In addition, clergy as perpetrators of sexual abuse and violence, against boys and women, are becoming increasingly visible, with accompanying revelations about church cover-ups of such crimes. The issue of collusion/separation between State and Church is a topic of increasing concern and attention, the complexities of which are too lengthy to address here. Suffice to say that there is a broad popular campaign in Latin America for a democratic State that ensures pluralism, free expression and protects against the incursion of monolithic religious perspectives in policy and law-making.

How is it that the widespread violence against women occurring in Latin America is not widely condemned by the Christian Churches? Why is it not a central concern of pastoral praxis and prophetic preaching, an area of visible public activism? The Latin American Catholic Church, for example, has taken a firm stand against the ravages of neo-liberal economic globalization in terms of the growing numbers of absolute poor, spoken out increasingly in many countries for the rights of groups marginalized within present socio-economic and political structures, including imprisoned gang members. Why, given the alarming increase in feminicide, have Churches not taken a vocal stand, even when the situation cries out for such a response?

In the face of such newly urgent questions to a centuries-old problem between religion and gender-based violence, women today are addressing and analyzing its roots, coming up with new formulations in order to live with greater peace, security and well-being. Women are assuming the role of critical religious leadership, no longer content to leave formulations and expressions of culture and religion in the hands of official leaders, many of whom continue to call upon religion and tradition in order to explain away inaction and impunity in the face of gender-based violence.[15] Women are daring to dream beyond the religious and cultural structures which underpin violence against women. This theological imagination and creativity, which challenges prevailing gender and religious systems and enhances women's agency, is critical to the transformation of the cultural and religious traditions which sustain violence against women.

A pivotal force of creative feminist theologizing in the face of violence against women in Latin America has been Brazilian Sister Ivone Gebara, arguably the continent's most well-known and influential ecofeminist theologian. Her theology, produced over the last 25 years, reflects the experiences of women of color of the favelas of Recife, where she lives, as well as the experiences of many other grassroots women throughout Latin America with whom she

15. In recognition of this destructive use of religion in women's lives, United Nations' documents on human rights over the last two decades, such as the 1993 Declaration on the Elimination of Violence Against Women (Article 4) and the 1995 Beijing Platform for Action (Chapter IV, 124a), clearly assert in relation to violence against women that States should not invoke 'custom, tradition or religious considerations to avoid their obligations with respect to its elimination'.

collaborates. Refuting the 'myth of masculine universality', Gebara emphasizes the need for broader frames of reference out of the histories of women and oppressed people[16] and draws upon an epistemological methodology that is gender-based, ecological, contextual, holistic, affective and inclusive[17] She grounds her epistemology in her understanding of reality as inherently dynamic and interdependent, as described by modern physics. Thus, she sees the acquisition of knowledge, including about God, as an ongoing process of continual change, profoundly historical and experiential, involving an inseparable connection between body and spirit, mind and emotion, subject and object, human and Earth/cosmos.[18]

Central to Gebara's theology then is a radical reformulation of the Aristotelian-Thomistic epistemological framework which she describes as hierarchical, anthropocentric and androcentric. She strongly rejects this very limited framework for being centered on the human as superior to the rest of creation, on the male as superior to the female, and for its general ranking of all persons and living things. In such a system, only knowledge of certain people is considered 'true' knowledge, that of propertied, white males who are at the top of the scale of creation with access to scientific, philosophical and theological learning. Other people and their knowledge are not honored; poor women of color, whose experience and knowledge Gebara privileges, are relegated in the Thomistic framework to the bottom of the epistemological ladder, associated with 'experiential' knowledge and the 'lowest levels of abstraction' and wisdom.[19]

While Thomas Aquinas emphasized the importance of experience and the body to the acquisition of knowledge, this applied only to certain truths discerned through natural reason. Truths pertaining to the faith were truths of a different sort, 'revealed' through Scripture and not solely through reason.[20] Gebara's concern is the way this distinction between natural and divine truth, inherited from Aquinas, has been utilized to stifle creativity and enforce unjust

16. Ivone Gebara, *Longing for Running Water: Ecofeminism and Liberation* (Minneapolis: Fortress Press, 1999), pp. 58–59.
17. Gebara, *Longing for Running Water*, pp. 57–65.
18. Gebara, *Longing for Running Water*, pp. 48–55.
19. Gebara, *Longing for Running Water*, pp. 25–26.
20. Gebara, *Longing for Running Water*, pp. 42–43.

power structures. 'Revealed truths…end up becoming truths that cannot be questioned in light of Christian communities' history and lived experience'. Doctrine, immutable, eternal and essentialist, is promulgated with 'teachings that sanction the power invested in male church authorities…to exercise control over what the faithful can and should believe'.[21] Gebara asserts of patriarchal theological discourse that when 'abstraction becomes an ideology that promotes the domination of the knowledge of some over others' then 'this abstraction is no longer knowledge but the politics of domination'.[22]

For women questioning gender-based violence throughout Latin America, chief among the biblical stories critical to re-examine are the creation stories of Genesis and the symbols of God, Eve, Paradise and the serpent. In fact, Genesis, particularly the story of Adam and Eve and the Fall, is often referred to as the main myth which has served to legitimize the subordination of women within Christian theological and popular discourse. Such a justification for gender inequity and violence has been based, according to Gebara, on 'an extremely limited interpretation of the myth in Genesis' but one that nonetheless has held sway over centuries in its explanation 'about the origins of the human race and evil'.[23]

A traditional biblical interpretation of the creation stories of Genesis has claimed that there are in fact two distinct natures by sex, and has associated female nature more closely with evil, indeed 'all but identifies woman with evil as if women incarnate evil'.[24] This arises particularly from the fact that Eve is associated more directly with the Fall, seen as more guilty of and closer to original sin. In contrast, man has been represented as made in the image of God and related to evil as a result of freedom, out of choice rather than out of his intrinsic nature. Woman's nature, secondary to man's 'normative' nature, is understood to be 'redeemed' by God through motherhood and marriage; in the complement of man or in 'a couple, she comes to share in the image of God' more fully.[25]

The denial of women as full human subjects can be traced to the symbol of Eve as mother of the living, symbol of 'the weakness of

21. Gebara, *Longing for Running Water*, p. 43.
22. Ivone Gebara, *Out of the Depths: Women's Experience of Evil and Salvation* (trans. Ann Patrick Ware; Minneapolis, MN: Fortress Press, 2002), p. 163.
23. Gebara, *Out of the Depths*, p. 5.
24. Gebara, *Out of the Depths*, p. 4.
25. Gebara, *Out of the Depths*, pp. 4–5.

the flesh, sensuality, voluptuousness, temptation and sin' with which women have become identified. Eve, as opposed to Adam, carries the burden of original sin through time.[26] The result is that 'all women then become Eve, responsible for the corruption of humanity, and in part, for the origin of evil'. Eve, and therefore all women, represent not just sin and evil, but also the dangerous energies of 'chaos and disorder', of the 'mysterious forces of life', of human power itself.[27] Both men and women fear Eve in fearing their own human power, body, sexuality and believe that women must submit to and be controlled by men.[28]

A feminist moral theology and re-interpretation of Genesis begins with that which has been rejected: the body, Eve's body, women's bodies. It entails a positive and open theology of sexuality which celebrates the body of both women and men, affirms sexuality as a 'divine energy' characteristic of all spirit/matter, reflective of the very dynamism of God and all creation, rather than strictly localized in woman, sin, evil. Such an outlook recognizes both the 'extraordinary creative beauty' of sexuality as well as its fragility and fallibility, both the 'wonder of the body…(and) the communion of bodies' as well as the limits and ambiguity of history. It questions an 'asexual creator God' and posits sexuality as 'constitutive' of human beings, rather than an 'accident' necessitating constant regulation.[29]

Indeed, Gebara rejects the notion of 'original sin' as the arrival of evil somehow from outside and by accident to affect original human nature.[30] There is no essential human nature which was once all good, like God, in a beginning time of original innocence and purity; there is then no such thing as a human 'fall', a radical break from God, Supreme Goodness.[31] Gebara rejects the concept of God as Supreme Goodness[32] separate from human beings and creation, judge over all history, a God who instills fear in Adam and Eve and punishes them and all subsequent generations for disobedience.

26. Gebara, *Teología a Ritmo de Mujer* (trans. Monica Maher; Madrid: San Pablo, 1995), pp. 72-73.
27. Gebara, *Teología a Ritmo de Mujer*, p. 75.
28. Gebara, *Teología a Ritmo de Mujer*, pp. 74-76, 80.
29. Gebara, *Teología a Ritmo de Mujer*, pp. 41, 77-79, 81, 85-86.
30. Gebara, *Longing for Running Water*, pp. 95-96, 162.
31. Gebara, *Longing for Running Water*, pp. 95, 163.
32. Gebara, *Longing for Running Water*, pp. 97, 163.

She re-reads Genesis from the perspective of non-separation between creation, God, and human beings, who together make up one Sacred Body, and for whom 'relatedness', as 'continual presence', 'mystery', 'attraction, flux, energy...passion', is the constitutive defining element.[33] She re-reads from the perspective that good and evil have always existed within the Sacred Body within an evolutionary process of creativity and destruction throughout space and time.

Within this ecofeminist framework then, there is no ideal ontological human perfection which was corrupted by original sin in a particular time and place called Paradise.[34] On the contrary, reflecting a modern scientific worldview, Gebara asserts that human freedom is expressed in a 'gradual, dialogical, spatiotemporal process' of evolutionary transformation and adaption.[35] Original sin is the particular expression of destructive energies within this process of the whole Sacred Body, the 'development within us and outside us of the capacity for destruction and exclusion'.[36] This capacity for evil manifests itself precisely in the kinds of dogmatic theological formulations that have perpetuated the narrow interpretation of the Genesis creation stories which justify violence toward women and require women's submission and silence. Such static and destructive doctrines, promulgated by powerful clerics in the name of God, act to stagnate the work of the Spirit.

Although Gebara clearly disagrees with traditional interpretations of Genesis 2–3, she still finds within these texts key symbolic references for the ongoing evolution of the human species. As a myth of origins, Genesis can catalyze in humans the memory of justice, can connect us to who we are, to the original equilibrium or harmony which is the natural state of all creation. Thus, although she rejects the notion of Paradise as traditionally conceived, Gebara embraces the symbol as having transformational potential to awaken in human beings the desire for happiness: 'In spite of the patriarchal model present in the Genesis myth of creation, it is important to remember that in this myth we existed, from the beginning, in a paradise'. Gebara in fact asserts paradise as existing both within and outside us. Within, paradise is the yearning for happiness, for

33. Gebara, *Longing for Running Water*, pp. 83, 103.
34. Gebara, *Longing for Running Water*, pp. 31, 96–97.
35. Gebara, *Longing for Running Water*, pp. 98.
36. Gebara, *Longing for Running Water*, p. 95.

justice, our hope, 'a dream of happiness'. Outside, paradise is the action toward this vision, political and spiritual project, never perfect or fully realized but always in creative process and 'blended' with suffering.[37]

Genesis is thus a key myth for maintaining hope alive in offering a reminder of the truth of 'our common origins' in the Earth, of original unity, the interconnection of all things, our co-existence with/in divinity. Genesis reminds us, ' "We are from the Earth", we are dust of the Earth. We are life, spirit, breath, breeze from the Earth. This is the place of our anchor...our Hope'. Our human hope then is anchored in this concrete place of origins, the Earth, the place where our dreams are realized. Gebara tells us 'how easy it is for us to forget our origins', and we must not forget.[38]

Overall, Gebara critiques traditional interpretations of Genesis as residing in a dualistic anthropology which sees women and men as unequal, and associates women with matter. These philosophical and religious hierarchical dualisms are problematic not only because they lead to an androcentric theological anthropology but also to a distorted concept of God, seen as instilling fear, inflicting punishment and wholly separate from the world. Thus, in interpreting Genesis, Gebara proposes a new concept of both human nature and God as constitutively relational, mysterious vital energy, and a view of common origins in which good and evil co-exist from the beginning of time in both human nature and God. This stands in contrast to traditional theology which sees God as Supreme Goodness, human beings as originally good and evil as arising by accident and associated with Eve/woman and body/sexuality.

Working with women to re-interpret texts from such a feminist perspective that critiques patriarchal biblical assumptions is critical. For the bodies of women, particularly women of color and women living in poverty, have been associated with nature and named as evil, used as special targets of economic and sexual exploitation. Indeed, the poorest women of Latin America, 'bear in their flesh the scars of the rejection of their bodies, of the guilty verdict pronounced on their flesh by the patriarchal system which has

37. Ivone Gebara, *Sacred Universe, Sacred Passion*, lecture presentations delivered at a conference sponsored by the Loretto Community, 1–6 June, 2001, Santa Cruz, CA (Nerinx, KY: Sisters of Loretto, 2001), p. 36.
38. Gebara, *Sacred Universe*, p. 35.

formed them'.[39] The denial of pleasure and imposition of guilt within women is a key to political, cultural and religious domination and control. In her efforts to educate 'against centuries of oppressive interpretations of the Bible', Gebara invites women to 'open a dialogue with the text' based on "lived experience and the questions it sets for us" so that the text can become a "possible ally" '.[40]

Gebara describes how Latin American women with whom she works have deeply internalized interpretations of Genesis and women's secondary status as natural and existing from the beginning of time. In one women's group discussion of Genesis 3, participants complained about their inferior social and political position yet at the same time did not see any options, believing that 'women should not be considered good...because a woman committed the first sin; this is how God... arranged it'. After acting out the biblical story together in socio-drama, the women decided that the 'most interesting character' in the text was in fact the serpent, followed by the woman and then the man. The least interesting was God.[41]

Gebara challenges others to 'take the risk of the serpent' of Genesis 3, to disobey the patriarchal law which demands 'childish submission and fear' and to dare tasting the fruit, in fact even to 'eat it with relish, passion, gluttony'. For, the serpent is 'the image of ourselves, of our power of transcendence and liberty', and the fruit must 'become our new flesh' in a slow 'transformation' of transcendence of patriarchal religious images and categories.[42] The symbol of the serpent, whose disobedience to the patriarchal God serves as the guidepost for women's courageous risk-taking, thus becomes a key symbol for the present evolutionary human journey which demands a new 'Copernican revolution',[43] a paradigm shift with respect to political, economic and ecclesial systems.

While being the myth whose interpretation provides the primary foundation for gender inequity and violence, Genesis 2–3 nonetheless then becomes an important text for women's

---

39. Ivone Gebara, 'The Face of Transcendence as a Challenge to the Reading of the Bible in Latin America', in Elisabeth Schüssler Fiorenza (ed.), *Searching the Scriptures*, I (New York: Crossroad, 1993), ch. 12, p. 172.

40. Gebara, 'The Face of Transcendence', p. 173.

41. Gebara, *Sacred Universe*, p. 8.

42. Gebara, 'The Face of Transcendence', p. 178.

43. Gebara, 'The Face of Transcendence', p. 177.

empowerment when re-read from an ecofeminist perspective. It can catalyze women's potential to challenge the oppressions which stem from precisely the patriarchal philosophical and religious tradition which it has served so well.

In one ecofeminist theological workshop in Chile facilitated by Gebara for women from throughout Latin America,[44] the biblical texts presented for re/interpretation were the creation stories of Genesis 2–3. Following critical reflection on the historical context of these texts, women were invited to re-enact the story, becoming each of the characters depicted. In one skit presented by women participants, the heroine was the serpent, symbol of women's collective wisdom and truth, represented by a group of women banded together. These serpent-women joined those playing Eve and Adam, working to overcome their divisions, so that they could dethrone Almighty God who ruled everyone abusively from on high, totally disconnected from Earthly reality. The goal was to persuade God to come down to join women's justice struggles, the focus on authority, power, right relation and collective self-determination.

These sorts of biblical re-enactments are typical of the way many grassroots women work with the Bible in the popular church in Latin America. Socio-dramas are used as a technique to allow women to connect to their own experiences, to visualize and embody outcomes different from the injustice of biblical stories as well as the stories of their own lives. In this way, women begin to question 'divine' law and authority justified within the text as derived necessarily from God, and thus to question sacred sanctions of violence and sacrifice in their own lives.

Demystification of the authority of certain biblical texts and textual interpretations goes hand in hand with demystification of the authority of certain symbols of God. Indeed, critical to biblical re-reading is always a reflection on and reformulation of images of God. For, traditional symbols of God have demanded of women that they forget themselves, that they sacrifice themselves for others' pleasures. One of the most important tasks then is to reformulate radically such divine images, including the image of God as liberator

44. The workshop was part of a two-week conference, 'Más allá de la violencia: solidaridad y ecofeminismo', 'Beyond Violence: Solidarity and Ecofeminism', 'Un Jardín Compartido' organizado por Colectivo Con-spirando, WATER y Coletivo Pé No Chao, Santiago de Chile, 27 de enero al 8 de febrero 1997.

or God simply with a feminine side; the task, according to Gebara, in fact requires passing through a period of 'purification' or 'atheism' so that new images can emerge.[45]

Popular educators of women's rights at *Católicas por el Derecho a Decidir* (CDD) in Mexico found it necessary to lead workshops solely on deconstructing the myth of Adam and Eve and re-imaging God, affirming that 'the experience of God is not the property of anyone' and that 'there is not just one way to express God'.[46] They place great emphasis on women's own narration as the starting point, facilitating the naming and claiming of women's own spiritual and mystical experiences. In workshops on sexual rights, CDD educators discovered that participants could not discuss pleasure until they had released traditional conceptions of God. So they began to ask women, 'How would you live if God didn't exist?' At first, participants were scandalized, and then as they entered into the exercise, their imagination and creativity were unleashed and they were able to dream about different ways of living with greater happiness. After such dreaming, the facilitators asked the women to imagine what God would look like in this world of their dreams.[47]

In this way, women undertake a process to deconstruct images of God in order to embrace happiness, for God is not often seen as one who desires women's greatest well-being but who requires their self-denial and inflicts punishment for experiences of bodily pleasure. Women work hard to rid themselves of this God, separate from themselves and demanding sadness and sacrifice. Only by freeing themselves of the fear-inspiring God of Genesis 2–3, who punishes Eve's daughters for original sin and condemns women to suffer for their redemption, are women able to begin to imagine life as possibility for pleasure, happiness and fulfillment of dreams.

45. Gebara, 'The Face of Transcendence', pp. 176, 177.

46. Guadalupe Cruz y Laura Figueroa, elaboradoras, Católicas por el Derecho a Decidir, 'Descubrir a Dios creciendo con nosotras: construcción y desconstrucción de la imagen de Dios', *Christus: Revista de Teología y Ciencias Sociales* (Nov/Dec 2001): 30. Translation, Monica Maher. Cruz and Figueroa document a group process, weaving together the stories and words of many women. Besides Cruz and Figueroa, the others whose reflections form part of the whole are: Luz María Estrada, Carmen Marañón, Laura Villalobos, Rosa María Mendoza, Adriana Vázquez, Nishni Quetzal, Guillermina Plascencia, Rocío Magdaleno, Laura Manrique, Graciela Tapia, Bertha Vallejo, Victoria López, Alma Rosa Botello, Maritza Rodríquez, Norma Escamilla, Luis del Valle.

47. Guadalupe Cruz, phone interview with author, 8 May 2002.

Gebara aptly points out that although Eve is born of a man's dream, out of Adam's sleep, Eve herself does not dream; dreaming itself becomes dangerous, forbidden, feared, for 'dreams have the force to change history'.[48] And yet, 'our most profound dreams are housed in our divinities', who represent their realization.[49] Critical to women's recovery of dreams and the ability to dream then is recovery of a divinity which represents their experiences, hopes and desires. As Mexican women participants of CDD workshops state, 'We are finding new sense and meanings in our lives, and there lives God (in) that permanent search of what we want with our lives'.[50] To be in touch with one's dreams for happiness, for justice, is to be in touch with one's own spirituality. It is to find what Gebara calls the 'unity' of self,[51] what Guadalupe Cruz, lay Mexican feminist theologian, refers to as 'an encounter with your own presence'.[52] In the words of Mexican workshop participants, 'God is in us; we want God to be with us so that we can live as if God did not exist...we want the courage...not to flee from the world, not to flee from ourselves'.[53]

Gebara describes the transformation that has been happening within grassroots women's groups throughout Latin America as a movement that is unleashing 'theological creativity and freedom', enabling women 'the courage to speak of God in their own way, without being afraid they are getting him wrong'.[54] Women are daring to dream of God outside of traditional interpretations of Genesis 2–3, daring to speak of their own spirituality, 'of Spirit, breath of life, energy refusing to be locked in a box'.[55] Such creativity and honesty express itself in words which give life, both to other women and back to the text itself, which suddenly takes on new meaning. The Word becomes that which is spoken through them, with their own voices, a word of truth which shares honestly the pain and joy of living. What is most important according to Mexican workshop participants is 'not to speak a lot but to speak life'. These

48. Gebara, *Teología a Ritmo de Mujer*, pp. 78–79.
49. Gebara, 'The Face of Transcendence', p. 179.
50. Cruz y Figueroa, 'Descubrir a Dios creciendo con nosotras', p. 31.
51. Gebara, 'Option for the Poor as an Option for Poor Women', in Elisabeth Schüssler Fiorenza (ed.), *The Power of Naming* (Maryknoll, NY: Orbis Books, 1996), p. 144.
52. Guadalupe Cruz, personal interview with author, 26 August 2002.
53. Cruz y Figueroa, 'Descubrir a Dios creciendo con nosotras', p. 31.
54. Gebara, 'Option for the Poor as an Option for Poor Women', p. 147.
55. Gebara, 'Option for the Poor as an Option for Poor Women'.

are words which have 'gone through the body' of those who speak them, words which are 'not invented or copied words'. These are words which have the power to transform others, which are like 'yeast' for the bread of community, giving life and hope to others.[56]

Thus, simultaneous to women's spiritual reawakening comes social transformation. Gebara emphasizes that theological creativity arises side by side with political creativity, the emergence of women as moral agents and historical subjects who focus their energy on 're-creating the world'.[57] Awakening to the desire for joy and happiness, the corporeal memory of justice is particularly significant for women. No longer solely a source of sin and temptation, the body becomes a vehicle to salvation. The discovery by women of their bodies as places of power, beauty, thought, desire and decision is indeed 'a fundamental conquest for history'.[58] Gebara encourages women to listen to the wisdom inherent in the body, with her to embrace the 'erotic excitement of the earth' and the 'intensity of life which arises everywhere', seeking greater happiness, pleasure and 'joy of existing in justice and truth'.[59]

By resurrecting the dream and desire for joy and justice, women remember who they are, regain their self-esteem, and begin to generate energy to work for change for themselves and their communities. The awakening of passionate energy among women in this way is part of an urgent 'political and religious revolutionary process'. Such a process liberates 'untold forces' which 'come from the depth of human suffering' and challenges injustice towards new forms of human relations based on solidarity, unity, compassion.[60] This is an awakening of profound spirituality, a return to the 'original source', to interdependence, reciprocity, tenderness, love, mystery.[61] This is the return to God, an experience at once deeply spiritual and corporeal, profoundly passionate and pleasurable, both joyful and just. Women's experience of passionate joy is both an

56. Cruz y Figueroa, 'Descubrir a Dios creciendo con nostoras', pp. 31, 33.

57. Gebara, 'Option for the Poor as an Option for Poor Women', p. 147.

58. Gebara, *Vida religiosa: de teologia patriarcal a teologia feminista – um desafio para o futuro*, Coleção Mulher (São Paulo: Edições Paulinas, 1992), p. 52.

59. Gebara, 'The Face of Transcendence', p. 181.

60. Ivone Gebara, 'Women and the Mystery of Life' in Marc Reuver, Friedhelm Solms and Gerrit Huizer (eds.), *The Ecumenical Movement Tomorrow: Suggestions for Approaches and Alternatives* (Kampen: Kok Publishing Company in cooperation with Geneva: WCC Publications, 1993), pp. 195, 198–99.

61. Gebara, 'Women and the Mystery of Life', pp. 200–201.

expression of justice and a catalyst for further transformation toward justice. Such experiences are happening in women's lives throughout Latin America, including Honduras.

## Case Study: Dream Weavers in Honduras

*Programa Misericordia Tejedora de Sueños* (Mercy Weaver of Dreams Program) known popularly simply as *Tejedoras de Sueños* or Dream Weavers, is a ministry of the Mercy Community in the area of San Pedro Sula in northwestern Honduras. Founded after Hurricane Mitch in 1998, Dream Weavers provides education and training for economically marginalized women on issues including spirituality, gender, self-esteem, domestic violence and sexuality in an effort to strengthen their leadership and organizational capacities. This mission is reflective of the general vision of the Mercy Sisters, active in Honduras for almost fifty years, who profess to 'commit our lives and our resources to act in solidarity with the poor, especially women and children, and with women looking for fullness of life and equality in the church and society'.[62] Through the Dream Weavers Program, led today by Mercy Lay Associates, the Community works with women's groups from five urban barrios or poor neighborhoods offering workshops and retreats to more than 100 women.

The Dream Weavers' creed describes the work within a broad context of faith in women and women's solidarity, affirming: 'We believe in women, in the power of their struggles, in their capacity to administer their resources. We believe that solidarity between women is the fundamental basis for...improving their personal, familial and communal situation'. The creed focuses on the importance of education in order to support women's agency for change: 'We believe that when grassroots women...know their rights and understand their reality of gender and class oppression, the transformation of unjust structures is made possible'.[63]

The program affirms the importance of women's spirituality in this process of social transformation: 'We believe that for having

62. As stated in the Vision Statement of the Sisters of Mercy of the Americas, e-mail communication from Carmen Manuela Del Cid, 10 April 2003. Translation, Monica Maher.

63. Dream Weavers' Creed, e-mail communication from Carmen Manuela Del Cid, 24 April 2003. Translation, Monica Maher.

been connected to the creation and care of life, women have the capacity to live a creative spirituality that recognizes the dignity and value of each person, affirming each from their own experience of God to continue the search for alternatives that privilege human and planetary life'. Dream Weavers asserts this key role of women's spiritual awakening to their action, citing: 'When each woman discovers within herself the inner power capable of transforming the world, she runs to give the good news to her women sisters'.[64]

Dream Weavers is an outgrowth of the Mercy Community Women's Cooperative of the Municipal Neighborhood (COMFEL), which since 1992 has provided a means of economic empowerment for women of northern Honduras. Operating out of the same office, Dream Weavers is a collaborative program of social, spiritual and political empowerment for women. For, COMFEL staff found that even when equipped with the means for greater financial independence, coop members often did not act on their own behalf but remained bound by societal or family dictates, often using their money for their husbands' dreams, not their own.

Carmen Manuela Del Cid, feminist lay theologian and Coordinator of Dream Weavers,[65] explains that as women enter Dream Weavers, they do not begin immediately to dream but rather to learn the very capacity to dream. For according to Del Cid, 'women don't dream; they don't know how'. In northern Honduras, most women are pre-occupied not with the search for happiness but with survival. This is truer every day, as Honduras faces greater and greater financial crisis, with larger numbers living in greater poverty and abject misery. Del Cid describes it as 'living a collective depression... desperation' due to the deteriorating economic situation and the escalating violence. 'There is an insecurity in the street and in the home...if you call the police, they don't do anything. It is a great tension. There is no safe place'.[66]

In the face of this insecurity, Dream Weavers works with women so that they begin to 'learn to listen to themselves and each other,

64. Dream Weavers' Creed.
65. Carmen Manuela Del Cid was one of the first women to receive a master's degree in theology from the Universidad Centroamericana José Simeón Cañas (UCA), the well-known Central American Catholic University run by Jesuits in El Salvador. She was awarded the degree in 1994 after completing her thesis on feminist liberation theology.
66. Carmen Manuela Del Cid, personal interview with author, San Pedro Sula, Honduras, 13 February 2003.

rather than an outside authority'. The program works to 'take away from women the "I can't" ' approach to life so 'that they learn to say their own word', to speak for themselves. Even those women who know what they want still do not normally voice their desires and needs to their husbands, families or program personnel, for 'women feel that they don't have any options…women don't have control'.[67] The program thus works with women in groups so that they learn to identify and verbalize their desires, begin to dream of new possibilities for themselves and to believe in their capacity to act on and realize those dreams in order to have greater satisfaction and happiness in life. As Del Cid affirms, 'It is a great advancement to be able to name (your dreams) out loud and then act'.[68]

The experience of depression, insecurity and lack of control in women's lives of poverty in northern Honduras is fueled by feminicide. Although Mexico and Guatemala have received the most attention in Latin America for the highest levels of women-killing, Honduras is also experiencing the crisis. According to media reports, in the six-month period, January to June 2003, 146 women in the San Pedro Sula Valley lost their lives: 71 murdered through shooting and stabbing; 42 through alleged accidents and 33 as yet under undetermined causes.[69] A few months later, in the early morning hours of August 4, 2003, an entire family of nine, including five women and an infant, were murdered in their home in the Rivera neighborhood of San Pedro Sula where Dream Weavers works.[70] In Honduras as a whole, there were about 300 reported cases of feminicide in 2003–2004.[71]

67. Carmen Manuela Del Cid, personal interview with author, San Pedro Sula, Honduras, 14 February 2003.

68. Del Cid, personal interview.

69. 'Investigación: Encuentran otras dos mujeres muertas', *La Prensa*, San Pedro Sula, Honduras, 20 julio 2003, Sección Pasiones, p. 44.

70. Women's Group 5 de Mayo, weekly meeting, la Rivera, San Pedro Sula, Honduras, 4 August 2003.

71. Carmen Manuela Del Cid, 'Feminicidio en Honduras', presentation at the panel on 'Crossing Boundaries: the Politics of 'Femicides' in the Americas', International Forum of the Association of Women's Rights in Development (AWID), Bangkok, Thailand, 27 October 2005. Del Cid cites 163 reported cases in 2003, 130 in 2004, and 170 in 2005; these are statistics she gathered from newspapers and they include girls and adult women. Boletina Dignas Solidarias (Associación de Mujeres por la Dignididad y la Vida) cites more than 300 feminicides in Honduras between 2003–2004, Boletina Electrónica No. 50, Noviembre 2004, San Salvador, El Salvador, http://www.isis.cl/Feminicidio/doc/ accessed 31 January 2006.

Although homicides are increasingly on the rise in Honduras, the crimes of feminicide have stood out for the lack of investigation by authorities and the common public perception of the responsibility of victims for the violence perpetrated against them.[72] Unlike most homicides, these murders are also marked by great brutality: torture of the victims before death, including rape and repeated shooting or stabbing, as well as dismemberment and mutilation after death. In addition, extensive media coverage of women's murders often sensationalizes the crimes, offering graphic descriptions and images of women's mutilated bodies as a kind of public entertainment.

In Honduras, many of those murdered are young women employees of off-shore factories or 'maquilas' of multinational corporations, or else the same age as these employees, approximately 16 to 35. Newspapers often report that the women killed were out for a night of leisure, to have fun, to dance. They are women who symbolize a new kind of economic and personal freedom in an increasingly stratified socio-economic system with growing absolute poverty and many disenfranchised men. Indeed, the pandemic of feminicide points to a new surge of male violence being unleashed on women of the same age as those employed within the industrial free zones, a small sector of the working class population more readily able to acquire formal sector employment. Many of the young women factory workers have become the sole supporters of their extended families, earning cherished incomes through bearing the sacrifices of long hours, tough working conditions and low wages demanded by the neo-liberal economic model. At the same time, they and other young women live with greater physical insecurity because of rising levels of feminicide which place them by class and age at greater risk.

Feminist activists in Honduras compare the assassinations to those in Ciudad Juarez, Mexico, a town known, like San Pedro Sula, for the multinational factories or maquilas where many women

72. Carmen Manuela Del Cid, 'La justificación de la violencia desde la perspectiva teológica', paper presented at the panel, 'Las Causas del Feminicidio', Foro de Mujeres por la Vida', San Pedro Sula, Honduras, 30 de julio 2003. Del Cid states that the common patterns among the recent crimes perpetrated against women are the hatred with which they are committed, the perception by police of the culpability of victims, and the minimal efforts of authorities to investigate.

work.[73] Honduran feminists emphatically reject an analysis that explains away the crimes based on the psychopathology of individual men or solely on the increase in gang violence. Indeed, issues related to perpetrators' criminality are diverse, complex and still unclear; their relationship to victims varied: partners, friends, acquaintances or strangers. Feminists see the causes as broad and structural, related to the extreme pressures of a society in transition economically, politically, socially. Rapid urbanization, migration and neo-liberal economic globalization have resulted in the sudden presence of many young, rural women looking for work in the maquilas of San Pedro Sula. Often in the city for the first time without any social support, they are particularly visible and vulnerable to exploitation.[74]

According to Dream Weavers' Coordinator Del Cid, the deadly consequences for women of what she names a 'crisis of masculinity' in northern Honduras are grounded in a religious conceptual framework very prevalent in popular thinking and discourse. This theological construct emerges out of Genesis, blames Eve for Adam's Fall, blames all women for men's failures, depicts women's bodies as dangerous and in need of control. This is a deeply ingrained 'belief in the inferiority of women' as 'an innate fact of nature' and in 'the eternal guilt of Eve…guilt that is passed from generation to generation'. Even the social problem of violence against women is attributed to women, 'Our body 'because of Eve' is transformed into an instrument of temptation for men, and if we are attacked in whatever form, it will always be our fault'. In general, women are 'seen as 'an eternal threat' since it was because of Eve (that) Adam lost his paradise'.[75]

In an era and region of growing religious fundamentalisms, women easily become scapegoats, the ones to blame for a breakdown in social and economic systems. They are seen as the bearers of social order/morality and thus a great threat to that order when

73. Comparison to Honduras made by Jessica Sánchez, 'El cuerpo como espacio de poder y ejercicio de violencia', and Maritza Paredes, 'La violencia y el asesinato de mujeres desde la perspectiva de los derechos humanos', papers presented at the panel, 'Las Causas del Feminicidio: Situación actual de la violencia contra las mujeres en la Región del Valle de Sula', Foro de Mujeres por la Vida, San Pedro Sula, Honduras, 30 de julio 2003.

74. Mirta Kennedy of Centro de Estudios de la Mujer-Honduras (CEM-H) clearly explains the reality in this way; private conversation, San Pedro Sula, Honduras, 7 October 2004.

75. Del Cid, 'La justificación de la violencia desde la perspectiva teológica'. Translation, Monica Maher.

they step out of traditional gender stereotypes, even when it is to hold up extended families economically. Biblical justification for violence against women as a kind of easy solution for social problems is striking. Such arguments point out in a dramatic way the intersection between women's economic, sexual and religious rights, the sobering impacts of capitalist globalization and religious fundamentalisms on women's lives.[76] A network of women's groups which coalesced in 2003 in northern Honduras as the *Foro de Mujeres por la Vida* (Forum of Women for Life), to express solidarity with women in Iraq and subsequently to address feminicide in Honduras, reflects this intersection of issues with participation of activists from Dream Weavers, the women's rights movement, women's labor rights groups and independent human rights monitors of the maquilas.

Indeed, as Del Cid points out, the 'crisis of masculinity' in Honduras is in fact a 'reflection of a crisis of a whole political, economic and ideological-religious system sustained on oppression of sex, race and class'. From her perspective, the murders of these women 'carry a message' for all women who are entering wider spaces outside the home, spaces of work and social organization. Alongside the broad economic and social changes which open new public avenues to women is also arriving strong public pressure to return home: 'the deaths are an effort to convince us that the safest place for us is the house'. Del Cid thus sees feminicide as a social phenomenon aimed at all women who step out of traditional gender roles prescribed by religion, 'in these (murdered) women they are punishing all of us women who in some way are leaving behind the canons established and legitimized by the divine order'. She asserts that, 'masculine domination and control (have) become legitimized as the will of God'.[77]

76. Mirta Kennedy of Centro de Estudios de la Mujer-Honduras (CEM-H) emphasizes the negative roles of economic and religious fundamentalisms. In her estimation, every three days two women in Honduras are assassinated by a male aggressor: one in a situation of domestic violence and the other in a situation not associated with domestic violence (totaling about 242 women per year). Mirta Kennedy, 'Violencia contra mujeres en el escenario de la globalización: proponiendo alternativas desde el feminismo', presentation at the Central American Feminist Encounter 'Citizenship and Women's Political Participation', panel on 'Neoliberal Globalization and Political Strategies of the Feminist and Women's Movements: Lay State, Sexual and Reproductive Rights, Free Trade Agreements, Poverty and Violence Toward Women', 23 May 2004, Tela, Atlántida, Honduras.

77. Del Cid, 'La justificación de la violencia desde la perspectiva teológica'.

Del Cid's statements reveal the way religious fundamentalisms are being questioned by Latin American women in addressing gender-based violence, specifically feminicide. In an area where hundreds of women have been raped, murdered and mutilated in the last several years, women are challenging Christian arguments that portray them as inheritors of Eve's eternal guilt for the Fall of humankind and thus dangerous and deserving of punishment. In an area where neo-liberal capitalist globalization is creating low-paying factory jobs for young women, feminist activists are challenging moralistic discourses that blame 'indecent' women for rising levels of violence and demand they return home. In an area where murdering women is often not considered a 'serious' crime, feminist coalitions are insisting that women aren't throw-a-way people, that their lives do matter.

While the transnational feminist campaign, 'For the Life of Women, Not One More Death', addresses these murders at the political and legal levels, faith-based feminists like Del Cid are approaching the violence from the perspective of religious values and beliefs as well. This is a movement which arises out of women's struggles in their local areas, struggles for racial, economic and gender equity, for survival in a context of increasing suffering and death.

In the popular education programs of Dream Weavers, women receive training to strengthen their economic, political as well as religious agency. The latter takes the form of an ongoing series of workshops on feminist biblical interpretation, spirituality and sexuality, and the history of women's religious leadership. It is a process which opens space to question the 'unquestionable' and to ask the forbidden: whether Eve's curiosity to know herself and the world was not a sin but a positive example for all women of creative protagonism; whether Mary Magdalene, not Peter, was the founding rock of Christianity and the Apostle of the Apostles; whether body pleasure may be, not sinful, but sacred; whether women are by nature not distinct and complementary, but equal to men. Through such reflections on silenced and taboo topics, women find voice, courage, wisdom…begin to view life with suspicion. Women wake up.

'For the first time', says Del Cid, women begin 'realizing that they belong to and support a religious structure that historically has marginalized them'. 'The sustaining lie(s) of a discriminatory and oppressive religious power' begin 'to crumble'.[78] Women see into the silence, omission, negligence and collusion of religious authorities and teachings in maintaining and supporting a culture of violence toward women. Indeed, churches in Honduras have made no public statements or organized any campaigns against feminicide. The Catholic Church has led campaigns and issued condemnations against the proposed death penalty, human rights' violations of imprisoned gang members, poverty and public violence in general. Evangelical churches have launched visible public campaigns against gay/lesbian rights. No churches to date have addressed the injustice of feminicide as a systemic public problem. In the face of such silence and inaction, the ongoing work of faith-based feminists and grassroots women activists, like those associated with Dream Weavers, is that much more significant.[79]

The feminist theological training at Dream Weavers reflects a transnational movement throughout the continent. The Collective Con-spirando in Santiago, Chile has been a center of this grassroots activism over the past decade. As a key center of popular education and publication on issues of ecofeminism, spirituality and theology, Con-spirando collaborates closely with Ivone Gebara. She asserts the collective to be 'the liveliest ecofeminist group in Latin America'[80] and presently serves on the editorial board of the quarterly magazine. Through Con-spirando workshops, many faith-based feminists, including Del Cid, have had the opportunity to discuss and document their ideas. Increasingly, part of Con-spirando's mission is precisely the networking of women in the region.

The broad purpose of this movement is the transformation of the cultural and religious myths and archetypes which underlie and justify the subordination of women as part of the natural order of creation.[81] Theoretical understanding of women's oppression is not

78. Carmen Manuela Del Cid, 'Memorias Peligrosas…Mujeres Poderosas', *Con-spirando* 49 (Spring 2005), pp. 22–24. Translation, Monica Maher.

79. When a woman cathequist was killed in the poor neighborhood of La Rivera, local Catholic nuns living there organized a march to denounce the murder; others, including many lay and religious women, joined the protest.

80. Gebara, *Longing for Running Water*, p. 14.

81. In 2000, Con-spirando began to sponsor a yearly 'Escuela de Etica y Espiritualidad Ecofeminista', 'School of Ecofeminist Ethics and Spirituality', which gathers women from throughout Latin America for two weeks of study, focusing on cross-cultural explorations of creation myths, images, symbols and female archetypes.

enough, since patriarchal patterns of power are deeply embedded in personal and social psyches. The roots of women's subordination and empowerment lie in symbolic structures which legitimize social and ecclesial orders. Addressing violence against women must therefore include addressing religious symbols and traditions in order to establish the psycho-social conditions which will make possible a new way of interacting between genders, classes and races. Feminists of faith are responding to the waves of feminicide as a call to more concentrated and collective work at this level of religious symbol and myth in order to create a world in which such violence does not occur. As Del Cid asserts, 'These deaths are a call to transform oppressive beliefs, values and norms into new forms of relating between genders, new forms of relating to our bodies, new forms of perceiving Divine Revelation from our embodiment'.[82]

Creativity in reinterpreting symbols and stories from the perspective of women's embodiment emerges naturally within women's collective experience and moral wisdom in trainings. Attention is often given to sources of inspiration not visible within the mainstream hegemonic tradition. One example of how this creativity unfolds is evident in a recent workshop on legend, myth, story and women's sexuality facilitated for over 150 women by Capacitar in Argentina,[83] and later re-created at a Mercy Dream Weavers retreat in Honduras. After discussing the personal and social impact of the Adam and Eve story, women studied the Song of Songs as an alternative creation myth marked by mutuality between humans, environment and God. They approached the text with all of their senses, absorbing the message of the text with sight as well as touch, taste, smell and sound, and then expressed the meaning through skit, song and dance. Women affirmed the Song of Songs as holding a much more life-giving view of women's sexuality than Genesis 2–3. In small group discussion, women embraced the presence of God 'as love' throughout the text, noting

82. Del Cid, 'La justificación de la violencia desde la perspectiva teológica'.
83. The two-day workshop was entitled, 'Mujer y Sexualidad: Mitos, cuentos y leyendas', 'Woman and Sexuality: Myths, Stories and Legends', held 9–10 April 2005 in Bella Vista, Argentina. It was sponsored by the Mercy Sisters and facilitated by Capacitar, a popular education organization closely affiliated with Con-spirando in Santiago, Chile.

that though God was not mentioned by name, the passages were filled with descriptions of erotic love as narrated through the voice of a woman.

This is the kind of theologizing from the body, from women's experiences, from an affirmation of sensuality and sexuality that is happening throughout the continent. In addressing and reformulating hegemonic religion, women begin to take more interest in their own lives, come to believe in the power of God as residing within themselves individually and collectively, a God who is the very motor in their work for the human rights of women.[84] Women come to believe in their own power to transform a world of violence into a world of greater justice, compassion and tenderness. In the face of rising levels of feminicide, economic globalization, and religious fundamentalisms in Central America, local women leaders are working on developing a network to support a public spirituality of women's rights, economic solidarity and religious diversity.[85] Theological creativity and political activism/agency emerge side by side.

This positive interface of religion and women's rights is a phenomenon occurring not only in Latin America but throughout the world. One clear example of the international and inter-religious aspect of this movement is the Chiang Mai Declaration, formulated in March 2004 at a meeting of religious and women's rights leaders from around the globe. The Declaration identifies the damaging role religion has played in denying women's rights and explores how 'the positive powers of religion could be engaged to advance the well-being of women'. It affirms 'that when women and religious

84. Guadalupe Quezada, p. 53, sharing her experiences of theological workshops of Católicas por el Derecho a Decidir in Mexico City said, 'I discovered my potential as a woman, I discovered this spirituality in me…you don't know how it filled me, strengthened me…' 'God is a being who lives within us, within me, this motor that pushes me to keep fighting in this way of thinking, trying to learn in this struggle for the re-vindication of the human rights of women. This is what gives me passion, with this I identify'. Group Interview with author, 27 August 2002, Mexico City, Mexico. Translation, Monica Mahler.

85. The idea for such a network emerged out of a workshop sponsored by Centro de Estudios de la Mujer-Honduras. It is based on the recommendations of participants in this workshop, 'Religion, Spirituality and Women's Rights', facilitated by the Mercy Weaver of Dreams Program in Tegucigalpa 25–26 February 2005; local women leaders came from Mexico, Honduras, Nicaragua, Guatemala, and El Salvador.

traditions collaborate, a powerful force for advancing women's human rights and leadership will be created'.[86]

This powerful force, as creative feminist theologizing, has been moving throughout Latin America and beyond in a transnational journey filled with dynamism and hope. Through trusting their own collective experience and imagination, increasing numbers of women are defying patriarchal gods whom they have been taught demand female silence, submission and sacrifice. In the face of rising levels of feminicide, women are celebrating themselves and their bodies not as a source of sin and an obstacle to salvation, but as the very source of spirituality and life. In the face of rising religious fundamentalisms, women are taking on the skin of the serpent, the flesh of the fruit of Genesis 3, daring to dream, slowly transforming themselves and oppressive cultural and religious traditions toward a life of greater justice, joy and solidarity.

86. 'Women and Religion: An Agenda for Change', a declaration approved unanimously by the participants at the meeting of *Women and Religions in a Globalized World: Conversations to Advance Gender Equity*, convened by the International Inter-Religious Peace Council and The Center for Health and Social Policy in Chiang Mai, Thailand from 29 February to 3 March 2004.

# GOD-TALK AND THE SEXUAL POLITICS OF MEAT

## Carol J. Adams

> The animal victim has a secure hold upon the modern psyche. Images
> of dead or dying animals are so abundant that the animal victim has
> become a virtual institution in modern thought... Every animal we
> see is likely to appear intrinsically defeated, a victim of human
> dominance.
>
> Marian Scholtmeijer

A dog was taken to the local vet in a very rural county in a southern
state. She had been hit by a car, limped to the only home she knew,
after which her 'owners' took her to the vet. While she was there,
the vet discovered damage to the dog's anus. The dog's tail had
been pulled six inches away from where it should be. There was
long-term damage and the damage revealed sexual abuse. It turned
out she had been used in a sodomy ring that was thought to be
servicing 17 to 23-year-old boys.

Naturally we wonder *Who would do such things?* Our revulsion
confirms our own moral sensibilities—because *we would not.*

A dairy cow in production for the cow-milk industry[1] is in
'negative energy balance'—she's producing ten times more milk
than she would were her milk feeding her own offspring, and she
is also pregnant. She cannot eat enough to support that kind of
production, and she is losing weight during the lactation cycle. The
last two months of her pregnancy she is 'reconditioned', that is,
she is stopped from producing milk so that she can 'dry' off and
gain weight.

---

1. 'Cow-milk industry' is a term coined by Joan Dunayer in her book *Animal
Equality* (Derwood, MD: Ryce Publishing, 2001), p. 131.

If her work schedule followed the calendar year, it would look like this:

- January 1: The cow gives birth. Within 24 hours her calf is taken from her so that the milk can go to human beings. Dr Temple Grandin took Oliver Sacks, the writer and medical authority, to a dairy farm. When they arrived, they could hear bellowing. Dr Grandin said, 'They must have separated the calves from the cows this morning'. They learned this was true. Sacks reports what happened:

  > We saw one cow outside the stockade, roaming, looking for her calf, and bellowing. 'That's not a happy cow', Temple said. 'That's one sad, unhappy, upset cow. She wants her baby. Bellowing for it, hunting for it. She'll forget for a while, then start again. It's like grieving—mourning—not much written about it. People don't like to allow them thoughts or feelings'.[2]

- March: The cow is forcibly impregnated, but the cow-milk industry continues to take milk from her.
- October: When she is seven months pregnant, she is dried out and fed high-energy concentrates to get weight back on her.
- January: She gives birth.

Because of the relentless physical demands upon them, though cows could live until 25 years old, they are depleted by the time they are four or five. Older cows often experience metabolic problems. If because they are sick, ill, exhausted, and unable to walk, though they are supposed to be euthanized, they often are not—it has still been more profitable to slaughter them. According to a report in the *Journal of Animal Science*, by the time they are killed, nearly 40 per cent of dairy cows are lame.[3]

What separates the cow from the dog? More specifically, what distinguishes the sexual abusers of this dog from those who drink the milk of pregnant cows? This essay will propose some answers to these questions, while raising several others. It will introduce a conceptual framework for understanding the fate of cows and other animals used by humans for food. It will offer insights into the disappearance of violence against animals as an ethical issue. We

---

2. Oliver Sacks, *An Anthropologist on Mars: Seven Paradoxical Tales* (New York: Vintage Books, 1996).

3. D.L. Roeber *et al.*, 'National Market Cow and Bull Beef Quality Audit—1999: A Survey of Producer-Related Defects in Market Cows and Bulls', *Journal of Animal Science* 12.2 (2001).

will see how — in a world structured upon inequality — God-talk and the fate of animals become linked.

## Feminized Protein

Other than the bee's production of honey, the only beings who produce food from their own body while living are females of child-bearing age who produce milk and eggs. Female animals are oppressed by their femaleness, becoming essentially surrogate wet-nurses. These other animals are oppressed as *Mother* animals. For this reason, I call the foods they are forced to produce for humans, *feminized protein*.

Barbara Noske applies the Marxian analysis of the workers' alienation from production to the life of terminal animals (those intended by humans to become food).

Noske points out that for cows, sows, chickens, and female sheep, their reproductive and productive labor has merged. Their bodies must reproduce so there are always 'supplies' in the meat production system, so that there will be 'meat' for humans, so that there will be cow's milk for humans, so that there will be eggs for humans.

> While for the [human] male home and work are separate, and for the [human] female work is in the home as well, animal 'workers' cannot 'go home' at all. The modern animal industry does not allow them to 'go home' — they are exploited 24 hours a day. In the case of animals the 'home' itself has been brought under factory control... Indeed, it is often the sphere of reproduction (mating, breeding, the laying of eggs), which the capitalist seeks to exploit... When alive the body and the bodily functions of the terminal animals are 'put to use in one capacity only...the *total* animal is being subordinated to this one activity'.[4]

The dairy cow has been forced to specialize in producing milk, thus, having become a laborer in milk production, when she no longer can so labor, her 'productive life' is over.

## False Mass Terms

God-talk never involves a mass term. Objects referred to by mass terms have no individuality, no uniqueness, no specificity, no particularity. Mass terms refer to things like water or colors; no matter how much you have of it, or what type of container it is in,

---

4. Barbara Noske, *Beyond Boundaries* (Montreal, New York, London: Black Rose Books, 1989), pp. 17-19.

it is still water. You can add a bucket of water to a pool of water without changing it at all. When humans turn a nonhuman into 'meat', someone who has a very particular, situated life, a unique being, is converted into something that has no distinctiveness, no uniqueness, no individuality. When one adds five pounds of meatballs to a plate of meatballs, it is more of the same thing; nothing is changed. But to have a living cow and then kill that cow, and butcher that cow, and grind up her flesh, you have not added a mass term to a mass term and ended up with more of the same. You have destroyed an individual. What is on the table in front of us is not devoid of specificity. It is the dead flesh of what was once a living, feeling being.

The crucial point here is that humans make someone who is a unique being and therefore not the appropriate referent of a mass term into something that is the appropriate referent of a mass term, which is why the words *chicken, lamb,* and *turkey,* refer both to living and dead animals.[5]

Chickens are prime examples of the results of mass term treatment. Usually, chickens are not seen as individuals, living or dead. Three hundred million laying hens in the United States are crowded into wire cages (3 to 5 of them per cage) that do not allow them room enough even to stretch out their wings. A free bird would spend about sixty percent of her day foraging. Instead, they are deprived of nest boxes, dust bathing material, perches, and of course, foraging opportunities.

When alive, tens of thousands of broiler chickens are crowded together in completely or partially enclosed buildings. Bred to gain weight quickly, they would usually weigh a pound and a half at three months old. Now they weigh nearly 10 pounds. They are so heavy they cannot hold themselves up. When they stand they tremble. A 'broiler' chicken at maturity has an average of half of a square foot of space in which to live. In that microwave, the chicken had more room than she ever did when alive!

Dogs kept as pets are not seen as mass terms, they each are given his or her own name to signify individuality. When they experience treatment as though they were mass terms, outrage is often expressed. Cows, though, are viewed as mass terms. Rarely given

5.  This discussion of false mass terms is taken from 'Eating Animals' in my book, *Neither Man nor Beast: Feminism and the Defense of Animals* (New York: Continuum, 1994), pp. 27-30.

individual names, they instead are rendered interchangeable. Their association with femaleness, with the lowered status of females, contributes further to their degradation. They then become unworthy of our attention: *'just* a cow, *just* a chicken'.

*Animal* is the anonymous, generic being, a mass term. Human is an individual, God the unique and the ineffable.

## The Absent Referent

Behind every meal of animal products is an absence: the suffering and death of the nonhuman whose place the product takes. Without animals there would be no flesh, cow's milk or egg eating, yet animals are absent from the act of consumption because they or their reproductive functions have been transformed into food. The *absent referent* is that which separates the consumer from the nonhuman and the nonhuman from the end product.

There are actually three ways by which animals become absent referents. One is literally: through flesh eating they are literally absent because they are dead. For feminized protein, cows and chickens are the absent referents laboring to produce and reproduce. Another aspect of the absent referent is definitional: many animals who are consumed are called by new names. For instance, we no longer talk about baby animals but about *veal*. The word *meat* has an absent referent, the dead animals.

The function of the absent referent is to keep some*thing* from being seen as having been some*one*, to keep our 'meat' separated from any idea that she or he was once a nonhuman, to keep the 'moo' or 'cluck' or 'baa' away from the meat, to keep feminized protein conceptually split from the captivity of the female animals forced to produce them.

The absent reference announces the destruction of the subject status of a living being. With dairy production, if there is no 'cow' conceptually, there is no suffering, no lameness, no cries for the one-day old veal calf, no butchering, just the end product—the milk, and then the hamburger from the worn-out cow's body.

The third way the absent referent functions is metaphorical. Animals' oppression becomes a metaphor for someone else's experience, not the animals. Once the existence of flesh and animal products is disconnected from the existence of a nonhuman who was used and eventually killed to become that product, 'meat' becomes unanchored by its original referent (the nonhuman), becoming instead a free-floating image, a metaphor, unbloodied by suffering.

In this metaphorical sense, the meaning of the absent referent derives from its application or reference to something else.

Through the structure of the absent referent, which lifts out of the literal oppressive framework a metaphorical meaning, (for instance, a woman is 'a piece of meat') the originating oppression is intensified while also being rendered invisible. A 'higher' or more imaginative function than its own existence might merit is applied.

When in August 2005, Amnesty International proposed using photos of naked girls wrapped in cellophane, sold as pieces of meat to publicize their anti-woman trafficking campaign, actual animals sold as pieces of meat were the absent referents. 'Meat' was a metaphor for someone else's experience. It is true that trafficking in women and girls is a very serious worldwide problem. Every year, an estimated four million women and girls are bought and sold worldwide, either into forced prostitution, slavery or forced marriage. Girls are forced into prostitution, into sweatshops, and into domestic servitude.[6]

The problem for Amnesty International was that their advertising campaign showing women and girls as meat *reproduced* a worldview rather than *challenging* it: feminists pointed out to Amnesty International that 'cellowrapped women, being abused is part of the porn scene'. Animals' fate as meat had already been used to represent women's sexual inequality. Women and animals had already been linked through the absent referent.

This essay posits that a structure of overlapping but absent referents links violence against women and animals, and that God-talk has a role in this. I am concerned with the conditions for violence. These conditions flourish when we structure our world hierarchically. Here is a simple way of showing it:

God
Human beings
Subhumans
Animals
Insects
'Material' nature—Earth, 'dirt'

6.  For further information see http://www.crlp.org/pdf/pub_fac_adoles_trafficking.pdf.

We might speculate that the further down the great chain of being one is placed, the less the barriers to violence.

In *Culture and the Ad*, William O'Barr observes that hierarchy, dominance, and subordination are the most frequently depicted qualities of social relationships in advertisements.[7] Rarely are ads egalitarian. Ads *advance* someone over something. Amnesty International, in trying to challenge dominance against women and girls placed its representation in the midst of subordination—the interconnected subordination of women to men and of animals to humans. Cultural dualisms inscribe this dominance and subordination.

Dualisms reduce diversity to two categories: A or Not A. They convey the impression that everything can then be appropriately categorized: *either it is A or Not A.*

| A = Dominant | Not A = Subordinate |
|---|---|
| MAN/male | woman/female |
| CULTURE | nature |
| HUMAN | nonhuman/animal |
| 'WHITE' | people of color |
| MIND/reason | body/emotion |

*The not A side is defined as being* not A, *that is:*

*not* man: woman
*not* culture: nature
*not* human: animal
*not* white: 'colored'
*not* mind: body

Even though humans are animals, culture arises from nature, nature is known and structured through culture, men and women are overwhelmingly similar, and there is no historical or biological reason to believe that there is a true 'white' or true 'black', these dualisms impose an order on our world, that we experience as 'true', as 'real'.

Ecofeminist philosopher Val Plumwood calls dualism 'the logic of colonization'.[8] Dualisms in our culture are not only oppositional— either *this* or *that*, either *A* or *not A*. Dualisms are hierarchical, *this*

7. William O'Barr, *Culture and Ad: Exploring Otherness in the World of Advertising* (Boulder, CA: Westview, 1994), p. 4.
8. Val Plumwood. *Feminism and the Mastery of Nature* (London and New York: Routledge, 1993), p. 41.

over *that*, A over *not A*. Through dualistic thinking, humans are conceptualized both as 'not animals' and as 'better than animals'. *Animal* is the status we humans wish to avoid. Animal is the despised, the rejected, the *brute*, that which must be controlled, transcended, overcome to be 'human'.

In a similar manner, dualisms give higher value or status to that which has historically been identified as 'mind', 'reason', and 'male' than to that which has historically been identified as 'body', 'emotion', and 'female'. As Plumwood points out, the mind or 'reason' is constructed to exclude nature, so nature (and nonhuman animals) are constructed as mindless.[9] Such radical exclusiveness positions nature as oppositional and alien to humans. The result is that differences are 'naturalized' so much so that construction of humans' notion of themselves is based on 'hyperseparation'.

Historically, men positioned themselves as being morally superior to women and a male-identified humanity similarly positioned itself as being morally superior to nonhumans (with whom women become equated on the Not-A side of the dualism).

## Consuming the Female

In *The Sexual Politics of Meat* I propose a connection between the abuse of farmed animals and male dominance, arguing that women and animals become interchangeable objects of oppression through the structure of the absent referent.[10] A patriarchal, sexualizing discourse is used about animals. Animals, especially those used, farmed, or hunted by humans are feminized, or described using female metaphors. Through advertisements, all farmed animals are described and depicted as though they are female.

In the pursuit of ever larger 'turkey breasts', the size and the shape of turkeys have been altered. Through genetic selection, larger breasted turkeys have been chosen over and over again in breeding, so that turkeys have become top heavy in terms of shape and much larger than normal. They have such huge chests that when they start to approach 'slaughter' weight, their legs are unable to hold their bodies up, and their skeletons can't support their body mass. Consequently, they develop leg problems, arthritis, and often fall

9. Plumwood, *Feminism*, p. 107.
10. See chapter 2, 'The Rape of Animals, the Butchering of Women', in *The Sexual Politics of Meat* (New York and London: Continuum, 1990, 2000).

over. The breasts of both the male and the female are so big that the male cannot mount the female anymore to reproduce.

Even if the turkey being eaten was male, the human consumer is told they are consuming fragmented female body parts.

Species is gendered (animals are feminized) and gender, that is woman, who carries gender identification, is animalized. Man transcends species; woman bears it. So do the other animals. All cattle can be called cows. Bull can be called 'cows'. Steer—castrated bulls—can be called cows.

Andre Joly, a linguistic scholar, demonstrates how in talking about the fate of animals we invoke femaleness. In a discussion of which pronouns one should use in reference to animals—whether one should call animals 'it', 'she', or 'he', animals' lesser status is dramatically captured. Joly observes that the use of the word 'it' 'signifies basically that the animal is excluded from the human sphere and that no personal relationship of any kind is established with the speaker'. The use of the word 'it' obviates any need to identify the sex of an animal.

Yet, there are times when one uses 'he' or 'she' for an animal regardless of whether the animal actually is male or female. What grammatical rules decide this? Joly explains it this way: 'Now any animal, however small or big, and irrespective of its sex, may be considered as a *major power* (he) or a *minor power* (she)'. 'He' is used when 'whatever its size, the animal is presented as an active power and a possible danger to the speaker'. 'She' on the other hand signals a *'minor power'*. This explains why whales are called 'shes' and we hear from the crow's nest the call 'There she blows!' As Joly points out, 'sportsmen will often speak of a *hare* and a *fish* as *she*'. He continues:

> In fact, *she* has acquired a very specific function in Modern English: as it expressly used to refer to an *animal regarded as a minor power*. This accounts in particular for the 'professional' use of *she*. Sportsmen, whalers, fishermen are in special relation to the animal. Whatever its size or strength, it is regarded as a potential prey, a power as that has to be destroyed—for sport or food—hence a dominated power.[11]

The generic animal, unlike *mankind*, is female.

11. Andre Joly, 'Toward a Theory of Gender in Modern English', in Andre Joly and T. Fraser (eds.), *Studies in English Grammar* (Paris: Editions Universitaires, 1975), p. 273.

While complex forces are at work in these oppressive structures, we cannot ignore the role of religion in sanctioning, if not originating, the problem through its hierarchical structures.

## Hierarchy and God-Talk

It is in the metaphoric arena that the fate of animals and God-talk becomes associated. As Sallie McFague has observed, all language about God is metaphoric.[12]

Animals are female; God is male: Joly's insights help us understand how these interlocking assumptions interact.

While Joly does not make this explicit, God, as a major power — as *the* most major power — inevitably must be referred to as male, for male in our culture represents the major power. In the following chart, I depict the resulting hierarchical structure in which major powers are placed above minor powers:

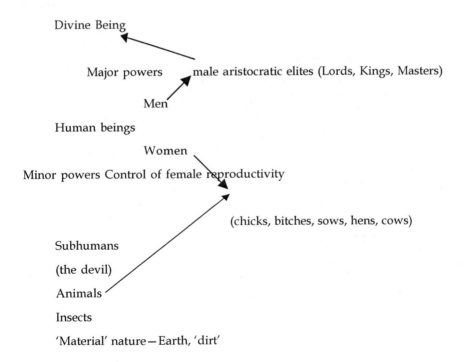

12. See Sallie McFague, *Models of God: Theology for an Ecological, Nuclear Age* (Philadelphia: Fortress Press, 1987).

Respectful language that refers to powerful men moves upwards in the hierarchy, and becomes the language that refers to God. Rather than that group of beings to which humans belong, animal becomes what the aristocratic male elite are not.

Exploitative language moves women and nonhumans downward. Women are called by the names of other beings who are not free to determine their own identity, 'pets', (sex) kitten, (Playboy) bunny, dog, beast, bird, bitch, heifer, sow, lamb, cow. Derogatory language that associates females with their loss of power over reproduction, connects women downward with other female animals.

Both instances that open this essay involve female animals, explicit sexual abuse in one case, manipulation of reproduction in the other, as well as the thwarting of the maternal desire to nurse one's child. There we find the *lived* expression of the downward movement of femaleness. Consider the terms that exist in the English language for female animals whose reproductive labor serves human interests: *biddy, sow, bitch, hen, cow*: Not a positive word among them. These terms are as much critical of the *femaleness* of the animal as of the species they represent and are reproducing. And this critical stance toward femaleness bleeds upward to human females:

As a term for a woman, *cow* is, in anthropologist John Haverson's words, "thoroughly derogatory", characterizing the woman as fat and dull. Exploitation of the cow for her milk has created a gender-specific image. Kept perpetually pregnant and/or lactating, with swollen belly or swollen udder, the 'dairy cow' is seen as fat. Confined to a stall, denied the active role of nurturing and protecting a calf — so that milking becomes something done *to* her rather than *by* her — she is seen as passive and dull. The cow then becomes emblematic of these traits, which metaphor can attach to women.[13]

When a man refers to a woman (or women as a group) as a cow, a bitch, a chick, the words are a distancing device that simultaneously objectify women, equate them with animals, and elevate men above women.

Men move upward, women downward:

| | | | | |
|---|---|---|---|---|
| men | → | major power | → | God |
| women | → | minor power | → | animal |

13. Joan Dunayer, 'Sexist Words, Speciesist Roots', in Carol J. Adams and Josephine Donovan (eds.), *Animals and Women: Feminist Theoretical Explorations* (Durham, NC: Duke University Press, 1995), p. 13.

Once this relationship is recognized, we see that the objection to nonsexist language for the Godhead is not only because of tradition, or ideas about women, but about women's association with animals. One reason there is resistance to language about women in references to God, is because women are unequal, having been associated with the other animals, so women's inequality would lower God not just to the level of hu/mankind but below it.

### Evil

According to the Bible the Fall of *mankind* and the introduction of death is blamed on a woman and a nonhuman, a snake.

In a hierarchically-structured culture, evil clearly resides below. Someone is nothing but 'dirt'.

When one turns from God, one *falls*. Falls where? Downward. To the dirt. One does not fall up. When God cursed the snake in Genesis 3, the snake lost the ability to walk, and so must move along the earth, must live in the dirt, must eat dust.

If we prefer definitions of human beings that establish the idea that the human transcends animality, then anything associated with animality or animal-like behavior will be denied, feared, avoided, controlled, and destroyed.

Depicting someone as an animal is one way to dehumanize and thus demonize them.

In between animals and humans, in the hierarchy: the devil. The devil (a human-animal being), who walks upright, with facial characteristics of a human being, but with horns, cloven hoofs and a tail.

Religious beliefs about evil accept the hierarchy described above. Women's bodies in the Christian tradition have been deeply connected to images of sin, sex and death.

Women who consorted with the devil were labeled witches. Witches were accused of having animal 'familiars' who aided them in doing evil.[14]

### Dominion: Major Powers over Minor Powers

One of the primordial acts of creation according to Genesis 1 is the separation of humans from the rest of creation.

14. See Anne L. Barstow, *Witchcraze: Our Legacy of Violence against Women* (New York: HarperCollins, 1994), p. 193 n. 24.

As justification for the treatment of animals, the idea of 'dominion' in Gen. 1. 26 is often invoked. The scholarly debate about the meaning of the term—whether the word means 'rule' or 'govern'[15] or has a stronger meaning'[16]—many commentators agree that the term uses royal language. Humans are to be like 'kings' over the other animals. Some argue that dominion carries no idea of exploitation, therefore, indeed 'man would lose his 'royal' position in the realm of living things if the animals were to him an object of use or of prey'.[17] However the debate about whether *dominion* allows violence against animals evolves, the metaphoric reliance on major powers and minor powers is implicit in the word 'rule'.

Clare Palmer identifies the metaphors implicit in this passage:

> God is understood to be an absentee landlord, who has put humanity in charge of his [*sic*] possessions… Within the framework of this model, God's actions and presence are largely mediated through humans. This is so both in the feudal perception, where God the Master leaves man [*sic*] in charge of his [*sic*] estate, and also in the financial perception, where God, the owner of financial resources, puts them in the trust of humanity, the investor, to use for him [*sic*] as best it can.[18]

15. James Barr suggests that *rada* was generally used about kings ruling over certain areas. 'For instance in 1 Kgs. 4 the verb is used to express Solomon's dominion (expressly a peaceful dominion) over a wide area'. James Barr, 'Man and Nature—the Ecological Controversy and the Old Testament', *Bulletin of the John Rylands University Library of Manchester* (1972), p. 22. Mary Phil Korsak translates the word 'govern' in the version printed in *Genesis: A Feminist Companion to the Bible*. Mary Phil Korsak, '…et GENETRIX', in Athalya Brenner (ed.), *Genesis: A Feminist Companion to the Bible* (Sheffield: Sheffield Academic Press, 1998), p. 27. C. Westermann suggests that the use of *rada* ('have dominion, govern') 'can be compared with what is said in 1.16 about the sun and the moon, which are to 'govern' the day and night'. Quoted in Barr, 'Man and Nature', p. 23.

16. Gerhard Von Rad states that 'the expressions for the exercise of this dominion are remarkably strong: *rada*, 'tread, 'trample' (e.g., the wine press); similarly *kabas*, 'stamp'. Gerhard Von Rad, *Genesis: A Commentary* (Philadelphia: Westminster Press, 1961, 1972), p. 60.

17. Barr, 'Man and Nature, p. 23.

18. Clare Palmer, 'Stewardship: A Case Study in Environmental Ethics', in I. Ball *et al.* (eds.), *The Earth Beneath: A Critical Guide to Green Theology* (London: SPCK, 1997), p. 74, quoted in 'Guiding Ecojustice Principles', by The Earth Bible Team, in Norman C. Habel (ed.), *The Earth Bible Volume One, Readings from the Perspective of Earth* (Sheffield: Sheffield Academic Press; Cleveland, OH: The Pilgrim Press, 2001), p. 50. The use of [sic] to correct for the lack of generic language is the choice of the Earth Bible Team.

No matter what the term *dominion* means in Gen. 1. 26, the hierarchy of separating God from creation and humans from the rest of creation is established there.

*Hyperseparation and Sacrifice*

The hierarchical differentiation of God from creation and humans from the other animals actually generates a hyperseparation that is guarded with vigilance. The hyperseparation instituted in Genesis 1 regarding humans and nonhumans will be recapitulated within human society, through associating women with animals' bodies.

With a skateboard, one moves over the world, at times even gravity appears a force that can be mastered, or used, as one sails over cars or stairs. The skate boarder soars above creation. In a skateboard ad, this mastery is celebrated. Man is in possession of the natural world.

Reading is one of the acts that distinguishes humans from nonhumans. That the man is the only individual reading the paper reinforces several dualisms: man over woman, human over animals, mind over body, reason over emotion.

Irving Goffman observes that advertisements contain rituals of subordination, which involve 'lowering oneself physically in some form of prostration' — lying, kneeling, on beds, on floors.[19]

The man is the major power. The hierarchy that advertisements re-present to us is one in which major powers dominate minor powers and the metaphorical obliterates the literal.

It has been suggested that the ritual sacrifice of animals for religious purposes in which a priestly male figure or hierophant oversaw the sacrifice led to flesh eating: at some point they began to eat the sacrificed animal's charred body. But today, animals are not being killed by hierophants, by respected and powerful males, but by oppressed people mediating our relationship to the other animals. Eighty per cent of slaughterhouse jobs — called 'the most dangerous job' — are held by immigrants, men of color, and women.[20]

One current formulation attempts to account for animals' victim status: *I thank the animal for its sacrifice of its life for me.* It is a simple move of a major power explaining away his power.

19. Irving Goffman, *Gender Advertisements* (New York: Harper and Row, 1979).
20. Eric Schlosser, *Fast Food Nation: The Dark Side of the All-American Meal* (New York: HarperCollins, 2002), pp. 169-90.

The language of sacrifice imputes moral agency to animals where none has actually been allowed to be exercised. (When animals *can* escape from being slaughtered they do.)

This moral agency is imputed *after* the fact—in the face of the steak dinner, the eater rewrites history: an animal who did not even know the current consumer is said to have chosen to be eaten by that specific person. Because of the hierarchy in which we look up but not down, in which hyperseparation locks us into a lack of empathy for those who are different from us, we never stop to say, *I might wish the sacrifice of animals' life is about more than a steak dinner for supper.*

By borrowing the language from Native hunting cultures without acknowledging the differences between those cultures and the dominant culture that most speakers are a part of, it decontextualizes 'sacrifice' while enacting colonialist presumptions.

Feminists critique the language of sacrifice on many accounts, arguing that the notion that suffering is redemptive is problematic, for instance, trapping many battered women into believing their suffering is to redeem the batterer. Some theorize that sacrifice originated in a patriarchal culture in which expiation for being 'of woman born' must occur. From advertisements, it is clear that it is assumed the sacrifice is being made by *female* animals.

It is anthropocentric: The only volition or independence animals in bondage are imputed to have is the desire and decision to sacrifice their bodies to meat eaters. Yet, many of these animals can barely walk. 'Broiler chickens', bred to gain weight quickly, would usually weigh a pound and a half at three months old. Now they weigh nearly ten pounds. They are so heavy they cannot hold themselves up. When they stand they tremble.

Because of the use of antibiotics in their feed, pigs, too, are brought to 'slaughter weight' more rapidly. The rapid rate of growth causes skeletal deformities, arthritis, limb deformities, and joint problems. Pigs grow to be so big their trotters cannot bear them. The pigs develop so much muscle that they become too stiff and are unable to move.

Sacrifice itself is hierarchical. Those with dominance are never invited to experience sacrifice, to say, *I shall sacrifice my old ways of eating flesh and feminized protein for you animals to free you from bondage.*

The language of sacrifice is never actually engaging with individual animals.

All of culture moves away from the literal; metaphoric language is the way our language literally moves away from it—just as God is described as moving away from the human and creation. To take something literally is not to get it. The literal is nature; the literal is animals. The animals, like the rest of nature, are the raw materials upon which we construct our lives, literally, and upon which we construct our meanings of who we are human, human and not animal.

Just as killing animals is what we can do to them, the figurative is what human language does with the natural, the literal, making them absent referents.

To release nonhuman animals from being the raw material for our lives would mean disordering the ladder of superiority. It would require restoring the absent referent.

*That is why the animals exist.* Yes, but how did they come into existence? Because the female of the species is caught in reproductive slavery.

To Marian Scholtmeijer's statement that 'Images of dead or dying animals are so abundant that the animal victim has become a virtual institution in modern thought', we must add this insight: especially when the dead animal is depicted as female. 'Every animal we see is likely to appear intrinsically defeated', Scholtmeijer asserts, 'a victim of human dominance'.[21] Farmed animals are likely to appear intrinsically female *and* defeated — victims of human dominance, to be sure, victims of that and much more.

---

21. Marian Scholtmeijer, *Animal Victims in Modern Fiction: From Sanctity to Sacrifice* (Toronto, Buffalo, London: University of Toronto Press, 1993), pp. 10, 11.

# SACRED MUSIC AND VIOLENCE

## June Boyce-Tillman

### 1. Introduction

> At the age of eight a singer was required to sing *O Jesus I have promised* in the Church Hall as part of a play. Various children came forward, both girls and boys. I was selected for the role. When I offered myself as a chorister for the liturgy I was told that only boys sang in CHURCH. No explanation was offered. I could only assume that a [male] God preferred the sound of boys' voices.

This is but one of a number of stories that could be told about institutional violence within Church structures.[1] It will come as no surprise to find that music which has for so much of its history been central to worship is caught up in this structural violence. There is much writing on peace keeping and music. 'Music leaps across language barriers and unites people of quite different cultural backgrounds. And so, through music, all peoples can come together to make the world a more harmonious place' said UN Secretary-General Kofi Annan.[2] Both this and its converse will be examined in this article for like all powers it can be used for many purposes. It can create peace and harmony but it can also initiate conflict, exclusion and humiliation. It can heal and soothe but it can also wound deeply and lastingly. It can unite but it can also very effectively divide.

---

1.   In the New Year 2006 *The Church Times* chose to collect similar stories to illustrate this. Paul Handley, 'Going to Church? Wear your thickest skin', *Church Times*, 30 December 2005, pp. 12-14.
2.   Kofi Annan, http://www.un.org/app. s/sg/sgstats.asp?nid=1166

## 2. The Spirituality of Music – Theoretical Framework

Throughout the history of Western music spirituality and music have been associated — from the ancient goddess traditions,[3] through Plato[4] and Hildegard.[5] In the hands of the philosophers of the Enlightenment the link between music and the spiritual became weakened and the search for the spiritual became an essentially human search located in the unconscious.[6] It became associated with notions of self-fulfilment and self-actualization.[7]

This chapter draws on this history to establish the five domains of the music experience.[8] Drawing on these it is clear that the musical experience is one of encounter and I am using the frame of the 'I/ Thou' experience described by Martin Buber[9] included by Nel Noddings[10] in her category 'spiritual' and elaborated by writers such as McDonagh,[11] Levinas[12] and Derrida:[13]

3.  Sophie Drinker (first published 1948, reissued 1995), *Music and Women, The Story of Women in their Relation to Music* (City University of New York, The Feminist Press).

4.  Joscelyn Godwin, *Music, Magic and Mysticism: A Sourcebook* (London: Arkana, 1987), pp. 3–8.

5.  June Boyce-Tillman, *The Creative Spirit – Harmonious Living with Hildegard of Bingen* (Norwich: Canterbury Press, 2000b).

6.  Jonathan Harvey, *Music and Inspiration* (London: Faber and Faber 1999).

7.  Abraham H. Maslow, 'The Creative Attitude', in Mooney and Razik (eds.), *Explorations in Creativity* (New York: Harper and Row, 1967), pp. 40–55; b. hooks, 'What's Passion Got to Do with It?', in *Outlaw Culture: Resisting Representations* (New York: Routledge, 1994), pp. 30–42.

8.  To take Allegri's choral piece *Miserere* from sixteenth century Italy, in the area of Materials it consists of a choir. In the area of Expression it is peaceful with fluctuations as the plainchant verse come in. In the area of Construction it is an alternating psalm with full harmonic verses and plainchant alternating verses. This is intimately related to its role as a psalm liturgically. In the area of Value it is held as a masterpiece within the Western canon of music and is frequently recorded and achieved a place in classical music charts and it represents an important statement about the Christian's attitude to penitence based on a Jewish psalm, especially as expressed at the beginning of the penitential season of Lent. It has a declared Spiritual intention. I have written in more detail about this in June Boyce-Tillman, 'Towards an Ecology of Music Education', *Philosophy of Music Education Review* 12.2 (Fall 2004), pp. 102–25.

9.  Martin Buber, *I and Thou* (trans. Walter Kaufmann; New York: Charles Scribner's Sons, 1970).

10.  Nel Noddings, *Happiness and Education* (Cambridge: Cambridge University Press, 2003).

11.  Enda McDonagh, *Vulnerable to the Holy in Faith, Morality and Art* (Dublin: The Columba Press, 2004), p. 142.

12.  Emmanuel Levinas, *Totality and Infinity: An Essay on Exteriority* (trans. Alphonso Lingis; Pittsburgh: Duquesne University Press 1969), p. 33.

13.  Jacques Derrida, *Margins of Philosophy* (Chicago: University of Chicago Press, 1972), p. 19.

it can also happen, if will and grace are joined, that as I contemplate the tree I am drawn into a relation, and the tree ceases to be an it.[14]

The domains that I have developed reflect the varied focus of the experiencer during the experience (which here includes a variety of ways of musicing—listening-in-audience, composing/ improvising, performing/improvising). They are:

- Expression—anOther self
- Values—anOther culture
- Construction—the world of abstract ideas
- Materials—the environment

All music consists of organizations of concrete Materials drawn both from the human body and the environment. These include musical instruments of various kinds, the infinite variety of tone colours associated with the human voice, the sounds of the natural world and the acoustic space in which the sounds are placed. The area I have called Expression is concerned with the evocation of mood, emotion (individual or corporate), images, memories and atmosphere on the part of all those involved in the musical performance. This is where the subjectivity of composer/performer and listener intersect powerfully. The listener may well bring extrinsic meaning to the music—meaning that has been locked onto that particular piece or style or musical tradition because of its association with certain events in their own lives. Popular music, in particular, often conjures up a range of associations. The phrase 'They are playing our tune' reflects the association of certain emotional events with certain pieces. This experience of encounter in music may be the music itself or another person within the musical experience as this is an area of empathy, imagination and identity creation. Singing songs from different cultures can, for example, give children a chance to empathize with cultures different from their own. I set a prayer from the black township of Gugulethu in *The Healing of the Earth* and when I ask children to sing it I tell them the story of how I collected it. One child said: 'When I sing that song to myself I think that somehow I am part of those people you talked about so far away'.[15] And so music becomes an antidote to violence.

14. Martin Buber, *I and Thou* (trans. Walter Kaufmann; New York: Charles Scribner's Sons 1970), p. 57.

15. In my two collections of songs from various cultures I give the background to the songs contextualizing the material. (J. Tillman, *Light the Candles* [Cambridge: Cambridge University Press, 1987a]; J. Tillman, *The Christmas Search* [Cambridge: Cambridge University Press, 1987b]).

In the area of Construction, effectiveness often depends on the right management of repetition and contrast within a particular idiom. The way in which contrast is handled within a tradition— how much or how little can be tolerated—is often carefully regulated by the elders of the various traditions—be they the composers or the cathedral organists of the Anglican tradition or the master drummers of Yoruba traditions—and they are usually male.

The area of Values is related to the context of the musical experience and links the experience with culture and society. All musical experiences are culturally related. The musical experience contains both implicit (within the music) and explicit (within the context) Value systems. However, these two areas of Value interact powerfully. Notions of internal values are a subject of debate in musicological circles[16] but as soon as a text is present—either in the music or associated with it[17]—Value systems will be declared, like the language of church liturgy and hymnody.

Whereas these four domains exist as overlapping circles in the experience, Spirituality, I am suggesting, exists in the relationship between these areas. I am defining it as the ability to transport the audience to a different time/space dimension—to move them from everyday reality to 'another world'. The perceived effectiveness of a musical experience—whether of performing, composing or listening—is often situated in this area.[18] Indeed, some would see music as the last remaining ubiquitous spiritual experience in a secularized Western culture.[19]

What accounts by composers, listeners and performers show is that the domains interact within the experience.[20] This identification

16. Susan McClary, *Feminine Endings* (Minnesota: University of Minnesota Press, 1991), Susan McClary, *Conventional Wisdom* (Berkeley: University of California Press, 2001).

17. Andrew Blake, *The Land without Music: Music Culture and Society in Twentieth Century Britain* (Manchester: Manchester University Press, 1997), p. 7.

18. The relationship of the aesthetic/spiritual and the commonplace is carefully explored in Philip W. Jackson, *John Dewey and the Lessons of Art* (New Haven and London: Yale University Press, 1998).

19. J. Boyce-Tillman, 'Sounding the Sacred: Music as Sacred Site', in Karen Ralls-MacLeod and Graham Harvey (ed.), *Indigenous Religious Musics* (Farnborough: Scolar, 2001), pp. 136–66.

20. 'The variation between different ways of experiencing something, then, derives from the fact that different aspects of different parts of the whole may or may not be discerned and be objects of focal awareness simultaneously...the unit of phenomenographic research—is an internal relationship between the experiencer and the experienced' (Marton and Booth 1998, pp. 112–13).

of the domains of the experience allows us to deconstruct the experience and to see how violence might arise for the listener or performer and how the Other may be rejected because it appears hostile to them:

- Associations attached with the instrument or vocal qualities used (like the association of the mbira (thumb piano) instrument in central Africa with the ancestor worship traditions
- The association of sacred music with unhappy memories in the area of Expression
- The perception of the construction being too simple or too complex especially in cross-cultural work
- The values encapsulated in the words being perceived as exclusivist in some way, as in the area of inclusive language in liturgy

If we regard the spiritual experience as central of the musical experience, how can we best facilitate it? What constitutes a relationality that will facilitate the spiritual experience? The spiritual experience is defined as a time when in the experience of the experiencer there is a perfect fit between all the domains.[21] This can happen gradually as this account shows:

> For the first twenty-five minutes I was totally unaware of any subtlety…whilst wondering what, if anything, was supposed to happen during the recital.
>
> What did happen was magic!
>
> After some time, insidiously the music began to reach me. Little by little, my mind all my senses it seemed — were becoming transfixed. Once held by these soft but powerful sounds, I was irresistibly drawn into a new world of musical shapes and colours. It almost felt as if the musicians were playing me rather than their instruments, and soon, I, too, was clapping and gasping with everyone else… I was unaware of time, unaware of anything other than the music. Then it was over. But it was, I am sure, the beginning of a profound admiration that I shall always have for an art form that has been until recently totally alien to me.[22]

It can be represented like this:

21. This is an area where spirituality, religion and culture interact powerfully (Ainsworth Smith 1998, Sullivan 1997, pp. 9–10).
22. Ian Dunmore, Sitar Magic, *Nadaposana One* (London: Editions Poetry, 1983), pp. 20–21.

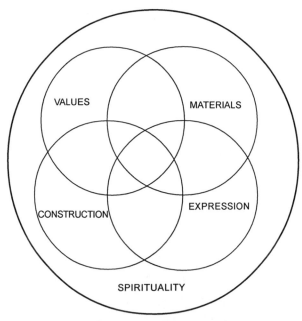

Figure 1: The complete spiritual experience

The converse of this is where there is so much dissatisfaction in one area or between two areas that there is no spiritual experience at all. For example, while in Greece I encountered a group of Greek Orthodox worshippers who were deeply racist and homophobic. When I turned on the television on the Sunday morning there was Greek Orthodox chanting. I had in the past found this a wonderful experience but now the Value systems that I had encountered interfered with the experience. In this story we encounter the distinction made by Marton and Booth[23] between reflected upon and unreflected-upon experience and the role of meta-awareness in the musical experience. So this meta-awareness or reflection which expands our knowledge about the music can disrupt a piece that previously could be relied upon to produce a spiritual experience. They can similarly be reinforced by these associations as in the case of a feminist's relationship to pieces by women. If these relational associations are benign to the experiencer then the level of absorption will be increased; if hostile, the music will be perceived as violent. This is particularly true for groups marginalized and subjugated in patriarchal church structures.

23. Ference Marton and Shirley Booth, *Learning and Awareness* (Mahwah, NJ: Lawrence Erlbaum Associates, Publishers, 1997).

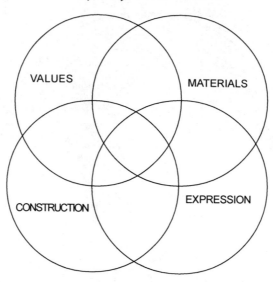

Figure 2.

To examine the problems implicit within sacred music and why it fails to conjure up the spiritual for many people, indeed is seen as a negative experience, we need to look in more detail at the area of Values. To do this we will look at a Foucauldian frame.

*Ways of Knowing*

This frame suggests that certain ways of knowing become subjugated in a particular society. These subjugated ways are also linked with certain groups of people who do not hold positions of power as the following diagram from Carter Heyward shows (see figure 3).

The following diagram shows some of the values that have become subjugated in Western culture. They are on the right-hand side of this list:

Individualism/community
Public/private
Product/process
Disembodied/embodied
Rational/intuitive
Challenge/Nurture
Unity/Diversity
Excitement/Relaxation

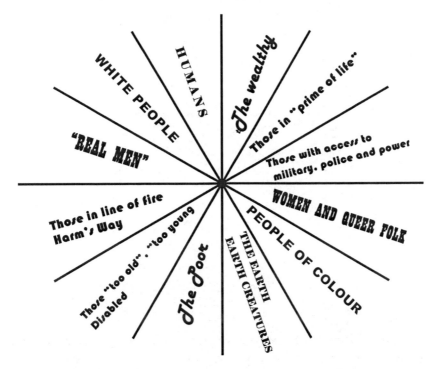

Figure 3. Carter Heyward

These polarities are drawn as ideally having a constant flow between them. Balance is defined as being when that flowing is fluid and dynamic.[24] The dominant culture will validate one of the poles more highly than the other. In the following sections we shall examine how violence is created when this dynamism is broken and how music might restore it.[25] So we have a theology of music and wellbeing based on a right relationship between dominant and subjugated values — the establishment of a creative flow.

*Community/individualism*

The need of human beings for community in Western society is to be found in many sources today — political, psychological, religious,

24. These are explored more fully in this article June Boyce-Tillman, 'Theologising the margins', *British Journal of Feminist Theology* 12.2 (2005).

25. This is based on Hildegard's theology of virtue. She sees virtue and vice has inextricably linked, the vice being a twisted form of the virtue. (June Boyce-Tillman, *The Creative Spirit – Harmonious Living with Hildegard of Bingen* [Norwich: Canterbury Press, 2000b]).

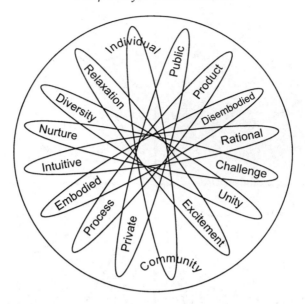

Figure 4. Value Systems

to name but a few and at its best music is about community creation and so supports this subjugated value system. Most religious traditions have used music to create unity with one another and the Divine and in indigenous traditions the natural world:

> Whenever two or more of us join together in chant... The boundaries that separate me from you, and us for others, through the magic of chant, meet and dance and merge in the communion of sound.[26]

However, there is a negative side to this and musical community and music in this context can also be seen as a totalizing force.[27] George Kent in his article *Unpeaceful Music* identifies how music can be used to support collusion, where co-operation is at the expense of a third party:

> Just as soldiers generally are motivated not so much by hate for the enemy as by the need for approval by their peers, racists and neo-Nazis also act hatefully mainly to win the approval of others in their cohorts... The best contrast to nationalistic music is We Are the World, conveying the message that we are all one, universally. Our merit is

26. Robert Gass and Kathleen Brehony, *Chanting: Discovering Spirit in Sound* (New York: Broadway Books, 1999), p. 158.

27. Jacques Attali, *Noise: The Political Economy of Music* (Minneapolis: University of Minnesota Press, 1985), p. 6.

based not on invidious comparisons with others, but on joining with others to constitute us, together.[28]

Here we encounter a sense of community in which music plays a part created by identifying a differentiated Other community rather than by inclusion. This draws on René Girard's theories of violence as mimetic and the theory of scapegoating. Girard's theory is that desire—as distinguished from needs—is mimetic and culturally constructed. Desire is based on imitating the desires of others and this leads to competition for the same end which can be acquisitive (directed to an object) or metaphysical (for well-being or fulfilment.[29] When community is threatened by this the community is restored by creating a common scapegoat by means of shared desires which is ritually sacrificed in order to maintain community solidarity. His understanding of the sacred was:

> as the means by which society's mimetic rivalry and its consequent aggression is contained... The expelled victim...acquires a 'sacred' numinosity, even a divine status... Key religious phenomena such as prohibitions (taboos), rituals (sacrifices) and myths all have the function of helping the community to 'contain' its mimetic violence... Violence is the heart and soul of the sacred. [This] constitutes a theory of religion and social origins.[30]

The Christian tradition has demonstrated these tendencies. Christians of all traditions have reinforced their shared desires by means of music and non-Christians have been a scapegoated Other with militaristic hymns like *Onward Christian soldiers*. There is also a certain mimetic metaphysical rivalry between Christian traditions concerning wellbeing and fulfilment—whether it is the conversion experiences of the evangelicals in hymns like *Jesus Calls Us* or the sacraments of the Roman Catholic Church, in *Tantum Ergo Sacramentum*; this can seen to be operating through the music. The Church with the cathedral-type choir distinguishes itself from the one down the road with worship songs and a music group. So the different denominations within Christianity are identified by their

28. George Kent, 'Unpeaceful Music', in Olivier Urbain (ed.), *Music for Peace* .
29. Michael Kirwan, *Discovering Girard* (London: Darton, Longman and Todd, 2004), p. 14.
30. Kirwan, *Discovering Girard*, pp. 38–39.

music — the Salvation Army by its bands, the monastic tradition by its plainchant.

Using the model of those groups of people subjugated by Western culture above we can see how when the musical community of the Church has developed its totalizing tendencies, it has excluded a number of these groups. One of these groups is women. The issue of inclusive language has been central to the feminist agenda and is still unheeded by the Church in general. Theorists like Lacan[31] saw the maleness of the phenomenon of language itself. Nowhere has this been more true than the language of hymnody, where the language has been assertively male:

> For all of my childhood and early adult years, I sang hymns and said prayers that made no reference to my own identity. The only reference to my gender was in the introduction to the children's address, which was to 'boys and girls' and the occasional hymn which used the non-gender-specific 'children'. Once again, pre-pubescent females were all right, but mature women were hidden, excluded by the language.[32]

This not only affected the human but also the Divine. There is a need for a feminine divine as in Janet Wootton's hymn *Dear Mother God*.[33]

Western imperializing tendencies have also resulted in violence to other musical traditions. *African Sanctus* was the work of the composer/explorer David Fanshawe, who was given a Winston Churchill scholarship in 1972 to collect the tapes that form the African elements in the piece. It had the intention of merging Western with African traditions.[34] At the level of Materials the work uses tapes of African singers and players alongside rock and classical instruments from the West. The Expression mixes the characters of the various African traditions, the Christian Mass with that of opera and commercial music. The forms reflect the interplay of the African tapes with the Western forms of David Fanshawe's own tradition. They are fitted into Western shapes and structures. The recipient

31. Jacques Lacan (Juliet Mitchell, and Jacqueline Rose, eds.), *Feminine Sexuality: Jacques Lacan and the École Freudienne* (Basingstoke: Macmillan; New York: Pantheon Press, 1982).

32. Janet H. Wootton, *Introducing a Practical Feminist Theology of Worship* (Sheffield: Sheffield Academic, 2000), p. 30.

33. June Boyce-Tillman and Janet Wootton (eds.), *Reflecting Praise* (London: Stainer and Bell, No 1, 1993).

34. David Fanshawe, *African Sanctus,* Sleeve notes 6558 001 Philips label, 1963.

of the royalties was David Fanshawe. Although it is clear[35] that the African performers gave permission for their pieces to be used , there is no record of any of the royalties being given to them. (This is in marked contrast to systems being developed by ethnomusicologists.) Indeed Western notions of ownership of music are in direct conflict with the collective ownership that characterizes the societies from which he collected the material. There is a notion of spirituality in the composer's intentions which relate to praise of the 'One God'. This is very much within the frame of monotheistic religions which would have shaped Fanshawe's own thinking. The work clearly fits into a longstanding Western colonial tradition which has pillaged indigenous traditions; this is in contrast to such intercultural synthesises as carried out by Peter Gabriel's development of the Realworld Music label and the WOMAD (World of Music, Arts and Dance) organization specifically to bring musicians from all over the world.[36]

The place music has in a capitalist economy also disadvantages the poor:

> Another sense in which music might be deemed unpeaceful is that, arguably, it diverts resources away from the fulfilment of basic needs. Many of us may feel we need music in our lives, but in the grand scheme of things, where globally more than 800 million people don't get enough to eat, music as we now enjoy it something of a luxury. Many people have large collections of expensive compact disks they hardly ever use. The wants of those who have money trump the needs of those who do not.

Jacques Attali also sees how music has got caught in a society where 'the value of the object is not in the work itself, but in the larger whole within which the demand for commodities is constructed'.[37] All sacred music commercially produced and sold in the marketplace is caught in this consumerist model that disadvantages the poor. Also, in another area a similar charge could be levelled against the Church's cathedral choir traditions which cost a great deal to maintain. Although it has given 'poor boys' a chance through subsidized education, the argument here is that the

35. David Fanshawe, *African Sanctus* (London: Collins, 1975).
36. Peter Gabriel, http://realworld.on.net contacted November 2000.
37. Jacques Attali, *Noise: The Political Economy of Music* (Minneapolis: University of Minnesota Press. 1985), p. 103.

maintenance of expensive traditions of this kind reinforces global inequity.

The process of commodification in commercial recordings has led to the trivialization of music so that 'it is stockpiled until it loses its meaning'.[38] George Kent goes on to illustrate this with the theft of jazz from American blacks[39] but the same could be said of the recordings being turned out by cathedral choirs to finance their existence — that the recordings separated from their worshipping context represent a violence to the tradition by trivialization. I have a picture in my imagination of Hildegard of Bingen — the twelfth century abbess and producer of 77 liturgical pieces — sitting in the front of a Mercedes playing a recording of the pieces and saying 'But I wrote it for the feast of St Ursula'. The process of decontextualization would be completely beyond her comprehension. The CD as a phenomenon has a great deal to answer for in decontextualization.

This is linked with a certain violence done by these traditions to the less well-educated musically. A leader of a course on congregational singing claimed that:

> King's College, Cambridge has done for music what Barbie has done for women

Local parish churches have aspired to do what King's College Cambridge does, even though they have none of their resources, rather than develop traditions suitable for their own resources. The result of this is a continual and inevitable sense of failure — the effect of the perfection of this Cambridge is rooted in he fact that it is based on considerable expenditure. This pursuit of an unreachable perfection has done violence to the sense of self of numerous church musicians and non-musicians across the world.

Finally, there is earth and its creatures. Within Western theology, human beings became alienated from the natural world — or indeed superior to it. This resulted at best in a patronizing stewardship and at worst domination and outright rape. Many people are seeing the possibilities of including connection with environment as a therapeutic tool for people trapped in the splitting of this polarity.

---

38. Jacques Attali, *Noise: The Political Economy of Music* (Minneapolis: University of Minnesota Press, 1985), p. 5.
  39. Attali, *Noise: The Political Economy of Music*, pp. 103–105.

All music making using instruments involves human beings in contact with the natural world. It is one of the most intimate relationships human beings have with the environment other than eating it. In traditional societies a drummer would reverence the tree and the animal that give the material for his/her drum. Sadly, in the West the loss of the connection with the natural world has been reflected in the way we treat and regard instruments. We need to re-establish this reverence in relation to instruments in our Western fragmented culture.

To summarize, the Church has often manifested a certain twisted form of community more concerned with exclusion than inclusion in the totalizing form of dogma reflected in its hymnody. The degree of tolerance of diversity is an important element in the way a community defines itself. Many musicians have engaged in peace making projects to contain diverse elements respectfully within musical structures like Yair Dalal in Israel and my own pieces *The Healing of the Earth*[40] and *Peacesong*.[41]

The community of the Gospels is one of inclusion. This has been part of the feminist agenda from the beginning and the absence of this theme in traditional hymns has led to the popularity of my hymn *We Shall Go Out* with its closing line:

> Including all within the circles of our love.

One of the significant challenges for the Church and indeed contemporary society is the establishment of an identity within an inclusive community.[42]

*Unity/Diversity*

All descriptions of creativity and particularly its processes include a measure of chaos or darkness—a time when the whole appears to fragment before it re-establishes itself again in a different configuration. So the flow between these two polarities produces creativity. But the Cartesian view of the unified, separated self,

40. June Boyce-Tillman, *The Healing of the Earth* (London: The Hildegard Press, 2001b).

41. June Boyce-Tillman, *Peacesong* (London: The Hildegard Press, 2006).

42. There have been some examples of this, including the Inauguration of John Sentamu as Archbishop of York with its huge variety of musical styles and traditions.

central to the project of Western rationalism has often done violence
to diversity:

> Thou whose Almighty Word
> Chaos and Darkness heard
> And took their flight.
> (John Marriott, Thomas Raffles)

Here we see the images of order, light and truth inextricably
linked. Feminist and liberation theology[43] has problematized such
thinking following in the steps of postmodern and postcolonial
theorists who see such thinking as linked with all great colonial
enterprises and yet these hymns are still regularly sung. This
thinking perpetuated the more violent aspects of social policy and
also to people undergoing times of fragmentation in their lives—
people who are often pathologized as mentally sick for there is a
rhythm to the integration and de-integration.[44] This process of
working with the broken middle can be facilitated by music. Most
musical forms allow for juxtaposition and simultaneous combination;
it therefore can accommodate difference and differing degrees of
unity:

> What we need is to fumble around in the darkness because that's
> where our lives (not necessarily all the time, but at least some of the
> time, and particularly when life gets problematical for us) take place;
> in the darkness, or, as they say in Christianity 'the dark night of the
> soul'. It is in these situations that Art must act and then it won't be
> judged Art but will be useful to our lives.[45]

Gillian Rose develops the notion of working in what she calls
'the broken middle':

> In the middle of imposed and negated identities and truths, in the
> uncertainty about who we are and what we should do… She commends
> us to work with these contradictions, with the roaring and the roasting
> of the broken middle, and to know that it is "I".[46]

---

43. Hannah Ward and Jennifer Wild (eds.), *Human Rites* (London: Mowbrays, 1995a).

44. Sue Jennings, *Introduction to Developmental Play Therapy: Playing and Health* (London: Jessica Kingsley, 1999), p. 45.

45. Cage quoted in Malcolm Ross, *The Creative Arts* (London: Heinemann, 1978), p. 10.

46. Nigel Tubbs, 'What is Love's Work?', in *Women: A Cultural Review*, 19.1 (October 1998), p. 34.

Some philosophers like Rosi Braidotti[47] in her seminal text, *Nomadic Subjects*, and psychologists in an age of globalization are looking towards the concept of a multiple self. I have found in my workshops that the acceptance of multiplicity within the self as being natural can be an experience of great freedom.

To summarize, the Church has not been comfortable in dealing with people who are phases of deintegration, often excluding them from public worship. However, small informal liturgies have been more able to accommodate these times. The music used here is often much more informal and inclusive. Things are tried out. Risks are taken. There is space for crying and more space for chaos which is no longer subject to violence in a fascist pursuit of order. The Church needs to rethink its violent thinking towards a darkness and confusion.

### Public/private

The public face of religious traditions is often male, particularly when we look at those holding positions of musical authority. In fact, music is no different from areas like the priesthood where violence has been done to women's authority. The result has been that they have not been able to claim a place such as this for the self-expression:

> I'd like to think that when I sing a song, I can let you all know about the heartbreak, struggle, lie and kicks in the ass I've gotten over the years for being black and everything else, without actually saying a word about it.[48]

However, the hymn was one area where some women's voices have been heard. In the Victorian period there were a number of women hymn writers who found considerable acceptance for their theological ideas in the form of the hymn: Fanny Crosby, Charlotte Elliott and Frances Alexander are few of a considerable number who still find a place in contemporary hymn books.

The advent of feminist theology gave women hymn writers another impetus to get their voices heard since the 1980s. At the same time, there was the foundation of a number of such groups as Women in Theology and Catholic Women's Network which needed

47.  Rosi Braidotti, *Nomadic Subjects* (New York: Columbia University Press, 1994).

48.  Ray Charles from Dudley Moore (1992 first published 1986), *Off Beat; Dudley Moore's Musical Anecdotes* (London: Robson Books), p. 123.

a new hymnody. It was my reason for embarking on the process of writing hymns. Collections including women's material started appearing in the late 1980s.[49] Publishers are now more interested in issuing collections by women writers. Books of alternative liturgies like *Human Rites*[50] and Catholic Women's Network's *Making Liturgy: Creating Rituals for Life*[51] include some material by women but usually without music.

*Reflecting Praise*,[52] a hymn book celebrating the work of women past and present, as well as men who use 'softer' , feminine or inclusive images for God, was the first collection concentrating on women's contribution to hymnody with both words and music. It was initiated by Women in Theology as a vision of the two editors, Janet Wootton and June Boyce-Tillman. It included material from the past as well as material from a variety of Christian traditions and other faith traditions. It included black spirituals and a variety of idioms and accompaniments. In the US, collections *Voices Found*,[53] appeared — a collection of hymns with similar aims to *Reflecting Praise*. Its origins, however, are very different in the Women's Liturgical Music Project run by Lisa Neufeld-Thomas:

> I don't want to become identified with a really radical approach. I think that it puts women off — sort of mainstream women who really do need to have texts that celebrate women, and if we came across as a radical group, they would not pay any attention.[54]

Not only has it been difficult to get women's material used in worship but also to play public roles in the most prestigious places of worship:

> In the privileged world of the male cathedral chorister and public schoolboy a system envied the world over has been created which makes full use of a boy's musicality and intelligence. From the age of

49. H. Ward, J. Wild and J. Morley (eds.), *Celebrating Women* (London: SPCK, 1995b [1986]).

50. Hannah Ward and Jennifer Wild (eds.), *Human Rites* (London: Mowbrays, 1995a).

51. Dorothea McEwan, Pat Pinsent, Ianthe Pratt and Veronica Seddon, *Making Liturgy: Creating Rituals for Life* (Norwich: Canterbury Press, 2001).

52. June Boyce-Tillman and Janet Wootton (eds.), *Reflecting Praise* (London: Stainer, 1993).

53. Lisa Neufeld-Thomas, *et al.*, *Voices Found: Women in the Church's Song* (New York: Church Publishing, 2003).

54. Interview with Lisa Neufeld Thomas May 2003, Philadelphia. This raises the complexity of the issue of women's contribution.

7 he can learn to sing, follow a part, become aware of other parts. He becomes aware of them fitting together, reading the full score as well as his line. On maturity he can learn to sing another part and will have learned another instrument, including the organ. He is in a wonderful position to observe conducting, accompanying and get ahead by copying his masters. He is an apprentice at a young age when the mind is ready to absorb all these skills. Musically, it is a wonderful set up, one denied to girls until comparatively recently. Yet some old fashioned attitudes prevail and one article I read recently in a magazine devoted to cathedral music suggested that girls should never be allowed anywhere near a cathedral. The reason given was that the boys-only system perpetuates itself and provides the tenors and basses of the future.

As an organ scholar, encouraged initially in a semi-rural parish and later in an urban one, I could not understand why I felt so inadequate besides men who appeared to know the ropes. Once I began to understand something of cathedral and public school education I began to realise where I had missed out. I regret never having learned an orchestral instrument for which, if I had been a boy in a cathedral choir or pupil in a better school, the opportunity would have been there.[55]

If girls are to be denied a cathedral style musical education where are female role models? Some parishes have fabulous mixed voice choirs from which girls can be inspired. Are women directors in public schools or state schools? They are more likely in state schools as heads of music. They do marvellous work in a variety of supportive and leadership situations. Are they in our cathedrals? One or two are beginning to be appointed. Do they conduct? Many operate at a local level, some at a national level, but until a woman conducts at the Last Night of the Proms women conductors will not have arrived… Opportunities are better now than they have ever been before, thanks to better communications, better musical activities and improving attitudes towards women already in positions of leadership.[56]

To summarize, music has huge potential for expressing private insight in public form. Women have been able to use the hymn form for this purpose but the limitation of public musical authority to men has done violence to women's ability to make themselves heard.

55. Story, Marilyn Harper, Co-ordinator of Academic Music, James Allen's Girls' School Organist, Christ's Chapel, Dulwich, London. Email communication, June 2002.
56. Story, Marilyn Harper, e-mail communication, June 2002.

*Product/process*

In a product based society literacy is dominant. The workplace is increasingly literate and the oracy[57] struggles to find any place in it. Literate musical traditions lay a high premium on musical notation. Characteristics of orate cultures are:

- The absence of a definitive form of any story or piece of music
- A fluidity in formal structures which are free flowing rather than linear and analytical
- Increased subjectivity
- Transmission by face-face contact not a book
- Open religion rather than a fixed revelation contained in a book.[58]

The devaluing of the oracy of process has done women no favours as many women's liturgy groups lack a person with sufficient musical education to be competent in musical notation.

The Church has played into the product-centred view and this is reflected in the words of hymns. People are seen in colonial evangelism as 'souls to be saved'. Christian doctrine has often, in such courses as the Alpha, been seen as a product to be consumed (not unlike the substances found on the shelves of a supermarket) rather than one to be wrestled with and contested. My mother was warned in the 1950s that her daughter asked too many questions in her confirmation class. I was given the Catechism to learn and accept; there was no compromise, no argument and the end of any debate was carefully contrived to produce that acceptance. Notions of a perfect product start to deconstruct notions of excellence, which have run through classical theology. A CSSM chorus runs:

> The best for God, the best for God, we want to be the very, very best for God.

I can still remember the moment, when playing for a group of eight-year-olds on a Christian mission in one of my more evangelical phases, I realized that this was not in tune with my understanding of the Christian Gospel, which was about God's acceptance of us

---

57. The words literacy and oracy refer to processes of communication. The terms literate and orate refer to societies which use either the written word or the spoken word as the prime means of communication.

58. Walter Ong, *Orality and Literacy: The Technologizing of the Word* (London and New York: Methuen, 1982), pp. 25–29.

wherever we happen to be in our journey. Notions of perfection often deny Christ's humanity.

Feminist theologians have challenged such a position from a number of perspectives. They have drawn on the development of process thought by such figures as Alfred North Whitehead.[59] Ruth Mantin[60] aims at seeing spirituality as process. Drawing on this, I used God as Verb:

CHORUS: And we'll go a-godding
To bring the world to birth

1. New life is calling;
   Help set it free.
   And we'll all go a-godding
   With a song of liberty.
   CHORUS

2. Hunger is calling,
   Find food to share;
   And we'll all go a-godding
   To reveal abundant care.
   CHORUS

The canonization of sacred texts, be they the Bible or books of liturgy sanctioned by Canon Law, has resulted in decontextualised liturgy and sacred texts that operate more like a museum of past treasures than a vibrant expression of contemporary concerns and spirituality. In 2002, I wished a College choir to sing a student's setting of an inclusive language Magnificat text based on that in the New Zealand prayer book as part of an evensong in a cathedral. I consulted the precentor who called a Chapter meeting. The upshot of it was that only the text of the 1662 prayer book could be set for choral evensong in that particular cathedral. We were an upper voice choir for which there is very little material. This young woman had set a text appropriate for her era that was rejected because it did not fit into what can only be called an imaginary museum of liturgical practice.[61]

59. Mary Daly, *Beyond God the Father; Towards a Philosophy of Women's Liberation* (Boston: Beacon Press, 1973); Mary Grey, *Redeeming the Dream* (London: Feminism, Redemption and the Christian Tradition, 1989).

60. Ruth Mantin, *Thealogies in Process: The Role of Goddess-talk in Feminist Spirituality* (Unpublished PhD Thesis, May 2002, Southampton University).

61. This setting of the liturgical text is the equivalent of the museum's hermetically sealed glass case proved a considerable problem for the Magnificat project described in Chapter 9. In this particular case we did manage to sing this setting, but as an anthem where the text is not controlled by canonical texts of liturgy.

In orate traditions, such a process cannot happen, because the means of preservation is simply not available. There is an ephemerality about oral traditions; there is less desire to retain material from particular situations which may be inappropriate for different contexts. We can see this in some contemporary women's approach to liturgy and their music.

The discovery of the evolving nature of the musical structure of traditional music has been an important contribution that traditional music have made to Western classical and popular music, even though in the colonial enterprise these were often downgraded in the face of the spreading of musically literate traditions. Judith Vander working on the songs of the Shoshone Indians saw the songs as characterized by inexact repetition.[62] This has been little explored in liturgical music, even though it is relatively easy to do over the repented chord patterns of chant like those of Margaret Rizza and the Taize community.

To summarize, Western culture is now trapped in a product-based society which has infused our liturgical traditions. Musical oracy is best seen in improvisatory traditions, particularly the totally free improvisation; this is more likely to be present in charismatic traditions. The perfectionism built into this system has been disempowering for participatory music making. The Church has accommodated to the perfectionism of the surrounding culture and moved increasingly to a literate musical culture, apart from the more informal groupings and those developing Gospel traditions.

*Excitement/relaxation*

Western society is frenetically exciting. The ultimate condemnation of the young is not that it is evil or wicked (both of which are now terms of endearment') but that it is 'boring'. Silence is an endangered species. In the rubric of some services now there is the instruction 'And now a time of silence will be kept'. This has often been so short in my experience that it has passed without my noticing. The patriarchal church has often presented us with a plethora of sounds and images, often communicated verbally, with little time to absorb, contemplate or reflect on them or indeed, to make them our own

62. Judith Vander, *Ghost Dance Songs and Religion of a Wind River Oshone Woman* (Monograph Series in *Ethnomusicology*, Number 4; Los Angeles: University of California, 1986).

by relating them to our own everyday experience. It often has little notion that the laity have anything that they might contribute to the process other than being swept into the activity themselves as prayer-leaders, Eucharistic ministers and so on. In this respect many churches resemble the surrounding culture. This is, in effect, a violence to the internal rhythm within the self which needs a balance of excitement and relaxation

And yet privately, people are buying meditative, slower material for their private use and attending classes in such slower disciplines as yoga. There is a contemplative Wisdom tradition within Christian, reflected in the silence of some monastic traditions but from the average churchgoer in the average congregation it is often remarkably well hidden. When we look at the practice of the alternative liturgy groups, we see silence is often prominent with regular times for reflection. There is often a rediscovery of meditative traditions of various kinds. The music used is often slow and functions as a raft for reflection and healing by the absorption of the ideas, sounds and images presented into the depth of one's being. Instruments that will relax and sustain, like the singing bowl, are popular. Many of the songs used have also been softer and slower and more meditative.

The louder instruments of our churches are also associated in the minds of many women with a triumphalist theology. Dominating the musical scene is the sound of the organ, which, although capable of soft gentle sounds and often used in this way, is usually characterized by non-organ lovers as loud and overbearing. When groups of worshipping women do have access to large liturgical spaces that include organs there is often a general resistance to using them as being the musical representation of a loud triumphalist theology.

In general, the instruments used for the informal private groups have to be portable—guitars and flutes have found a ready acceptance. Recently there has been a greater use of the power of the drum, but this has received a mixed reception. It is great energizing power and some women have wanted to reclaim it from the hands of the men who controlled it in many ritual traditions. Others have resisted its militaristic overtones.[63] A further problem

63. The drums have summoned people to war in many cultures including the West; however, it is actually simply an energizer and energy once raised can be used for destructive or constructive purposes.

is its appropriation from other cultures particularly the Native American or the African.[64] The reclaiming of energizing instruments and the use of them to empower action for social justice does need to be part of the feminist agenda.

To summarize, human beings need to establish a rhythm of excitement and relaxation in their lives. Loud and fast music induces arousal and slower softer music relaxation. Certain instruments have exciting or calming qualities. Feminist liturgies have tended to claim the softer gentler moods in the music they chose, rebelling against the more triumphalist dominant tradition which they feel has done violence to the softer gentler musical traditions.

*Challenge/Nurture*

The pursuit of excitement and the dominance of the archetypal myth of the heroic journey have led to a profoundly challenging society devaluing nurture. Jantzen highlights how far the Anglo-American approach to the philosophy of religion is based on violence and death rather than birth and growth. She bases her work on the philosopher, Hannah Arendt, to critique the necrophilic models of theology,[65] which have generated a culture valuing war and destruction. She suggests a model of theology based on natality rather than mortality which links with a well-established tradition of music associated with Mary, the Mother of Jesus:

> a symbolic which will lovingly enable natals, women and men, to become subjects, and the earth on which we live to bloom, to be 'faithful to the process of the divine which passes through' us and through the earth itself.[66]

There are examples in Church history where the Church has made a significant contribution to empowering the poor through music education but also examples where the less well-educated are excluded from Church traditions. Estelle Jorgensen[67] in a powerful article bringing together Paolo Freire's Pedagogy of Hope with the

64. Conversation with Mary Hunt, Harvard University, 1 May 2003.
65. Hannah Arendt, *The Human Condition* (Chicago: University of Chicago Press, 1958), p. 246.
66. Grace M. Jantzen, *Becoming Divine: Toward a Feminist Philosophy of Religion* (Manchester: Manchester University Press, 1998), p. 254.
67. Jorgensen Estelle, 'The Artist and the Pedagogy of Hope', *International Journal for Music Education* 27 (1996), pp. 36–50.

role of the artist in society and education in the arts, highlights the role of the itinerant singing masters in empowering the poor and the women in eighteenth century society. These delivered the only formal education open to groups of people from otherwise disenfranchised groups, especially women and girls who were excluded from much music making in the churches and communities.

However, in the name of music education and in the way we use music in churches we have sometimes cheated people out of their birthright to sing by the use of false challenges. The map of singing as presented in the average school is one of a restricted range of pitches and tone colours. We all have our own note, the note that is easiest for us to sing at any time. This has often not been validated by the dominant system particularly if it is a low note.[68] The map of singing presented in schools and offered as the model in churches was often too limited.

The task of the leader of singing including that in religious contexts is to find a pitch acceptable to a group, not choose one from pitched instruments like the piano. It is an intuitive process, demanding being in tune with the group. For the pitch will be lower if the group is tired, has colds or is depressed or when it is early in the day or Winter time.

The issue of tuning and perfection has led to a violent attitude on the part of professional church choir conductor who has often bullied his choir to perfection by means of public humiliation. This is part of the classical conducting traditions and has damaged a number of cathedral choristers:

> We can't afford to let these coarse and ignorant people keep running our orchestras [choirs] and our music as if they were their private property. This is not what they are here for, this is not what they are engaged to do.[69]

This is all the more tragic as music is a way of dealing with violence. There are many stories from the holocausts of people singing to retain their power and from the El Mozote massacre in El Salvador in 1981 comes the remarkable story of a young girl, an evangelical Christian who was raped several times in one afternoon:

68. June Boyce-Tillman, 'Getting our Acts Together: Conflict Resolution Through Music', in Marian Liebmann (ed.), *Arts Approaches to Conflict* (London: Jessica Kingsley, 1996), p. 215.

69. Louis Yffer, *Music is the Victim* (Melbourne: Bookaburra Press, 1995), p. 16.

She had kept on singing, too, even after they had done what had to be done, and shot her in the chest. She had lain there on La Cruz [the hill on which the soldiers carried out their killings] — with the blood flowing from her chest and had kept on singing — a bit weaker than before, but still singing. And the soldiers, stupefied, had watched, and pointed. Then they had grown tired of the game and shot her again, and she sang still, and their wonder turned to fear, until they had unsheathed their machetes, and hacked her through the neck, and at last the singing stopped.[70]

I met a nun who felt overwhelmed by her work in a community that concerned itself with violations of human rights. After the course in which she had sung some of her songs she said to me: 'I know what I had forgotten; I had forgotten to sing. If I remember to sing I can survive the stories that our community is receiving and even transform them in some way'. Here Pam Brown talks of its power to lift depression:

My son and I met days of depression together. We put on recordings of early blues, recorded by ancient men and women in the days of the hissing disc, put out the light and bayed at the moon in mournful accompaniment.

It always did the trick.[71]

In the Alister Hardy are many accounts of the relation of music, healing and spirituality which include notions of empowerment. This one from a woman in 1970 shows a healing miracle during a hymn:

After the address came the hymn 'All hail the power of Jesus' name'. During the singing of it I felt the power of God falling upon me. My sister felt it too, and said ' Floie, you're going to walk'. The Lord gave me faith then.[72]

In a service in Gugulethu, South Africa, I was present at a service where people could come forward for healing. The pastor relayed their request to the congregation. The congregation then sang to support the healing. What was interesting here was that the songs were not the soft gentle sounds that we associate with nurturing of

70. Mark Danner, *The Massacre at El Mozote* (New York: Vintage, 1994), pp. 78–79.

71. Pam Brown (b. 1928) quoted in Helen Exley, *Music Lovers Quotations* (Watford: Exley Publications, 1991).

72. RERC 0001301, Religious Experience Research Centre Accounts of Religious Experience, held at Lampeter University.

Western culture, but strong louder pieces accompanied by drumming patterns made on hymn books. The greater the need, the greater the strength of the singing of the thousand people present. I have seen similar phenomena in black funeral wakes in the UK.

There is also a need for texts challenging the injustices of patriarchal society. George Kent calls this Insurrectionary music. The vision of Galtung—an important founder of the peace studies movement—is:

> that peace is not about the absence of conflict, but about the handling of conflict in mature, productive ways, meaning mainly in non-violent ways. Music that is combative in tone may nevertheless be peaceful if it seeks justice and if it uses non-violent means in that pursuit. It is combative but nevertheless peaceful.[73]

Some would see such insurrectionary music as violent and in some cases it is. George Kent's solution is:

> I take the view that acting non-violently in support of justice is peaceful. It is a means for pursuing positive peace, which is not only the absence of violence but also the presence of justice. Thus, insurrectionary music that is claimed to be on the side of justice may or may not be peaceful, depending on whether it advocates violence.[74]

I have written texts of this kind, like the one written for Catholic women's ordination:

> Following the vision we will move forward
> Following the vision we won't look back
> Following the vision we will move forward
> Or ?Our?resolve will never slack, never ,never slack

To summarize, music can contribute effectively to reverse the violence of injustice if attention is paid to nurturing people's musical ability especially their right to sing. It can also challenge it through its texts drawing attention to injustices such as the tradition of the protest song.

### Rational/intuitive

Post-Enlightenment Western culture has valued reason and devalued intuition. The Enlightenment Project, based on 'I think therefore I

---

73. George Kent, 'Unpeaceful Music', in Olivier Urbain (ed.), *Music for Peace* 2005).
74. George Kent, 'Unpeaceful Music'.

am', saw the answer to successful human society as the dominance of reason over human beings' unruly passions and imaginings. The intuitive and experiential aspects of the Church were suppressed in favour of theological codifications and this included music. Hymns such as *Hark the Herald Angels Sing* – are often doctrinal statements rather than accounts of experience. The centrality of lived experience to feminist theology is reflected in feminist hymns. Mel Bringle's hymn draws, for example, from experiences of Alzheimer's:

> When memory fades and recognition falters,
> When eyes we love grow dim, and minds, confused,
> Speak to our souls of love, that never alters;
> Speak to our hearts by pain and fear abused
> O God of life and healing peace, empower us
> With patient courage, by your grace infused.[75]

In a widening of this exploration of experience, the role of the visionary experience is being re-evaluated and rediscovered. There are examples of women in Church history whose music came from visionary experiences. Hildegard's 77 songs were given as part of her visionary experiences and the visionary experience was the centre of Mother Ann Lee's leadership of the Shaker. During her time in prison in 1770, she received the visions that shaped Shakerism:

> The most astonishing visions and divine manifestations were presented to her in so clear and striking a manner, that the whole spiritual world seemed displayed before her.[76]

During her ecstatic experiences she felt a strong current of energy flow through her spine which was often expressed in songs. The tradition of vision songs continued as in the 1840's; many Shakers became vehicles for messages from Mother Ann, other early leaders, the heavenly Father, the Holy Mother Wisdom, angels, saints and so on. Mother Ann Lee and the Shakers stand as a challenge to the rationalism that was gaining ascendancy at that time. To a certain extent these traditions are taken up in the more charismatic traditions of the Church. Nevertheless, there are a number of places within

75. Mary Louise Bringle, *Joy and Wonder, Love and Longing: 75 Hymn Texts* (Chicago: GIA Publications, 2002).

76. Calvin Green and Seth Y. Wells, *A Summary View of the Millennial Church of the United Society of Believers (commonly called Shakers)* (Albany, NY: Packard and van Benthuysen, 1823).

Christianity where such phenomena would be met with scepticism and outright ridicule.

To summarize, Western rationalism has come to be at odds with intuition and its associated expressive and spiritual elements. This has led to violence to some more intuitive forms of creativity.

## Disembodiment/Embodiment

Christianity has deep in its conceptualizing a notion of body/soul split. The Enlightenment added a third element that could be split off — the mind or intellect. Few other human societies have achieved such an effective split. But music offers a great possibility for the uniting of body and soul but has, in Western culture, got trapped in this split. For it is in the alliance of music and dance that we see a clear example of the blend of body and soul; yet this has been a problem for Christianity. The circle dance has become a popular way of cementing group cohesion in women's liturgies. However, when women have contributed dance pieces to acts of worship, I have heard people remark that 'the woman's writhing body' has no place in public worship. This is remarkable as certain bodily movements have been validated for men by long liturgical tradition. The split of music and dance has done violence to women's bodies.

The development of trance and rave music traditions have seen music and dance rejoined with notions of transcendence and the music sometimes is seen in religious terms. They use very old techniques — the combination of prolonged periods of music and dance with hallucinogens. Matthew Collin sees its development as part of 'the restless search for bliss'.[77] However, the commodification of Western society has produced a situation where money is the only value system. This has opened the way for the exploitation of what is a fundamental need in human beings — the experience of transcendence. It has done violence to the human search for the experience of transcendence.

The rediscovery of drumming has helped people to rediscover the embodiment of performance. A student from a largely Western Classical background after a concert of African drumming told me. 'At first I hated it. I found it strange, different and fought the power of the drums. Eventually, I yielded to their power and I found my

77. Matthew Collin, *Altered State: The Story of Ecstasy Culture and Acid House* (London: Serpent's Tail, 1997), p. 316.

whole body taken over by the drums so that they seemed to play my body. Then I never wanted them to stop'.[78] This experience of music empowering the body has been problematic for Christianity which has systematically deprived people of the drums wherever it found them in the early colonial enterprise as a way of doing violence to their power.

To summarize: the traditional mind, body and spirit that has characterized Western culture has done violence to the human body especially those of women. But it can be healed by musical activities like dance and chanting. It has endeavoured to keep music as a mental/spiritual experience divorced from the body and physical empowerment which it has perceived as a threat to its powerful hierarchies.

## Conclusion

This chapter has set out a model of five lenses for examining the musical experience. It has used this lens as a way of examining the way in which the musical traditions have done violence to various value systems and those who would subscribe to them. It has shown how the values of patriarchal religion have been manifested in the musical traditions of Christianity and have done violence to a variety of groups, including women, and how this will have an effect on whether various groups regard the musical experience as spiritual. Although this is most clear in the words of hymns and songs especially in areas like inclusive language, this is also true of the hierarchical structures that characterize the performing and composing traditions, with their hierarchical views of collaboration and also the exclusion of the actual bodies of women from the public versions of these traditions. This essay has looked at the models of music used in feminist liturgies and the rediscovery or oral musical traditions in the light of their placing in less public spaces. It has seen the rediscovery of dance as a reinstatement of the body within the musical experience.

Galtung's definition of peace is as 'the capacity to transform conflicts with empathy, creativity and nonviolence'.[79] This chapter

78. Unpublished conversation with an undergraduate at King Alfred's University College, 1992.

79. J. Galtung, shared during a private telephone conversation with Olivier Urbain in January 2000.

has given some indication about how church music has been responsible for violence to subjugated peoples and cultures. It has also shown how—by embracing different value systems—it might be used to reverse and ameliorate the effects of the structural violence within the Church.

# Bibliography

Adams, Carol J., *Neither Man nor Beast: Feminism and the Defense of Animals* (New York: Continuum, 1994).

Adams, Carol J. and Marie M. Fortune (eds.), *Violence Against Women and Children: A Theological Sourcebook* (New York: Continuum, 1995).

Adelsberger, Lucy, *A Doctor's Story* (trans. Susan Ray; London: Robson Books, 1996).

Agamben, G., *Homo Sacer III: El poder soberano y la vida desnuda.*

Alter, Robert, *The World of Biblical Literature* (London: SPCK, 1992).

Althaus-Reid, Marcella Maria, *The Queer God* (London: Routledge, 2003).

Am Oved, *Our Tree on the Top of the Hill* (Tel Aviv: Am Oved, 1997 [7th edn 1992]).

Amit, Yairah, *The Book of Judges: The Art of Editing* (trans. Jonathan Chipman; Leiden, Boston, Köln: E. J. Brill 1999).

Arad, Yizhak, 'The Christian Churches and the Persecution of Jews in the Occupied Territories of the Soviet Union' in Carol Rittner, Stephen D. Smith and Irena Steinfeldt (eds.), *The Holocaust and the Christian World: Reflections on the Past, Challenges for the Future* (New York: The Continuum Publishing Group, 2000).

Ardy, Peter and Julie Arliss, *A Thinker's Guide to Evil* (London: John Hunt Publishing, 2003).

Aristotle, *Aristotle Horace Longinus; Classical Literary Criticism,* ed., T.S. Dorsch; (Harmondsworth: Penguin Classics, 1965).

Armstrong, Karen, *The End of Silence: Women and the Priesthood* (London: Fourth Estate, 1993).

Ashworth, Georgina (ed.), *A Diplomacy of the Oppressed: New Directions in International Feminism* (New Jersey: Zed Books, Atlantic Highlands, 1995).

Bainton, Roland, *Christian Attitudes Toward War and Peace: A Historical Survey and Critical Re-evaluation* (Nashville: Abingdon Press, 1960).

Bal, Mieke, *Death and Dissymmetry: The Politics of Coherence in the Book of Judges* (Chicago and London: University of Chicago Press, 1988).

Ballasuriya, Tissa, *The Eucharist and Human Liberation* (London: SCM Press, 1997).

Bard, Mitchell, *Forgotten Victims: American's in Hitler's Concentration Camps* (Boulder, C.O: Westview Press, HarperCollins, 1994).

Barker-Benfield, C.J., *The Horrors of the Half-Known Life: Male Attitudes toward Women's Sexuality in Nineteenth Century America* (New York: W. W. Norton, 1976).

Barstow, Anne Llewellyn, *Witchcraze: Our Legacy of Violence Against Women* (New York: Harper Collins, 1994).
_____ *'Jane'/Human Rights Watch. 'Rwanda: Women Speak' War's Dirty Secret: Rape, Prostitution, and Other Crimes Against Women* (Cleveland, OH: The Pilgrim Press, 2000).
Bartov, Omer and Phyllis Mack (eds.), *In God's Name: Genocide and Religion in the Twentieth Century* (New York and Oxford: Berghahn Books, 2001).
Bauer, Yehuda, *History of the Holocaust* (New York: Franklin Watts, 1982).
Bechtel, Lyn M., 'Shame' in Russell and Clarkson (eds.), *Dictionary of Feminist Theologies*, pp. 259-60 and 'A Feminist Reading of Genesis 19.1-11' in Athalya Brenner (ed.), *Genesis: A Feminist Companion to the Bible [Second Series]* (Sheffield: Sheffield Academic Press, 1998), pp. 108-28.
Belensky, Mary et al., *Women's Ways of Knowing* (New York: Basic Books, 1986).
Benjamin, Jessica, 'Master & Slave. The Fantasy of Erotic Domination' in Ann Snitow (ed.), 'Powers of Desire', *New York Monthly Review* (1983) pp. 280-99.
Berkovits, Eliezer, *With God in Hell: Judaism in the Ghettos and Death Camps* (New York and London: Sanhedrin, 1979).
Bettleheim, Bruno, *The Informed Heart* (London: Penguin, 1960).
Bicknell, Jon, *Sexy but True Love Waits* (London: Marshall Pickering, 1999).
Binney, Val, Gina Harkel and Judy Nixon, *Leaving Violent Men: A Study of Refuges and Housing for Abused Women* (Bristol: Women's Aid Federation, 1981, 1988).
Boal, A., *Theatre of the Oppressed* (London: Pluto Press, 2000).
Brenner, Athalya (ed.), *A Feminist Companion to Judges* (Sheffield: Sheffield Academic Press, 1993).
_____ *The Intercourse of Knowledge: On Gendering Desire and 'Sexuality' in the Hebrew Bible* (Leiden and New York: E. J. Brill, 1997).
_____ *Genesis: A Feminist Companion to the Bible [Second Series]* (Sheffield: Sheffield Academic Press, 1998).
_____ *Judges: A Feminist Companion to the Bible [Second Series]* (The Continuum International Publishing Group, 1999).
Brettler, Marc Zvi, *The Book of Judges* (London and New York: Routledge, 2002).
Bryne, Bridget, Rachel Marcus and Tanya Powers-Stevens, 'Gender, Conflict and Development', Volume II: Cambodia Case Study Report (Bridge, Brighton: 1995).
Buber-Neumann, Margaret, *Kafkova pritelkyne Milena* (Toronto, Canada: Sixty-Eight Publishers, 1982).
Bussert, Joy M.K., *Battered Women: From a Theology of Suffering to an Ethic of Empowerment*, (New York: Division for Mission in Northern America/Lutheran Church in America, 1986).
Butler, Judith, *The Psychic Life of Power* (Stanford, CT: Stanford University Press, 1997).
Campbell, Jacquelyn, (ed.), *Empowering Survivors of Abuse: Health Care for Battered Women and Their Children* (London: Sage Publications, 1998).
Carden, Michael, *Sodomy: A History of a Christian Biblical Myth* (London: Equinox Publishing, 2004).
Cargas, Harry J., *The Unnecessary Problem of Edith Stein* (Lanham, MD: University Press of America, 1994).
Carillo, Roxanna, *Battered Dreams: Violence Against Women as An Obstacle to Development* (New York: UNIFEM/Women Ink, 1992).

Chodorow, Nancy, The Reproduction of Mothering: Psychoanalysis and the Sociology of Gender (Berkeley, CA: University of California Press, 1978).

Cohen, Anthony P., *The Symbolic Construction of Community* (London and New York: Routledge, 2000).

Concha-Eastman, Alberto and Andres Villaveces, 'Guidelines for the Epidemiological Surveillance on Violence and Injuries', Pan American Health Organization. February 2001. www.paho.org/English/AD/SDE/RA/VIP_Guidelines.pdf

Cone, James, *A Theology of the Oppressed* (New York, Seabury Press, 1975).

Conway, Helen, *Domestic Violence and the Church* (Carlisle: Paternoster Press, 1998).

Copperman, Jeanette *et al* (eds.), *Generation of Memories: Voices of Jewish Women*, (London: The Women's Press, 1989).

Corker, Marian and Tom Shakespeare (eds.), *Disability/postmodernity: Embodying Disability Theory* (New York: The Continuum Publishing Group: 2002).

Cotterell, Peter and Max Turner, *Linguistics & Biblical Interpretation* (Downers Grove, IL: InterVarsity Press, 1989).

Davis, Kathy, 'Surgical Passing: or Why Michael Jackson's Nose Makes "Us" Uneasy', presentation, The Women's Library Symposium, 'Beauty and the Body', London, 11/06/04.

Delbo, Charlotte, *Auschwitz and After* (trans. Rosette Lamont; New Haven, C.T: Yale University Press, 1995).

Demetria, Martinez, 'Between Two Worlds', in Luis J. Rodriguez, *Hearts and Hands: Creating Community in Violent Times* (New York: Seven Stories Press, 2001).

Dent, M. J., *Jubilee 2000 and Lessons of the World Debt Tables* (Keele, Staffs: Keele University, 2004).

Dobash, Russell E. and Rebecca P. Dobash, *Violence Against Wives* (London: Open Books Publishing Ltd., 1992).

Donovan, (ed.) *Animals and Women: Feminist Theoretical Explorations* (Durham, NC: Duke University Press, 1995).

Douglas, Mary, *Purity and Danger* (London: Penguin Books, 1966).

Doward, Jamie, 'Homeless Crisis Fuelled by Domestic Violence', *The Observer* newspaper, London, England, 17/08/03.

Dunayer, Joan, 'Sexist Words, Speciesist Roots', in Carol J. Adams and Josephine Donovan (eds.), *Animals and Women: Feminist Theoretical Explorations* (Durham, NC: Duke University Press, 1995).

Dworkin, Andrea, 'The Bruise That Didn't Heal', Mother Jones, July 1978, (altered), paraphrased by Marie M., Fortune, 'Violence Against Women', in James B. Nelson and Sandra Longfellow, *Sexuality and the Sacred: Sources for Theological Reflection* (London: Mowbrays, 1994).

Ellis, Marc, *Toward a Jewish Theology of Liberation* (London: SCM Press, 1987).

_____ *Unholy Alliance: Religion and Atrocity in Our Time* (London: SCM Press Ltd., 1997).

Ellison, Marvin, *Erotic Justice: A Liberating Ethic of Sexuality* (Louisville, KY: Westminster John Knox Press, 1996).

Elshtain, Jean Bethke, 'Reflection on War and Political Discourse: Realism, Just War, and Feminism in a Nuclear Age' in Elshtain *et al*, *Just War Theory* (New York: University Press, 1992).

Exum, Cheryl, *Fragmented Women: Feminist (Sub)versions of Biblical Narratives* (Valley Forge, PA: Trinity Press International, 1993).

Farley, Margaret, 'New Patterns of Relationship: Beginnings of a Moral Revolution' in Walter Burkhardt (ed.), *Woman* (New York, Paulist Press, 1977).

Farley, Wendy, *Tragic Vision and Divine Compassion: A Contemporary Theodicy* (Louisville, KY: Westminster/John Knox Press, 1990).

Fields, Weston W. *Sodom and Gomorrah: History and Motif in Biblical Narrative* (Sheffield: Sheffield Academic Press, 1997).

Fioravanti, A., 'Reciprocidad y Economía de Mercado', *Allpanchis*, 5 (1973), pp. 121-31.

Flanders, Laura, 'Rwanda's Living Casualties' in Anne Llewellyn Barstow, *War's Dirty Secret: Rape, Prostitution, and Other Crimes Against Women* (Cleveland, OH: The Pilgrim Press, 2000).

Fortune, Marie M., 'The Transformation of Suffering: A Biblical and Theological Perspective' in Carol J. Adams and Marie M. Fortune (eds.), *Violence Against Women and Children* (New York: The Continuum Publishing Group, 1996).

Fox, Everett, *The Five Books of Moses: Genesis, Exodus, Leviticus, Numbers, and Deuteronomy: A New Translation with Introductions, Commentary, and Notes* (New York: Schocken Books, 1995).

Fraser, Giles, *Christianity and Violence: Girard, Nietzche and Tutu* (London: Darton, Longman and Todd, 2001).

Freedman, David, *Eerdmans Dictionary of the Bible* (Grand Rapids: Eerdmans, 2000).

Freire, P., *Pedagogy of the Oppressed* (London: Penguin, 1993).

Friedhelm Solms, Gerrit Huizer (Kampen: Kok Publishing Company in cooperation with Geneva: WCC Publications, 1993), pp. 198-99).

Gagnon, Robert A. J., *The Bible and Homosexual Practice: Texts and Hermeneutics* (Nashville: Abingdon Press, 2001).

Garber, Zev, 'Jewish Perspective on Edith Stein's Martyrdom', in Harry James Cargas, 1994.

Gebara, Ivone, 'Option for the Poor as an Option for Poor Women,' in Elisabeth Schüssler Fiorenza (ed.), *The Power of Naming* (Maryknoll, NY: Orbis Books, 1996).

_____ 'The Face of Transcendence as a Challenge to the Reading of the Bible in Latin America' in Elisabeth Schüssler Fiorenza (ed.), *Searching the Scriptures*, I, (New York: Crossroad, 1993).

_____ *Longing for Running Water: Ecofeminism and Liberation* (Minneapolis, MN: Fortress Press, 1999).

_____ *Out of the Depths: Women's Experience of Evil and Salvation*, (trans. Ann Patrick Ware; Minneapolis, MN: Fortress Press, 2002).

_____ 'Women and the Mystery of Life' in Marc Reuver (ed.), *The Ecumenical Movement Tomorrow: Suggestions for Approaches and Alternatives*.

Geertz, Clifford, 'Ideology as a Cultural System', *The Interpretation of Cultures* (New York: Basic Books, 1973).

Gila, Almagor [21st edn 1998] *The Summer of Avya: A Girl with a Strange Name* (Tel Aviv: 1985)

Gilbert, Martin, *Never Again: A History of the Holocaust*, Harper Collins in association with the Imperial War Museum, London, England, 2001.

Gilligan, Carol, *In A Different Voice, Psychological Theory and Women's Development* (Cambridge, Harvard University Press, 1982).

Gilligan, James, *Preventing Violence* (London: Thames and Hudson, 2001).

Ginsberg, Allen, *The Norton Anthology of American Literature*, 2.

Gnanadason, Aruna, *No Longer A Secret: The Church and Violence Against Women* (Geneva, Switzerland: World Council of Churches, 1993).

Godelier, M., 'Q'est-ce que définir une "formation économique et sociale": L'example des Incas', *La Pensée*, no. 159, October, 1971.

Goetting, Ann, (with Caroline Jory), *Getting Out: Life Stories of Women Who Left Abusive Men* (New York: Columbia University Press, 1999).

Goffman, Irving, *Gender Advertisements* (New York: Harper and Row, 1979).

Golden, Stephanie, *The Women Outside: Meaning and Myth of Homelessness* (Berkeley, CA: University of California Press, 1992).

Goldenberg, Naomi, 'The Divine Masquerade: A Psychoanalytic Theory about the Play of Gender in Religion' in Kathleen O'Grady, Ann L. Gilroy and Janette Patricia Gray (eds.), *Bodies, Lives, Voices* (Sheffield: Sheffield University Press, 1998).

Goodsir-Thomas, Ronwyn, 'Symbols', in Lisa Isherwood and Dorothea McEwan (eds.), *An A to Z of Feminist Theology* (Sheffield: Sheffield Academic Press, 1996), p. 224.

Gordon, Linda, *Birth Control in America* (New York: Penguin, 1990).

Gorringe, T., *God's Just Vengeance: Christ, Violence and the Rhetoric of Salvation* (Cambridge: Cambridge University Press, 1996).

_____ *Discerning Spirit: A Theology of Revelation* (London: Trinity Press, 1990).

Gottesman, Francis Murphy (New York and London: W.W. Norton & Company, 1979).

Greeley, Andrew, *American Catholics Since the Council: An Unauthorized Report* (Chicago: Thomas More, 1985).

Greenberg, Steven, *Wrestling with God and Men: Homosexuality in the Jewish Tradition* (Madison: The University of Wisconsin Press, 2004).

Grey, Mary, *Redeeming the Dream: Feminism, Redemption and the Christian Tradition* (London: SPCK, 1999).

_____ *The Outrageous Pursuit of Hope* (London: Darton, Longman and Todd, 2000).

Groom, Susan Anne, *Linguistic Analysis of Biblical Hebrew* (Carlisle: Paternoster Press, 2003).

Guadalupe Cruz y Laura Figueroa, elaboradoras, Católicas por el Derecho a Decidir, 'Descubrir a Dios creciendo con nosotras: construcción y desconstrucción de la imagen de Dios', *Christus: Revista de Teología y Ciencias Sociales* (nov/dec. 2001).

Guillebaud, Meg, *Rwanda: The Land God Forgot: Revival, Genocide and Hope* (London: Monarch Books, 2002).

Habel, Norman C., *The Earth Bible Volume One, Readings from the Perspective of Earth*, (Sheffield and Cleveland: Sheffield Academic Press and The Pilgrim Press).

Hall, Sidney G., *Christian Anti-Semitism and Paul's Theology* (Minneapolis, MN: Fortress Press, 1993).

Hanks, Thomas D. *God So Loved the Third World. The Bible, the Reformation, and Liberation Theologies. The Biblical Vocabulary of Oppression* (Maryknoll, NY: Orbis Books, 1983).

Haywood, Pippa (ed.), *Poems for Refugees* (London: Vintage, 2002).

Hearn, Jeff, *The Violences of Men* (London: Sage Publications, 1998).

Herman, J., *Trauma & Recovery* (New York: Basic Books, 1992).

Heyward, Isabel C., *The Redemption of God: A Theology of Mutual Relation* (Lanham, MD: University Press of America, 1982).

_____ *Touching Our Strength* (San Francisco, CA: Harper & Row, 1989).

Hoff, Lee Ann, *Battered Women as Survivors* (London: Routledge, 1990).

Holdsworth, Angela, *Out of the Doll's House* (London: BBC Publications, 1998).

Holland, Janet *et al.*, *The Male in the Head* (London: The Tufnell Press, 1998).

Hood, Helen, 'Speaking Out and Doing Justice: It's No Longer a Secret but What are the Churches Doing About Overcoming Violence?', *Feminist Theology* 11.2, (2003), pp. 216-25.

Howson, Alexandra, *Embodying Gender* (London: Sage Publications, 2005).

Human Rights Watch Division, *Seeking Protection: Addressing Sexual and Domestic Violence in Tanzania's Refugee Camps* (New York and London: Human Rights Watch, 2000).

Idel, Moshe, *Kabbalah, New Perspectives* (Tel Aviv, Israel: Schocken, 1993).

Isherwood, Lisa, *Liberating Christ* (Cleveland, OH: Pilgrim Press, 1999).

———— 'Marriage: Heaven or Hell? Twin Souls and Broken Bones', *Feminist Theology* 11.2 (2003), pp. 203-15.

———— *Erotic Celibacy: Queering Heteropatriarchy* (London: T. & T. Clark, 2006).

Isherwood, Lisa and Stuart, Elizabeth, *Introducing Body Theology* (Sheffield: Sheffield Academic Press, 1998).

Jantzen, Grace M., *Becoming Divine: Towards a Feminist Philosophy of Religion* (Manchester: Manchester University Press, 1998).

Johnson, Elizabeth, *She Who Is: The Mystery of God in Feminist Theological Discourse* (New York: Crossroad, 1994).

Johnson, James Turner, 'Historical Roots and Sources of the Just War Tradition in Western Culture' in John Kelsay and James Turner Johnson, *Just War and Jihad: Historical and Theoretical Perspectives on War and Peace in Western and Islamic Traditions* (New York: Greenwood Press, 1991).

Johnson, Vivian, *The Last Resort: A Woman's Refuge Guide* (London: Penguin Books, 1981).

Joly, Andre, 'Toward a Theory of Gender in Modern English' in Andre Joly and T. Fraser (eds.), *Studies in English Grammar* (Paris: Editions Universitaires, 1975).

Jones, Serena, *Cartographies of Grace* (Minneapolis, MN: Fortress Press, 2000).

Jukes, Adam, in Anne Borrowdale, *Distorted Images: Christian Attitudes to Women, Men and Sex* (London: SPCK, 1991).

Kaufman, Philip, *Why You Can Disagree and Remain a Faithful Catholic* (New York: Crossroad, 1991).

Keneally, Thomas, *The Great Shame: A Story of the Irish in the Old World and the New* (London: Chatto and Windus, 1998).

Kirkwood, Catherine, *Leaving Abusive Partners: From the Scars of Survival to the Wisdom for Change* (London: Sage Publications, 1993).

Korsak, Mary Phil, *At the Start: Genesis Made New* (trans. Mary Phil Korsak; New York: Doubleday, 1993).

La NacionLine *Lavagna prevé una dura discusión con el FMI*. Available, online at http://www.lanacion.com.ar/04/03/12

Langer, Lawrence L., *Versions of Survival: The Holocaust and the Human Spirit* (Albany, NY: State University of New York Press, 1982).

Laska, Vera, *Women of the Resistance and in the Holocaust: Voices of Eyewitness* (Westport, CT: Greenwood Press, 1983).

Leddy, Mary Jo, 'A Different Power' in Carol Rittner and John K. Roth, (eds.), *Different Voices: Women and the Holocaust* (New York: Paragon Press, 1993).

Levi, Primo, *The Drowned and the Saved* (trans. Raymond Rosenthal; New York and London: Abacus Books, 1988).

Loades, Ann, (ed.), *Feminist Theology: A Reader* (London: SPCK, 1996).

MacKinnon, Catharine A., 'Rape, Genocide, and Women's Human Rights' in Stanley G. French, Wanda Teays, Laura Martha Purdy, *Violence Against Women: Philosophical Perspectives* (Ithaca: Cornell University Press, 1998).

Main, Pauline *et al.*, (eds.), 'Letter on Violence to Women', Churches Together in Britain and Ireland, undated.

May, Larry and Robert Strikwerda, 'Men in Groups: Collective Responsibility for Rape' in Karen J. Warren and Duane L. Cady, *Bringing Peace Home: Feminism, Violence and Nature* (Bloomington: Indiana University Press, 1996).

McClintock, Karen, *A Sexual Shame: An Urgent Call to Healing* (Minneapolis, MN: Fortress Press, 2001).

McClory, Robert, *Turning Point: The Inside Story of the Papal Birth Control Commission* (New York: Crossroad, 1995).

McFague, Sallie, Models of God: Theology for an Ecological, Nuclear Age (Philadelphia, PA: Fortress Press, 1987).

Merleau-Ponty, Maurice, *Phenomenology of Perception* (New York: Routledge, 1962).

Meyers, Carol, *Discovering Eve: Ancient Israelite Women in Context* (New York and Oxford: Oxford University Press, 1998).

Mies, Maria and Vandana Shiva, *Ecofeminism* (London: Fernwood Publishing, 1993).

Miller, Alice, *Thou Shalt Not Be Aware* (London: Virago, 1986).

Mladjenovic, Lepa and Donna M. Hughes 'Feminist Resistance to War and Violence in Serbia' in Marguerite R. Waller, and Jennifer Rycenga (eds.), *Frontline Feminisms* (New York: Garland Publishing, 2000).

Moessner, Jeanne (ed.), *Through the Eyes of Women: Images of Pastoral Care* (Minneapolis, MN: Fortress Press, 1991).

Moltmann, Jürgen, *On Human Dignity: Political Theology and Ethics* (Philadelphia, PA: Fortress Press, 1984).

_____ *Creating a Just Future* (London: SCM Press, 1989).

Mortley, R., *French Philosophers in Conversation* (London: Routledge, 1991).

Morton, Nelle, *The Journey is Home* (Boston, MA: Beacon Press, 1985).

Müllner, Ilse, 'Lethal Differences: Sexual Violence as Violence against Others in Judges 19', in Athalya Brenner (ed.), *Judges. A Feminist Companion to the Bible [Second Series]* (London: The Continuum International Publishing Group, 1999, pp. 126-42).

Nelson, James B. and Sandra Longfellow (eds.), *Sexuality and the Sacred: Sources for Theological Reflection* (London: Mowbrays, 1994).

Newburn, Tim, and Elizabeth Stanko, *Just Boys Doing Business? Men, Masculinities and Crime* (London: Routledge, 1994).

Nissinen, Martti, *Homoeroticism in the Biblical World: A Historical Perspective* (Minneapolis, MN: Fortress Press, 1998).

Noonan, John T., *Contraception: A History of Its Treatment by the Catholic Theologians and Canonists* (Cambridge, MA: Harvard University Press, 1966).

Noske, Barbara, *Beyond Boundaries* (London: Black Rose Books, 1989).

O'Barr, William, *Culture and Ad: Exploring Otherness in the World of Advertising* (Boulder, CO: Westview, 1994).

Ofer, Dalia and Lenore Weitzman (eds.), *Women in the Holocaust* (London: Yale University Press, and Binghampton, NY: Vailbalou Press, 1998).

Pahl, Jan, (ed.), *Private Violence and Public Policy: The Needs of Battered Women and the Response of the Public Services* (London: Routledge & Keegan Paul, 1990).

Patai, Raphael, *The Hebrew Goddess* (New York: Ktav Publishing House, 1967).

Peach, Lucinda J., 'An Alternative to Pacifism? Feminism and Just-War Theory' in Karen J. Warren and Duane L. Cady *et al.*, *Bringing Peace Home: Feminism, Violence, and Nature* (Bloomington: Indiana University Press, 1996).

Pellauer, Mary D., Barbara Chester and Jane Boyajian (eds.), *Sexual Assault and Abuse: A Handbook for Clergy and Religious Professionals* (San Francisco, CA: Harper/Collins, 1987).

Plumwood, Val, *Feminism and the Mastery of Nature* (London and New York: Routledge, 1993).

Poling, James N., *The Abuse of Power: A Theological Problem* (Nashville, TN: Abingdon Press, 1991, 1993).

Prigerson, Holly G., Paul K. Maciejewski and Robert A. Rosenheck, 'Population Attributable Fractions of Psychiatric Disorders and Behavioral Outcomes Associated with Combat Exposure Among U.S. Men' in the *American Journal of Public Health*, 92.1 (2002).

Raab, Kelly A., *When Women Become Priests* (New York: Columbia University Press, 2000).

Radford, Jill and Diana E. H. Russell (eds.), *Femicide: The Politics of Woman Killing* (New York: Twayne Publishers, 1992), authors' preface, xi.

Radford, Lorraine, Marianne Hester and Chris Pearson, *Domestic Violence Fact Sheet*, (Bristol: Women's Aid Federation, 1998).

Raphael, Melissa, *The Female Face of God in Auschwitz: A Jewish Feminist Theology of the Holocaust* (London: Routledge, 2003).

Rehn, Elizabeth and Ellen Johnson Sirleaf, 'Women, War and Peace: The Independent Experts' Assessment on the Impact of Armed Conflict on Women and Women's Role in Peace-Building' (New York: UNIFEM Headquarters, 2002).

Richard, P., 'Challenges to Liberation Theology in the Decade of the Nineties' in G. Cook (ed.) *New Face of the Church in Latin America* (Maryknoll, NY: Orbis Books, 1993).

Ricoeur, Paul, 'Introductory Lecture' *Lectures on Ideology and Utopia* (ed. George H. Taylor; New York: Columbia University Press, 1986).

Ringelblum, Emmanuel, *Last Writings* Volume 2 (Jerusalem: K Yad Vashem, 1992).

Rittner, Carol and John K. Roth (eds.), *Different Voices: Women and the Holocaust* (New York: Paragon Press, 1993).

Rittner, Carol, D. Stephen and Irena Steinfeldt (eds.), *The Holocaust and the Christian World: Reflections on the Past, Challenges for the Future* (New York: The Continuum Publishing Group, 2000).

Rodrigue, George, 'Sexual Violence: Enslavement and Forced Prostitution' in Roy Gutman *et al.*, *Crimes of War* (New York: W.W. Norton and Company, 1999).

Rodriguez, Luis J. *Hearts and Hands: Creating Community in Violent Times* (New York: Seven Stories Press, 2001).

Roeber, D.L. *et al.*, 'National Market Cow and Bull Beef Quality Audit—1999: A Survey of Producer-Related Defects in Market Cows and Bulls,' *Journal of Animal Science* (2001).

Rogers, Rex S. and Wendy S. Rogers, *The Psychology of Gender and Sexuality* (Buckingham: Open University Press, 2001).

Roth, John K., *Holocaust Politics* (Louisville, KY: Westminster John Knox Press, 2001).

Ruddick, Sara, *Maternal Thinking: Toward a Politics of Peace* (Boston: Beacon Press, 1989).

Rudniska, Lea 'Dremln Feigle' in Eleanor Mlotek and Malke Gottlieb (eds,), *Mir Zeinen Do; We Are Here* (New York: Workmen's Circle, 943, 1983).

Ruether, Rosemary Radford, *Women and Redemption: A Theological History* (London: SCM Press, 1998).

_____ 'The Western Religious Tradition and Violence Against Women in the Home' in Joanne Carlson Brown and Carole R. Bohn, *Christianity, Patriarchy and Abuse: A Feminist Critique* (New York: The Pilgrim Press, 1989).

_____ *Goddesses and the Divine Feminine: A Western Religious History* (Berkeley, CA: University of California Press, 2005).

Russell, L. & S. Clarkson, *Dictionary of Feminist Theologies* (London: Mowbray, 1996).

Russell, Letty M., and J. Shannon Clarkson (eds.) *Dictionary of Feminist Theologies* (London: Mowbray).

Sacks, Oliver, *An Anthropologist on Mars: Seven Paradoxical Tales* (New York: Vintage Books: 1996).

Sajor, Indai Lourdes et. al., *Common Grounds: Violence Against Women in War and Armed Conflict Situations* (Philippines: Asian Center for Women's Human Rights, 1998).

Salgado, S., *Migrants & Refugees the Survival Instinct* (New York: Aperture, 2000).

Santos, Aida F., *Violence Against Women in Times of War and Peace,* Gender, Reproductive Health and Development Monograph Series (Quezon City, Philippines: Philippines Centre for Women's Studies, Ford Foundation, 2001).

Schecter, Susan, *Women and Male Violence* (Boston, MA: South End Press, 1982).

Schicke, Monika, *Cognitive Processing for Rape Victims* (Thousand Oaks, CA: Sage, Publications, 1993).

Schlosser, Eric, *Fast Food Nation: The Dark Side of the All-American Meal* (New York: HarperCollins, 2002).

Scholtmeijer, Marian, *Animal Victims in Modern Fiction: From Sanctity to Sacrifice* (Toronto, ON: University of Toronto Press, 1993).

Selby, P., *Grace and Mortgage: The Language of Faith and the Debt of the World* (London: Darton, Longman and Todd, 1997).

Sells, Michael A., *The Bridge Betrayed: Religion and Genocide in Bosnia* (Berkeley, C.A: University of California Press, 1998).

Sengupta, Somini, 'All Sides in Liberian Conflict Make Women Spoils of War', *The New York Times*, 20 November 2003.

Sieerakowiak, David, *The Diary of David Sieerakowiak: Five Notebooks from the Lodz Ghetto* (ed. Alan Adelson; New York: Oxford Press, 1996).

Silberman, Charles E., *Criminal Violence, Criminal Justice* (New York: Random House, 1996).

Sjöö, Monica & Barbara Mor, *The Great Cosmic Mother* (New York: HarperCollins, 1991).

Sobrino, J., *Christology at the Crossroads* (Maryknoll, NY: Orbis Books, 1978).

Speer, Albert, *Inside the Third Reich* (New York: Collier-Macmillan, 1970).

Spielberg, Steven and the Survivors of the Shoah Visual History Foundation, *The Last Days,* (London: Seven Dials, 2000).

Starhawk, *Why We Need Women's Action and Feminist Voices for Peace,* Sophia Newsletter, 1.3 (March 2003), pp. 2-4.

Stevens, Maryanne (ed.), *Reconstructing the Christ Symbol,* (New York/Mahwah: Paulist Press, 1993).

Stringer, Martin, 'Expanding the Boundaries of Sex: An Exploration of Sexual Ethics After the Second Sexual Revolution' in *Theology and Sexuality* (Sheffield, Sheffield Academic Press, 1997), pp. 27-43.

Stuart, Elizabeth and Adrian Thatcher, *People of Passion: What the Churches Teach about Sex* (London: Mowbrays, 1997).

Suchalla, Ann, *It's Time to Talk About It: Violence against Women in Culture, Society and the Church*, Wuppertal, Germany, 2000, (document of the World Council of Churches, Geneva, Switzerland.)

Sujo, Glenn, *Legacies of Silence: The Visual Arts and Holocaust Memory* (London: Philip Wilson Publishers, 2001).

Swiss, Shana, and Joan Giller, *Journal of the American Medical Association*, 270. 5 (August 4, 1993), pp. 612-15.

Tamez, Elsa, *Letter to All Christians*, 14 March 2003, Biblical University, San Juan, Costa Rica.

Taylor, John V. *A Matter of Life and Death* (London: SCM Press, 1986).

Thistlewaite, Susan Brocks, 'Every Two Minutes', in Judith Plaskow and Carol Christ, *Weaving the Visions: New Patterns in Feminist Spirituality* (New York: Harper Collins, 1989, pp. 302-11).

Thistlewaite, Susan and Mary P. Engel, *Lift Every Voice: Theologies from the Underside* (San Francisco, C.A: Harper, 1990).

Tichauer, Eva, *I Was # 20832 at Auschwitz* (trans. Colette Levy and Nicki Rensten; London: Vallentine Mitchell, 2000).

Tifft, L., *Battering of Women: The Failure of Intervention and the Case for Prevention* (Boulder, CO: Westview, 1993).

Todorov, Tzvetan, *Facing the Extreme: Moral Life in the Concentration Camps* (trans. Arthur Denner and Abigail Pollack; London: Phoenix, Orion Books, 1996).

Trible, Phylis, *Texts of Terror: Literary-Feminist Readings of Biblical Narratives* (Minneapolis, M.N: Fortress Press, 1984).

UNICEF website. http://www.unicef.org/protection/index_armedconflict.html

Vance, Jonathan F. (ed.), *Encyclopedia of Prisoners of War and Internment* (Santa Barbara, CA: ABC-CLIO, 2000).

Vandenberg, Martina, 'Women, Violence and Tajikistan'. Posted 20 February 2001. Eurasia Policy Forum website. http://www.eurasianet.org/policy_forum/vand022001.shtml

Warren, Karen and Duane L. Cady, 'Feminism and Peace: Seeing Connections', in Karen J. Warren and Duane L. Cady (eds.), *Bringing Peace Home: Feminism, Violence, and Nature* (Bloomington: Indiana University Press, 1996).

Weiss, Reska, *Journey Through Hell: A Woman's Account of her Experiences at the Hands of the Nazis* (London: Vallentine Mitchell and Co. Ltd, 1961).

Westhelle, Vitor, 'Creation Motifs in the Search for Vital Space' in Susan B. Thistlethwaite, and Mary P., Engel (eds.), *Lift Every Voice: Constructing Christian Theologies from the Underside* (Maryknoll, NY: Orbis Books, 1998).

Williams, Delores, *Sisters in the Wilderness: The Challenges of Womanist God-Talk*, (Maryknoll, NY. Orbis Books, 1993).

Wistrich, Robert S., *Hitler and the Holocaust* (London: Weidenfeld & Nicholson, 2001).

Women's International League for Peace and Freedom, 'Militarism and HIV/AIDS: The Deadly Consequences for Women'. Background paper for UN General Assembly Special Session on HIV/AIDS June, 2001. http://www.wilpf.int.ch/publications/2001hiv.htm.

Woolf, Virginia, *A Room of One's Own and Three Guineas* (Oxford: Oxford University Press, 1992).

_____ *Three Guineas* (London: The Hogarth Press, 1938).

World Council of Churches, *Decade Festival and Assembly, Churches in Solidarity with Women* (Harare, Zimbabwe: World Council of Churches, 1998).

Yahii, Leni, *The Holocaust: The Fate of European Jewry* (New York: Oxford University Press, 1990).

# INDEX

Printed in the United Kingdom
by Lightning Source UK Ltd.
127771UK00001B/193-234/P